RITUAL FAILURE

Sidestone Press

RITUAL FAILURE

ARCHAEOLOGICAL PERSPECTIVES

EDITED BY
VASILIKI G. KOUTRAFOURI & JEFF SANDERS

© 2017 The individual authors

First published in 2013 (softcover)

Published by Sidestone Press, Leiden
www.sidestone.com

Imprint: Sidestone Press Academics (peer-reviewed)
For more information and peer-review procedure see:
www.sidestone.com/publishing/

Lay-out & cover design: Sidestone Press
Photograph cover: © William Attard Mccarthy | Dreamstime.com

ISBN 978-90-8890-220-8 (Softcover)
ISBN 978-90-8890-479-0 (Hardcover)
ISBN 978-90-8890-221-5 (PDF e-book)

Contents

Introduction 7
Vasiliki G. Koutrafouri and Jeff Sanders

Foreword 11
Introductory thoughts on the theme of "Ritual failure. Archaeological perspectives"
Timothy Insoll

1 The passage of matter 23
Transformations of objects and ritual meanings in the Neolithic of the Near East
Marc Verhoeven

2 The sky almost never falls on your head – why ritual rarely fails 37
Jeff Sanders

3 Ritual failure in the business records of Mesopotamian temples 51
Michael Kozuh

4 Ritual failure and the temple collapse of prehistoric Malta 63
Caroline Malone and Simon Stoddart

5 From wells to pillars, and from pillars to...? 85
Ritual systems transformation and collapse in the early prehistory of Cyprus
Vasiliki G. Koutrafouri

6 When ancestors become Gods 109
The transformation of Cypriote ritual and religion in the Late Bronze Age
David Collard

7 Colonial entanglements and cultic heterogeneity on Rome's Germanic frontier 131
Karim Mata

8 The dead acrobat 155
Managing risk and Minoan iconography
Evangelos Kyriakidis

Discussion: Defining moments 165
Richard Bradley

Introduction

Vasiliki G. Koutrafouri and Jeff Sanders

This book presents a collection of essays on the theme of ritual collapse or transformation from an archaeological perspective. It was inspired by two works in anthropology, *The Dynamics of Changing Rituals* (Kreinath *et al.* 2004) and *When Rituals Go Wrong: Mistakes, Failure, and the Dynamics of Ritual* (Hüsken *et al.* 2007), which led to considerable office debate between the editors, and then further discussion during a dedicated conference session. The present collection of papers seeks therefore to address a gap in current archaeological discourse and hopes to have laid the foundation for further debate.

What is 'ritual failure'?

The definition and identification of 'ritual' in archaeology has always been a troublesome subject. Numerous archaeologists (*e.g.* Brück 1999; Bradley 2003, and many more) have had to confront this issue, spilling much ink in order to feel able to discuss the identification of their evidence as a result of ritual practices in the past. Colin Renfrew (1985, 18-20) was pioneering in confronting and addressing this subject, creating a list of criteria for identifying ritual using an explicitly processual approach. Marc Verhoeven (2002, 33-34) designed a methodological chart for identifying ritual archaeologically. Evangelos Kyriakidis (2008, 290, also in this volume) highlighted the lack of a theoretical and methodological consensus and stressed the hidden danger for the discipline of archaeology "*[…] of having an epistemology that is not derived from the ontology*". Vasiliki Koutrafouri (2009, 90-126) composed a definition for 'prehistoric ritual' within a post-structuralist and Pragmatics approach.

The reader of this volume will notice that the authors avoided engaging at length with "what ritual is", instead focusing on the theme of 'when and how ritual fails'. This was a conscious editorial decision for three main reasons. First of all, the contributors (and indeed editors) would unlikely agree on one definition. Secondly, as already noted, recent works (Verhoeven 2002; Kyriakidis 2008; Koutrafouri 2009, 13-129) have addressed this issue. Lastly, the editors aimed at minimising the focus on definitions in order to allow interpretative space for the exploration of the emerging theme of 'ritual failure' within archaeology. However, it should be highlighted that the types of ritual discussed in this collection can be described as religious ritual or as taking place within a religious context. Namely, the editors would favour definitions which account for cultural and contextual elements, while incorporating the idea of the 'sacred' or 'sacral' (Sanders 2006, 84), such as the influential definition provided by the anthropologist Clifford Geertz' (1973, 89, 90, 91-123, 127), considering it as both comprehensive and useful for the archaeological exploration of the subject.

As the focus of this work is 'ritual failure', however, and if such concepts are to be useful, a robust debate is required, as is some common ground. We had to consider what we mean by 'ritual failure' in archaeology and outline how it differs from aspects of change or transformation more generally. This book is therefore an attempt to address the topic of 'ritual failure' from archaeological perspectives. We wanted to explore ritual failure through archaeological evidence: What can archaeology contribute? How do we identify ritual failure? And in turn, explore how the concept of ritual failure can be employed to enrich archaeological approaches. Archaeology must engage with this debate as it has robust data to contribute. The papers included in this collection demonstrate potential ways in which archaeological evidence can be used to address this powerful, if nascent, topic.

Rituals form fundamentally resilient systems: therefore ritual failure represents a particularly emotive and powerful phenomenon. This work focuses on ritual practices as revealed through material traces. The various papers explore the failure, disruption and discontinuation of those customs by considering how this is revealed in the archaeological record. A number of other considerations follow on from this, including: in what ways such disruptions or discontinuities occurred; what risks were inherent in ritual practices; what the social implications were for ritual failure; and in turn which theoretical approaches provide the necessary tools for answering such questions. By focusing on these transitional periods in the early development or decline of a system, we can also explore wider questions of the nature and organisation of societies in general, shedding light on the social conditions that forced or introduced change. Therefore, answers to the question of "how such a strongly bonded institution such as 'ritual' can fail" is used in this book to better understand other themes as well, such as identity, and the social, economic and political organisation of a community. This collection therefore explores ritual endings both on a theoretical basis and from the practical perspective of the appearance and disappearance in the archaeological record of the remains of previously well-established ritual practices. Ritual practices in archaeology tend to be identified at their peak and therefore in an apparently crystallised form. Sometimes it is only the absence of evidence that indicates change. In some cases, religious systems appear to survive for millennia before disappearing or being replaced, and new ritual systems may also appear to us apparently 'fully formed'. How to approach such issues (amongst many others), is addressed by the papers in this book.

As a first archaeological attempt dedicated to explore the phenomenon of ritual failure, the editors of this book did not offer a strict steer to the authors. The contributors in this book were only asked to respond to the theme of ritual failure and were given free reign to explore this topic from their own perspective and through the prism of the evidence they selected. As this is a fresh theme for archaeology the idea was to let the authors engage with the concept of ritual failure from the perspectives they felt were most productive and meaningful archaeologically to them. Different approaches and ideas are to be encouraged as long as we can also explore the areas of common ground – the point of reference and vocabulary to enable the conversation to take place. The papers in this book explore ritual practices from different places and times. Some provide investigations of the dynamics that resulted in ritual systems coming to an end, and analyse those endings (and subsequent transformations), through combinations of theoretical and archaeological perspectives. Other papers, with central interests in themes beyond the limits of ritual, but focusing for example on transitional periods and how these occur in the archaeological record, examine how early signs of social change can be attested via the study of a 'sensitive indicator' such as ritual. All authors have worked on the exploration of ritual practices and associated social phenomena, and analyse these themes through archaeological case studies from sites with dates ranging from the Neolithic to the Roman, and extending from Babylonia to the Scottish islands. Some recast the concept itself in terms of change and transformation more broadly, others were more confident in identifying failure through the evidence.

The range of geographical and chronological topics, as well as theoretical approaches, in itself highlights the pervasiveness of the theme. However, as Timothy Insoll notes (and addresses through the provision of West African examples in this volume), the contributions primarily investigate European examples (along with the Near East), and tend to focus on islands. This may be reflective of a bias or of the type of evidence which archaeologists feel comfortable exploring. Future debates would be enriched by evidence and approaches from around the world. A recurring theme throughout the papers in this volume is that dynamic and complex models are needed. These must consider different social, geographical and chronological scales. Archaeological data has much to contribute to the development of such models, and can constitute the basis for the engagement with these wider considerations.

Hopefully it will be a long and fruitful conversation.

Acknowledgements

We would like to thank all of the contributors to this volume for providing stimulating ideas, encouragement and generosity of time. We are also grateful to Karsten Wentink, from Sidestone Press, for his invaluable guidance and advice throughout the publication process.

References

Bradley, R. 2003. A life less ordinary: The Ritualization of the Domestic Sphere in Later Prehistoric Europe. *Cambridge Archaeological Journal 13:1, 5-23.*

Brück, J. 1999. Ritual and rationality: some problems of interpretation in European archaeology. *European Journal of Archaeology 2:3, 313-344.*

Geertz, C. 1973 [1993]. *The Interpretation of the Cultures.* Selected essays. Fontana Press. Hammersmith, Lonfon.

Koutrafouri, V.G. 2009. *Ritual in Prehistory; Definition and Identification. Religious Insights in Early Prehistoric Cyprus.* Unpublished PhD Thesis, University of Edinburgh, also accessible from the Edinburgh Research Archive: http://www.era.lib.ed.ac.uk/handle/1842/3288.

Kreinath J. *et al.* 2004 (eds.). *The Dynamics of Changing Rituals. The Transformation of Religious Rituals within Their Social and Cultural Context.* Toronto Studies in Religion 29, New York: Lang Publishing.

Kyriakidis, E. 2007 (ed.). *The Archaeology of Ritual.* Cotsen Advanced Seminars 3. Cotsen Institute of Archaeology, University of California, Los Angeles.

Hüsken, U. 2007 (ed.). Ritual Dynamics and Ritual Failure, in Ute Hüsken (ed.). *When Rituals Go Wrong: Mistakes, Failure, and the Dynamics of Ritual.* Leiden, Boston: Brill, 337-366.

Renfrew, C. 1985. *The archaeology of cult: the sanctuary at Phylacopi.* British School of Archaeology at Athens. London.

Sanders, J. 2006. *Sacral Landscapes. Narratives of the Megalith in North-Western Europe.* Unpublished PhD Thesis, University of Edinburgh, also accessible online from the Edinburgh Research Archive: https://www.era.lib.ed.ac.uk/handle/1842/2671.

Verhoeven M. 2002. Ritual and its Investigation in Prehistory. in: Gebel, H.G.K. *et al. Magic Practices and Ritual in the Near Eastern Neolithic,* Proceedings of a Workshop held at the 2nd International Congress on the Archaeology of the Ancient Near East (ICAANE), Copenhagen University, May 2000. Studies in Early Near Eastern Production, Subsistence, and Environment 8. Berlin: Berlin *ex oriente*, 5-40.

Foreword

Introductory thoughts on the theme of "Ritual failure. Archaeological perspectives"

Timothy Insoll[1]

Introduction

The invitation to write some words of introduction to this volume was gladly accepted, as ritual failure is an intriguing, interesting, and innovative theme. Religions and the rituals that accompany them are by their nature primarily concerned with success. Where failure is a focus then it would usually be in relation to the failure of others, perhaps achieved via cursing or actions of evil intent. These processes are clearly evident archaeologically with, for instance, examples of curses incised on lead tablets recovered from various Graeco-Roman sites, as in a late Roman context at Trier, Germany. Prophylactic measures against such intentions have also been found widely in archaeological and architectural contexts in northern Europe, well-known being the so-called 'witch-bottles', frequently bellarmine, German stoneware jars or bottles of seventeenth or eighteenth centuries AD date containing items such as iron nails, hair, felt hearts, and nail-pairings (Merrifield 1987, 137, 163-175).

Ethnography further indicates that the manipulation of substances and objects perceived as having agency recurs in the pursuit of the failure of others. The agency of "objectification" is here defined following Gell (1998, 21) as social agency manifest and realised through the "proliferation of fragments of 'primary' intentional agents in their 'secondary' artefactual forms". A useful West African ethnographic example of this is provided by the *bocio*, "empowered cadaver", and *bo*, non-figurative empowerment objects, of southern Benin and Togo. These have multi-functional psychodynamic meanings, in part linked with alchemical processes protecting from and controlling sorcery and evil (Preston Blier 1995), and precisely meet the agency criteria previously defined. Carved wooden figures (*bocio*), and substances such as blood and other organic materials, selected animal remains (species and elements), and iron were treated in various ways with a particular emphasis placed on binding and tying of substances and objects so as to

---

[1] Department of Archaeology, Mansfield Cooper Building, University of Manchester, M13 9PL. Tim.Insoll@manchester.ac.uk.

maximise their agency and propensity for controlling, protecting, and cursing (cf. Preston Blier 1995; and for the general magico-religious significance of binding, Gell 1998, 102).

The objects and substances just described were evidently associated with causing failure or its prevention, but the key difference with the material discussed in this volume is that they functioned as part of established ritual processes, neither *bocio*, bellarmines nor Roman lead curse tablets provide instances of uncontrolled, inadvertent ritual failure that the case studies in this book, uniquely, focus upon from an archaeological perspective. However, there are seemingly numerous instances of unplanned ritual failure in the archaeological record, but apparently never previously conceptualised in such a way. Failed, abandoned, and outdated religions, cults, shrines, and the detritus of myriad rituals, desperate ritual actions to avert famine, disease, invasion or other catastrophes, these could constitute what is defined here as ritual failure. Considering ritual failure poses a challenge to ahistorical and static constructs of ritual practices and religious beliefs, and instead permits ritual agency and a more dynamic perspective to be adopted in archaeological interpretation (cf. Collard this volume).

Koutrafouri notes the disciplinary imbalance between anthropology and archaeology in studies of ritual failure (cf. Koutrafouri this volume). Some anthropologists have acknowledged and studied it as a phenomenon; archaeologists have not (*e.g.* Insoll 2004, 2011*a*; Kyriakidis 2007; Whitley and Hays-Gilpin 2008; Rountree, Morris, and Peatfield 2012). Yet even within anthropology, the allure of presumed ritual success has been the dominant focus of academic study, and ritual failure seems to be infrequently acknowledged, at least in a defined form as represented in the indexes of the small selection of seminal African anthropological texts sampled here (*e.g.* Fortes 1987; Goody 1962; Turner 1967, 1969; Evans-Pritchard 1937, 1956). This is not to say that it remains unacknowledged, but where discussed, as by Fortes 1987) in relation to the Talensi of northern Ghana (see also Insoll, MacLean, and Kankpeyeng *in press*), it is again, usually, in the context of considering personal ritual outcomes rather than as a diachronically treated multi-scale phenomena as in this book.

The theme of ritual failure

The papers in this volume, excluding a consideration of the Neolithic Near East, are concerned with parts of Europe, largely in prehistory. It would be interesting to see how the theme of ritual failure is expressed and can be approached in archaeological contexts outside the European and Near Eastern context, and to this effect, a couple of West African examples are considered below. Equally, the recurrence of island societies in the studies presented here is also notable (Cyprus, Crete, Malta, and at a larger scale, the British Isles). Perhaps they do provide a 'usefully closed context' to explore concepts such as ritual failure (cf. Malone and Stoddart this volume), but could the same point also be extended to an isolated chain of hills or a city-state? The variable geographical and environmental dimensions of ritual failure need further exploration.

The case studies in this volume clearly indicate the many dimensions of ritual failure and how it might be materially manifest. Koutrafouri provides a detailed investigation of ritual processes in early Cypriot prehistory and indicates how these can fundamentally change over time with ritual failure ultimately manifest because the world of prehistoric Cyprus changed and pre-existing rituals simply did not reflect this, or allow the individuals inhabiting it to express themselves. Here, rituals are seen as embedded in belief, and their failure is thus an outcome of changed beliefs and worldviews. In contrast, in the Cypriot Late Bronze Age, Collard identifies processes of ritual continuity and not collapse in the archaeological record. Mortuary ritual is seen as the primary ritual expression, allied with the consumption of stimulants, and possibly linked to a continuation of the importance of ancestral veneration through time. World change is again acknowledged, but existing rituals seem able to confront this and do not fail, and neither are they abandoned or radically altered, providing a different scenario to earlier Cypriot prehistory.

A third, midway, between ritual failure and continuity is provided by Mata's discussion of the Hercules *Magasanus* cult on Rome's Germanic frontier where the evidence suggests the formation of syncretic cults, and a heterogeneous cultic narrative revolving around what is described as the 'colonial entanglements' of the Roman Rhineland frontier. Compromise is key, and ritual failure is seemingly being deliberately averted as part of political strategy reflecting the tangled relationships that existed. Verhoeven advocates another direction in suggesting that 'transformation' rather than the termination implied by failure is manifest in the Neolithic Near East. Processes of discard, abandonment, and death are suggested as potential new beginnings not terminations, with fragmentation, enchainment, and object biography related to both remembering and forgetting allowing the exploration of complex material and ritual life cycles in the archaeological record. The whole concept of ritual failure is essentially questioned.

Sanders similarly, though more explicitly, challenges the concept of ritual failure in discussing the meaning of the Ballachulish figure of indeterminate Late Bronze Age – Iron Age date from western Scotland. The context of this spectacular artifact is interpreted as one of ritual closure; failure is described as an element of change rather than as a binary indicator of failure or success. This is a thought provoking idea but one that would need further empirical support before it could be more widely accepted, even if it is applicable to the archaeological context of Ballachulish Moss. Emic and etic perspectives on what constitutes ritual failure need acknowledging, but the archaeological record, as shown in this volume, does seem to provide some clear material examples of ritual failure, evident from both internal and external standpoints.

Conversely, Malone and Stoddart emphasise termination and ritual failure in prehistoric Malta. They link ritual failure to environmental and economic decline when ritual ceased either to be believable or efficacious. Hence the burial sites of the now useless ancestors were scattered with pieces of the temple statues as an act of closure. Transformation and fragmentation processes cannot seemingly be viewed in the context of mid-third millennium BC Malta as a positive process enchaining individuals and powerful artefacts (*e.g.* Chapman 2000; Chapman and Gaydarska 2007), but as a destructive way of bringing to an end something ineffectual. Ritual is posited as linked with cultural continuity and it failed as a mechanism for achieving this, hence it was abandoned and the associated material culture destroyed.

Kozuh also stresses the linkage between ritual and culture, and cultural expression and continuity, in first millennium BC Mesopotamia. The ritual ruptures described for Malta or early prehistoric Cyprus might be absent, with instead Gods stolen, or administrative breakdown leading to an absence of the required offerings, but the implications of the subsequent failed rituals could, nonetheless, be profound. To the extent that ritual failure was ultimately seen to equate with the abandonment of Mesopotamian values, and subject in the temple records to deep 'contemplation'. Kyriakidis draws attention in his discussion of Minoan Crete to another key aspect related to ritual failure, the inherent element of risk existing in rituals such as divination and sacrifice, *i.e.* that they might not succeed. Therefore ritual failure has to be conceived of almost on a sliding scale of effect, from personal failure, the ritual did not bring the desired results, through kin group, community, society, and so on. The key point being that ritual failure must be considered as complex and multi-scalar.

The case studies indicate that one interpretation of, and one meaning for ritual failure does not exist and in summary ritual failure can be seen as –

- A wholly neglected theme.

- Potentially variable in relation to geographical and environmental conditions.

- Of variable consequence seemingly dependent on the pragmatism of the ritual authorities and perceived degree of the continuity of 'culture' and 'identity' linked to ritual practice as a whole.

- Capable of being defined in the archaeological record to varying degrees.

- Requiring differentiation from ritual change, syncretism, closure, and transformation.

- Needing consideration, where possible, from both emic and etic perspectives.

- Multi-scalar, from the level of individual to society.

- Requiring further exploration in archaeological contexts.

Ritual failure in Iron Age West African archaeology

This complexity can be seen in Iron Age West Africa, and providing these introductory thoughts offers an opportunity to reassess aspects of the archaeological record of this region for examples of ritual failure. Ritual is a subject that has been previously neglected from the standpoint of 'failure' even when the salient ritual practices have been adequately archaeologically investigated and interpreted, which is, unfortunately, infrequently. Immediately, however, theoretical and methodological problems emerge akin to those identified above, as for instance in, first, differentiating between ritual closure and failure, or second, recognising the incorporation of new or exotic elements of ritual and associated material culture that could ultimately supplant existing systems and equipment, perhaps even abruptly, for reasons of prestige, or politics, related to the negotiation and maintenance of identities, but which might not be related to the failure of existing ritual.

Conant (1963) describes the latter processes in the ethnographic context of the Jos-Bauchi Plateau of northern Nigeria where ritual equipment was abandoned, and the associated rituals ceased for various reasons. For example, following Dass-Barawa, Bankalawa, and Jarawa chiefly conversion to Islam many of the title-holders would abandon their ritual equipment in the bush; sacred hoe blades, weapons, polished stone axe heads, divining paraphernalia, and dance costumes made of leaves and grasses were all left to rot. Alternative impetus for abandonment could be provided by moving settlement to a new area where a pre-condition of occupation might be the prior abandonment of existing ritual equipment and the acceptance of that of the host community, a factor functioning in helping to negotiate autochthon-incomer relations.

Significant here is that in neither instance do earlier rituals actually fail, but the disposal patterns, assuming preservation in archaeological contexts, could be interpreted as such. Rather, the same ethno-linguistic group is abandoning ritual and its associated material culture for reasons of prestige, and political and social accommodation. Genuine belief in the tenets of Islam by the authority figure represented by the chief might of course exist (cf. Insoll 2003), but this does not explain why those below him would abandon their ritual equipment as well. Thus the immediate ritual change represented by the dumping of ritual paraphernalia in the Jos-Bauchi area has to be viewed as ritual abandonment for more cynical earthly reasons rather than the failure of Gods, rituals, and beliefs. It also has to be recognised that this example is contextually specific. A model for ritual failure in the West African Iron Age archaeological record cannot be constructed from it, but it serves to reinforce how carefully interpretation in relation to this subject must proceed.

The Sao

Clearer indications of ritual failure are seemingly provided by the archaeology of the Sao of southern Chad and northern Cameroon whose highpoint has been dated to between the tenth to sixteenth centuries AD (Lebeuf, Treinen-Claustre, and Courtin 1980). The Sao are thought to have been the indigenous inhabitants of the areas west and south of Lake Chad. 'Sao' probably masks significant social complexity, but certain generalities emerge. They were farmers, followers of complex indigenous religions, lived in agglomerated settlements frequently represented archaeologically by mounds, and had varying degrees of political centralisation (Holl 1994; Jansen and Gauthier 1973; Insoll 2003).

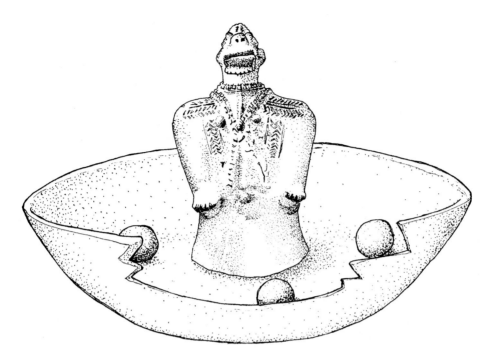

Figure 1. The central figurine recorded in the Sao Tago site, Chad (after Lebeuf and Masson Detourbet 1950, 69, 131).

The Sao produced ceramic figurines (Lebeuf 1962; Lebeuf and Masson Detourbet 1950), and these have been interpreted as linked with healing and medicine (Insoll 2011*b*, 148), as well as ancestor cults, 'totemism', and spirit beliefs related more generally to Sao ritual and religion (Lebeuf and Masson Detourbet 1950, 128-129). Figurines were incorporated into ritual practices focused on what seem to have been shrines. At the site of Tago, for instance, three figurines with human torsos, arms and heads represented were recorded grouped together and oriented to the east. One of the figurines had been placed upon part of a funerary jar accompanied by four balls of fired clay put at the cardinal points (Figure 1). Further groups of hundreds of figurine fragments, animals, people, masked dancers, as well as pieces of ochre, stone rubbers, and faunal remains interpreted as the residue from sacrifices and offerings, were recorded arranged in three semi-circles to the side of and behind the central figurines (Lebeuf and Masson Detourbet 1950, 68-70).

Complex ritual practices and presumably accompanying religious beliefs are thus attested but this did not help the Sao to survive. Tago and many other sites indicate that they disappeared as a recognisable entity. Large scale campaigns began to be directed against the Sao, primarily for the purposes of obtaining slaves, from the neighbouring Islamised polity of Kanem-Borno in the fourteenth century, a date when the first historical references to the Sao appear in the Arabic sources (Lange 1989; Insoll 2003, 278). As a reaction to this it would seem that the Sao intensified their ritual activities as indicated by changes in funerary practices, three phases of which are apparent as, for instance, in the Kotoko-Logone region. First, burial of the corpse simply stretched out full length in the ground was evident (*c.*

late twelfth century AD); second, corpses were placed in a foetal position within large pots (*c.* late fifteenth century AD); and third, jar burials disappear and corpses were once again placed at full length in graves (Jansen and Gauthier 1973, 9; Insoll 2003, 279).

It is phase two that is significant in assessing ritual failure, the jar burial era, for the presence of exotic grave-goods in these burials, such as imported glass and carnelian beads, suggests that Sao contacts with their northern Muslim neighbours, the likely source of these imports, were not only violent ones, but also that more peaceful trade and exchange relationships existed. Tago is unfortunately undated, other than to the first half of the second millennium AD, but it is not improbable that it too could be linked with this phase of ritual intensification. Support for this assertion being given by the fact that the degeneration and disappearance of Sao 'art' forms, such as the figurines, did not occur until the sixteenth century. This was linked with the third burial phase and both this and the disappearance/alteration of figural representation have been interpreted as indicative of Islamisation (Jansen and Gauthier 1973, 9).

The concept of ritual failure has permitted this brief re-evaluation of aspects of Sao archaeology and it would appear that Sao ritual failed to confront, halt, or incorporate the new religion, Islam, facing Sao societies. Enhanced ritual activities were seemingly attempted to try and achieve this but these failed and indigenous beliefs and ritual practices were either abandoned, or perhaps syncretised with Islam to varying degrees. A narrative invoking Kanem-Borno Muslim conquest of Sao lands accompanied by large scale destruction of Sao shrines and other ritual sites seems improbable, instead older rituals could not compete, were abandoned, and as such failed.

Koma Land

Even more complex and less easy to reconstruct are the varied reasons for the decline and disappearance of the ritual practices represented in the mound sites of Koma Land in northern Ghana, but this too can be approached from the perspective of ritual failure. The archaeological region referred to as Koma Land is situated within the basins of the Kulpawn and Sisili rivers and covers an area of *c.* 100 x 100 km (Kankpeyeng, and Nkumbaan 2009). Two forms of mound sites have been recorded in Koma Land, stone circle mounds and larger house mounds, sometimes with accompanying burials. Koma Land was initially the focus of research in the 1980s by James Anquandah (Anquandah 1998), with renewed research taking place since 2006 under the direction of Benjamin Kankpeyeng (cf. Kankpeyeng and Nkumbaan 2009), and the participation of this author in the project since 2010 (cf. Insoll, Kankpeyeng, and Nkumbaan 2012).

The people who generated the mounds were seemingly settled agriculturalists keeping domestic animals (*e.g.* cattle, sheep, and goats), and processing cereals such as millet with the large numbers of grinding stones recorded (cf. Anquandah 1998). They also worked iron and produced pottery and participated in trade and exchange as suggested by the small number of figurines found depicting people

Figure 2. Pointed anthropomorphic figurines in-situ, Yikpabongo, Koma Land (photo. T. Insoll).

riding camels and horses, and the small quantities of trade goods (glass beads and cowry shells) recovered (Anquandah 1998, 78-82; Insoll, Kankpeyeng, and Nkumbaan 2012, 26). The main period of occupation and use of the sites has been dated to between the sixth and twelfth centuries AD (Kankpeyeng and Nkumbaan 2009, 200; Kankpeyeng, Nkumbaan, and Insoll 2011, 209).

Like the Sao, the populations that formerly inhabited Koma Land produced clay figurines. These have been recovered in significant numbers from the stone circle mounds, along with other categories of material such as clay models of ritual "gongs" (Kankpeyeng and Nkumbaan 2009, 201), grinding stones, considerable quantities of pottery, some animal and human remains, iron bracelets and utilitarian artefacts, ceramic disks possibly used as stoppers for gourds that themselves have not survived, clay models of gourds, and small numbers of objects such as glass beads, cowry shells, and a stone lip plug (Anquandah 1998; Kankpeyeng and Nkumbaan 2009; Insoll, Kankpeyeng, and Nkumbaan 2012). Initially interpreted as burial mounds (Anquandah 1998, 82-86), it has been subsequently suggested that the stone circle mounds might represent the remains of shrines, multi-functional, but possibly utilised within the context of medicine or healing, and used for the disposal of powerful materials (Kankpeyeng, Nkumbaan, and Insoll 2011, 209)

The clay figurines are of various types; human, animal, part human and part animal, and anthropomorphic cone figurines (Anquandah 1998; Kankpeyeng and Nkumbaan 2009). Besides complete examples, many of the human figurines are recovered in fragments resulting possibly, in part at least, from deliberate fragmentation processes. The interpretation has been proposed (Insoll,

Kankpeyeng, and Nkumbaan 2012, 40-41) that both whole and fragmentary figurines, and selected body parts such as skulls, jawbones, and teeth, seem to have been used in enchainment processes linking kin groups and individuals through ancestors perhaps represented by the figurines, which also may have been used in constructing personhood of 'partible' form (cf. Fowler 2004).

The offering of libations might have been a key component of ritual practice directed at some of the figurines. Certain figurine forms that are pointed at their base, perhaps to facilitate insertion in the earth, suggest this (Figure 2). Subsequently, ritual attention/libations could then have been offered to these figurines via a crouching position (Insoll and Kankpeyeng *in press*). Libations are also suggested by cavities sometimes pierced into figurines recorded singularly or in combination from the ears, nostrils, mouth, or top of the head (Insoll, Kankpeyeng, and Nkumbaan 2012). These cavities might also have been used for the insertion of substances, possibly within the framework of protecting or healing, which would link to the previously suggested interpretation for some of the mounds as shrines (Kankpeyeng, Nkumbaan, and Insoll 2011). Perhaps also, crucially, some of the figurines might have been regarded as active agents, empowered via substances, and akin, though not directly analogous with the *bo* and *bocio* previous described.

Further ritual complexity is seemingly added by the presence of bird figurines with human faces that have been interpreted as relating to exorcising witchcraft (Kankpeyeng, Nkumbaan, and Insoll 2011, 211), and by animal forms that have been suggested as representing "animal totemic forms" (Anquandah 1998, 159). The latter interpretation has been questioned based on the precise ethnographic parallels drawn (Insoll 2011*c*, 1013), but the animal forms could still be significant in suggesting symbolic or metaphorical links with, predominantly, wild animals (Insoll 2011*c*, 1013; Insoll, Kankpeyeng, and Nkumbaan 2012).

Ultimately these complex ritual practices ceased and the area was abandoned, possibly from the thirteenth-fourteenth centuries AD. This rupture is also indicated by the current population of the region who are unconnected with the makers of the figurines, having only been settled in Koma Land for about 120-130 years (Kröger 2010, 1). Various reasons have been suggested for why depopulation occurred, including diseases like river blindness, changing climate, or perhaps migration as a correlate of insecurity caused by slave raiding, possibly to supply northern trans-Saharan markets such as Gao and Timbuktu in Mali (Kankpeyeng and Nkumbaan 2009; Insoll, Kankpeyeng, and Nkumbaan 2012, 28). These causes of decline and abandonment could have functioned singularly or in combination. Ritual failure should also be added to the list for it is evident that the complex ritual practices and beliefs that had sustained the population for several centuries ultimately failed. It can be suggested, albeit from a largely unverifiable emic perspective that the rituals and the beliefs that accompanied them ultimately did not protect from raiders and misfortune, provide sustenance, or cure diseases. Ritual failure was potentially part of the package that contributed to the disappearance of the inhabitants of the region now known as Koma Land.

Conclusions

It has to be remembered that not all abandoned or destroyed ritual materials or sites, or indications of ruptured, terminated, or replacement ritual practices in archaeological contexts need be indicative of failure, and differentiating failure from, for example, ritual closure, might not be straightforward. Equally, the variable nature of the available evidence is significant both in assessing ritual failure and the degree to which rituals in totality can be reconstructed. This is apparent in the studies in this book most of which have rich data sets to draw upon. For example, Kyriakidis utilises Minoan iconography that he describes as depicting reality, real events, rather than imaginary ones. Thus the intricacies of bull leaping or ritual procession can be examined in precise detail. Similarly, Kozuh draws upon the cuneiform records of Mesopotamian temples, a source allowing a detailed evaluation of ritual failure, perhaps not permitted via purely archaeological evidence.

Excluding iconography or historical sources, the archaeological material drawn on in this book is also generally rich, as with Koutrafoura's early prehistoric Cypriot case study and Collard's later Bronze Age evidence from Cyprus that permit an evaluation of ritual to an exceptional degree. This author also draws upon two figurine centred case studies as these too enhance the possibilities for ritual interpretation including its failure. The data from third and fourth millennia BC Malta is also extensive. Although the reliability of earlier archaeological methodologies and interpretations weakens the value of some of the data from Crete, Cyprus, or Malta (cf. Malone and Stoddart this volume), the evaluation of ritual failure, as a concept, its forms and materiality, remains to be further explored in more empirically challenging archaeological contexts. Yet this is shown to be possible, as with Sanders's focus on the single figure from Ballachulish, that was not even excavated archaeologically but recovered by workmen, as he describes, further increasing the interpretive challenges faced.

These points acknowledged, the theme of ritual failure provides an alternative interpretive perspective for viewing relevant aspects of the archaeological record at multiple levels from landscapes, to sites, assemblages, and even individual artefacts, through challenging the (often unacknowledged) assumption of ritual efficacy and in so doing making us think about and interrogate our archaeological material in new ways. It is thus hoped that it is a theme that will be further engaged with by archaeologists in the future.

Acknowledgements

I am grateful to Vasiliki Koutrafouri for the invitation to contribute to this volume and to Rachel MacLean for comments on the paper, though all errors and omissions remain my own.

References

Anquandah, J. 1998. *Koma-Bulsa. Its Art and Archaeology*. Rome: Istituto Italiano Per L'Africa e L'Oriente.

Chapman, J. 2000. *Fragmentation in Archaeology*. London: Routledge.

Chapman, J. and Gaydarska, B. 2007. *Parts and Wholes. Fragmentation in Prehistoric Context*. Oxford: Oxbow Books.

Conant, F.P. 1963. The Manipulation of Ritual among Plateau Nigerians. *Africa* 33, 227-236.

Evans-Pritchard, E.E. 1937. *Witchcraft, Oracles, and Magic among the Azande*. London: Oxford University Press.

Evans-Pritchard, E.E. 1956. *Nuer Religion*. London: Oxford University Press.

Fortes, M. 1987. *Religion, Morality and the Person*. Cambridge: Cambridge University Press.

Fowler, C. 2004. *The Archaeology of Personhood*. London: Routledge.

Gell, A. 1998. *Art and Agency. An Anthropological Theory*. Oxford: Clarendon Press.

Goody, J. 1962. *Death, Property and the Ancestors*. Stanford: Stanford University Press.

Holl, A. 1994. The Cemetery of Houlouf in Northern Cameroon (AD1500-1600): Fragments of a Past Social System. *African Archaeological Review* 12, 133-170.

Insoll, T. 2003. *The Archaeology of Islam in Sub-Saharan Africa*. Cambridge: Cambridge University Press.

Insoll, T. 2004. *Archaeology, Ritual, Religion*. London: Routledge.

Insoll, T. 2011a. (ed.). *The Oxford Handbook of the Archaeology of Ritual and Religion*. Oxford: Oxford University Press.

Insoll, T. 2011b. Introduction. Shrines, Substances and Medicine in sub-Saharan Africa: Archaeological, Anthropological, and Historical Perspectives. *Anthropology and Medicine* 18, 145-166.

Insoll, T. 2011c. "Animism and Totemism", in: Insoll, T. (ed.). *Oxford Handbook of the Archaeology of Ritual and Religion*. Oxford: Oxford University Press, 1004-1016.

Insoll, T. and Kankpeyeng, B. In Press. Reconstructing the Archaeology of Movement in Northern Ghana. Insights into Past Ritual, Posture, and Performance?, in: Ogundiran, A., and Saunders, P. (eds.). *Materialities, Meanings, and Modernities of Rituals in the Black Atlantic*. Bloomington: Indiana University Press.

Insoll, T., Kankpeyeng, B., and Nkumbaan, S. 2012. Fragmentary Ancestors? Medicine, Bodies and Persons in a Koma Mound, Northern Ghana, in: Rountree, K., Morris, C., and Peatfield, A. (eds.). *Archaeology of Spiritualities*. New York: Springer, 25-45.

Insoll, T., MacLean, R., and Kankpeyeng, B. In Press. *Temporalising Anthropology. Archaeology in the Talensi Tong Hills, Northern Ghana*. Frankfurt: Africa Magna Verlag.

Jansen, J. and Gauthier, J-G. 1973. *Ancient Art of the Northern Cameroons: Sao and Fali.* Oosterhout: Anthropological Publications.

Kankpeyeng, B., and Nkumbaan, S. 2009. Ancient Shrines? New Insights on the Koma Land Sites of Northern Ghana, in: Magnavita, S., Koté, L., Breunig, P., and Idé, O. (eds.). *Crossroads/Carrefour Sahel.* Frankfurt: Africa Magna Verlag, 193-202.

Kankpeyeng, B., Nkumbaan, S., and Insoll, T. 2011. Indigenous Cosmology, Art Forms and Past Medicinal Practices: Towards an Interpretation of Ancient Koma Land Sites in Northern Ghana. *Anthropology and Medicine* 18, 205-216.

Kröger, F. 2010, *First Notes on Koma Culture.* Berlin: Lit Verlag.

Kyriakidis, E. 2007. *The Archaeology of Ritual.* Los Angeles: Cotsen Institute of Archaeology.

Lange, D. 1989. Preliminarires pour une Histoire des Sao. *Journal of Africa History* 30: 189-210.

Lebeuf, J-P. 1962. *Archéologie Tchadienne.* Paris: Hermann.

Lebeuf, J-P. and Masson Detourbet, A. 1950. *La Civilisation du Tchad.* Paris: Payot.

Lebeuf, J-P., Treinen-Claustre, F. and Courtin, J. 1980. *Le Gisement Sao de Mdaga.* Paris: Societe d'Ethnographie.

Merrifield, R. 1987. *The Archaeology of Ritual and Magic.* London: Batsford.

Preston Blier, S. 1995. *African Vodun. Art, Psychology, and Power.* Chicago: University of Chicago Press.

Rountree, K., Morris, C., and Peatfield, A. 2012 (eds.). *Archaeology of Spiritualities.* New York: Springer.

Turner, V. 1967. *The Forest of Symbols.* Ithaca: Cornell University Press.

Turner, V. 1969. *The Ritual Process.* Harmondsworth: Penguin.

Whitley, D. and Hays-Gilpin, K. 2008 (eds.). *Belief in the Past.* Walnut Creek: Left Coast Press.

Chapter 1

The passage of matter

Transformations of objects and ritual meanings in the Neolithic of the Near East

Marc Verhoeven[1]

Abstract

On the basis of a discussion of formation processes, fragmentation and the relationship between material culture and memory, this contribution explores the symbolic transformations of objects of stone and bone with probable ritual and religious significance in the Neolithic of the Near East.

Keywords: *transformations, formation processes, fragmentation, memory, ritual, Neolithic, Near East.*

Introduction

The concept of ritual failure is mainly based on the idea of collapse and termination of the social and symbolic functions and meanings of ceremonial practices. At first sight, the shift from the general use of evocative and dominant ritual symbolism in the Pre-Pottery Neolithic in the Near East to the employment of rather inconspicuous objects in the subsequent Pottery Neolithic would be an example of such a ritual collapse (Simmons 2007; Verhoeven 2002*a*; 2002*b*).[2] However, notwithstanding major changes, in the Pottery Neolithic some of the earlier practices were continued.[3] In this case, and I suspect in many others too, it is more appropriate to speak of a *transformation* instead of a termination of ritual. With this idea in mind, this paper deals with the life cycle of (ritual) objects, particularly with the way in which materials and meanings were transformed. Briefly discussing formation processes, fragmentation and the 'objectification' of

---

[1] RAAP Archaeological Consultancy, the Netherlands, marc.verhoeven@yahoo.com.
[2] Examples of ritual objects in the Pre-Pottery Neolithic are decorated human skulls, statues and large stone pillars decorated with animals, while in the Pottery Neolithic small human and animal figurines made of clay are typical.
[3] *E.g.* the use of figurines and the manipulation of (human) skulls.

memory, this contribution focuses on symbolic transformations of objects of stone and bone with probable ritual and religious significance after their 'first life' in the Neolithic (*c.* 8500 and 6000 cal BC) of the Near East (Syria, Turkey and Israel).

Formation processes

Broken and abandoned objects (discard and refuse) have received much attention in processual archaeology (see *e.g.* Binford 1983; Goldberg *et al.* 1993; Rathje and Murphy 1992; Schiffer 1987), mainly in the context of the study of the formation of the archaeological record, *i.e.* of formation processes. A wealth of valuable data about the life cycles of objects has been generated by these studies. However, an over-enthusiastic systematization, based on a natural science approach, has in many instances led to a too rigid formulation of predictable laws of human and artefactual behaviour. As a consequence, and despite their importance, formation processes are not regularly dealt with anymore. Nevertheless, many archaeologists still think in terms of traditional formation processes theory, as indicated in figure 3. Here we see a flow model of the life cycle of artefacts as formulated in the 1970s by Michael Schiffer (Schiffer 1972). A basic distinction has been made between the so-called systemic and archaeological contexts, *i.e.* between living and 'dead' cultural systems. Within the systemic context objects are procured, manufactured, used, recycled and eventually discarded. In the archaeological context the discarded objects become refuse, which designates the end of their 'life'.

In figure 4 the former scheme has been adapted, focusing on discard and refuse. Three important adjustments have been made. First, in order to avoid the – often negative – modern/Western connotations, the terms discard and refuse have been changed into the more neutral terms broken and abandoned. Second, as will be shown in this paper, such objects often continue to have value in society; therefore abandoned/broken objects have been included in the systemic context. Third, it is indicated that – like all things – such objects are not only functional implements; they have symbolic dimensions as well. In other words, they are not only used; they are also interpreted and experienced, by people both in the past and in the present. In fact, precisely due to their 'death' and (deliberate) destruction, abandoned structures and broken artefacts may be transformed into important meaningful and symbolic elements. Moreover, according to animistic beliefs, in many cultures all over the world material objects, whether complete or broken, are regarded as being very much alive and active, especially in the contexts of cosmology, religion and ritual (see *e.g.* Willerslev 2007). The following sections present some approaches that explicitly pay attention to such transformations as well as to the symbolic and cognitive dimensions of material culture.

Fragmentation and enchainment

In his book *Fragmentation in Archaeology*, Chapman (2000) has analysed the meanings of broken objects in prehistoric societies in southeastern Europe. In general, fragmentation or breakage is due to accidents, may occur after deposition or is deliberate, often resulting in structured depositions. It is important to

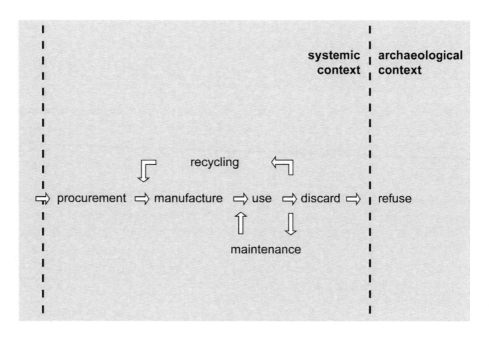

Figure 3. Formation processes: simplified flow model of the life cycle of artefacts in systemic and archaeological contexts (based on figure 1 of Schiffer 1972).

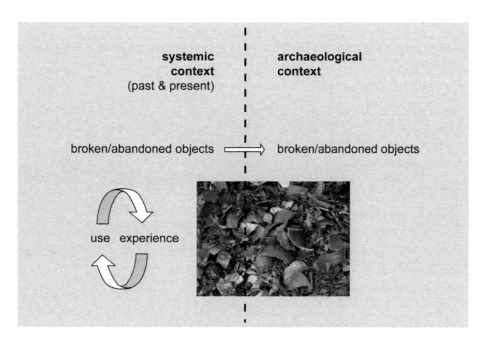

Figure 4. Formation processes: the role of broken and abandoned objects.

distinguish between broken but *complete* objects (such as in burials) and broken and *incomplete* objects. The latter are the subject of Chapman's study. There are four traditional explanations for the presence of such objects in the archaeological record. First, such items may be the remains of accidental breakage, or are broken as a result of use. Second, objects may have been deliberately buried because they were broken. Especially Garfinkel (1994) has advocated such a view, arguing that broken special and ritual objects in the Neolithic and Chalcolithic of the Near East were too sacred to just dispose of, and were therefore deliberately deposited. Third, objects may have been ritually 'killed' and then deposited. The reasons for this practice include fear of pollution, reluctance of reuse, and avoidance of association with objects of the deceased (Grinsell 1960). Fourth, it has been argued by some that objects were broken in order to disperse fertility in the settlement and its surroundings (*e.g.* Japanese Jomon figurines).

Alternatively, Chapman (2000) proposes that deliberately broken objects were primarily used in so-called *enchainment*. Enchainment denotes the succeeding chain of personal relations through the exchange of objects (Chapman 2000, 5).[4] More generally, the notion is based on the belief that in many societies – past and present – people and objects are not strictly separated (as in modern Western society), but are closely related instead. People adopt qualities of objects and *vice versa*. Thus people are objectified and objects are personified. As long as the object remains inalienable these links continue, even when objects are exchanged. In this respect, anthropologist Weiner (1992) writes about the paradox of 'keeping-while-giving' in a study on exchange in Oceanic societies. Meant is the transfer of social and supernatural values, which can benefit exchange partners.

A matter of memory

The problem with enchainment is that in many cases (*e.g.* pottery fragmentation) it is virtually impossible to distinguish between deliberate and non-deliberate fragmentation. The idea, however, does make us aware of the crucial role of material culture in the construction of memory.

Clearly, memory and remembrance, which can be personal or collective, are things of the human mind. It is also clear from recent studies, however, that memories are embedded and supported within a material framework.[5] Whether in theoretical terms it is called *habitus* (Bourdieu 1977), *structuration* (Giddens 1979), *objectification* (Miller 1987), *dwelling* (Ingold 2000) or *engagement* and *materiality* (Boivin 2008; DeMarrais *et al.* 2004; Meskell ed. 2005; Miller ed.

---

4 According to Chapman (2000, 6), enchainment works as follows: First, two people involved in establishing a social relationship and/or an economic transaction agree on an object appropriate to the interaction and break it in parts, each keeping one or more parts as a token of the relationship. The fragments are then kept until reconstitution of the relationship is required. Finally, parts may be deposited in a structured manner. *Pars pro toto*, then, each part of a broken objects stands for both the artefact and the persons related in the exchange. In other words, fragments of objects not only refer to their complete form, but also to past makers and owners.

5 As denoted by *materiality*, a term nowadays in vogue for the well-established post-processual notion that material culture is active, see *e.g.* Hodder 1982.

2005), it is clear that there is an active and dialectical relationship between objects and people. Objects shape people as much as people shape objects. By means of interacting with objects, *i.e.* by social practice and by dwelling among them, humans learn about their specific traditions and culture. Given its immediate presence and protective nature, the house is a principal location for engendering such knowledge (habitus), but in fact we pick up clues about expected behaviour in many other contexts. Ultimately the transmission of information by material culture and our lives are based on experience and remembrance; if we would forget all we encounter and perceive, we would not live very long or well (see *e.g.* Butler ed. 1989; Casey 1987; Coleman 1992; Connerton 1989; Le Goff 1992; Van Dyke and Alcock eds. 2003 and Williams ed. 2003).

Especially in non-literate prehistoric societies, in which writing as a basic information system was lacking, material culture must have been of the utmost importance for the constitution of persons and society. Monuments, for instance, as a material presence of the past, recall histories and evoke memories. As Alcock notes, monuments are a form of *inscribed memorial practice*, favouring a conservative transmission of cultural information (Alcock 2002, see also Bradley 1998). *Incorporated memorial practice*, on the other hand, denotes performative ceremonies, which generate sensory and emotional experiences that result in habitual memory. Especially the use of spectacular or dramatic sensory and emotional media results in the creation and transmission of memories. According to Whitehouse (2004) this is the result of the *imagistic mode of ritual*, characterized by a low frequency and high arousal. *Doctrinal rituals*, on the other hand, are marked by a high frequency and low arousal.

The apparently deliberate conflagration of a Pottery Neolithic settlement (*c.* 5970 cal BC) at Tell Sabi Abyad I in northern Syria as part of an extended funerary and abandonment ritual is a good example of the imagistic mode. The probably most important effect of the ritual was the impression of a very dramatic act in memory, as the heat, colours and smell produced by a large fire provided an intensive stimulation of the senses. This plurality and intensity of experience probably also played a role on a cognitive level, as there was a sense of order, with things that were intentionally brought to an end, but also a sense of disorder, with all the chaos that the fire engendered (Verhoeven 2010, 39). An example of doctrinal ritual practice would be the production and use of small figurines, including the deliberate breakage of these which has been attested at many Neolithic sites (*e.g.* Verhoeven 2007). The relatively high frequency and low arousal of such practices does not mean that they were insignificant with regard to the transmission of memories. Rather, they were probably triggers for emotions and experiences at the level of the individual and the small group.

Deliberately broken and destroyed objects thus have the capacity to act as 'vehicles for evoking remembrance', to paraphrase Jones (2004, 167, see also Jones 2007). It is important to realize that it is not necessarily the object itself, but the *action* in which the object is involved that is most significant. For example, many ceramic anthropomorphic figurines from the Upper Palaeolithic Pavlovian (29,000-25,000 years ago) of Central Europe were left broken in fireplaces. It has been argued that it was their destruction, *i.e.* their explosion in the fire, that made them meaningful, instead of their physical presence, and that they were not meant to be viewed (Verpoorte 2001). In a similar vein, with regard to human figurines with apparently removable heads at Neolithic Çatalhöyük (*c.* 7400-6000 cal BC)[6] in central Turkey, Meskell (2008, 381) has suggested that the potential of figurines to change identity by means of manipulation of their heads indicates that they were part of processes and not just static forms. Such figurines, and indeed many other objects, probably acted as vehicles for story-telling and remembrance, *i.e.* history-making (Meskell 2008, 379). As Jones points out, it is important to realize that material culture does not simply 'freeze' or 'fix' memory to be recalled later. Rather, remembrance is a dialogue between object and person, which can differ according to circumstances and contexts. Finally, I would like to point out that, apart from remembrance, we should pay attention to forgetting. We shall see that, just like the creation and maintenance of memory, activities focused on forgetting and the act of forgetting itself have important cultural implications.

Stones and bones

The above discussion has indicated that broken, abandoned and destroyed artefacts can continue to have a role after their initial 'life'. In fact, in many instances it is precisely due to their 'death', breaking, destruction, and so on, that they become meaningful. In the following, this will be exemplified with a number of examples of the changing symbolic and probably ritual and religious significance of objects of stone and of bones.

Stones

Nevali Çori is a site located in the Taurus foothills in southeastern Turkey and dating from the Pre-Pottery Neolithic B (PPNB, *c.* 8500-7900 cal BC). Excavations at the site have revealed large stone buildings that were marked by terrazzo floors, interior benches, niches, large anthropomorphic T-shaped pillars and large stone sculpture depicting both humans and animals. Undoubtedly, we here have the remains of ritual buildings (Hauptmann 1993; 1999; 2007; Hauptmann and Özdoğan 2007). There were three such buildings, which were fitted together like a Russian matryoshka doll. The final building 3 was set within the walls of the former building 2, which seems to have been built on building 1 (Hauptmann 1999, figs. 7-9). Interestingly, most of the large stone sculpture was broken and from secondary contexts, as it was found embedded within the walls and buried in the benches of buildings 2 and 3 (see Lichter 2007, catalogue figure nrs. 96-99, pages 289-290). For instance, the famous 'snake head' (part of a larger statue), depicting a stylized human head with a snake at the back, was found in a niche in the east wall of building 3. Likewise, two so-called birdmen, representing creatures both human and bird-like, had been

---

6   Çatalhöyük dates from the Late Pre-Pottery Neolithic B (PPNB) and Early Pottery Neolithic.

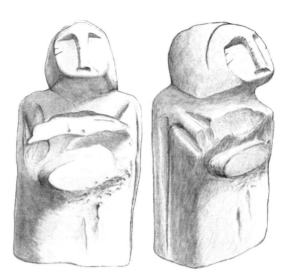

Figure 5. The 'birdman' from Nevali Çori, which was embedded in a stone bench on the east side of the most recent phase (III) of the ritual building at the site. The two protrusions at the front are generally interpreted as folded wings. Middle PPNB, c. 8500-7950 cal BC. Height: 23.1 cm, width: 11.6 cm. Redrawn from figure 12 from Hauptmann 1999.

incorporated into a wall of building 3 (Figure 5). An approximately one-metre high so-called totem pole, again consisting of a combination of a human and a bird, was found embedded in a bench of building 2.

It is very likely that this broken and secondarily-used stone sculpture stems from earlier phases of the building (Hauptmann 1999, 74-76). The fact that buildings 2 and 3 were built within the confines of predecessors, and not next to it or in another place, strongly suggests that they tapped into the power of former structures. Thus, preceding buildings and their sculpture were probably remembered for the performances and rituals carried out within their confines. Old and often broken sculpture was hidden in plastered walls and in benches of new buildings. As Garfinkel has argued (see above), this might have been done because these objects were too significant to be merely disposed. It is as if the new structures needed to be 'injected' with the ritual power of former structures. Some of the sculpture was present but invisible. However, if something is invisible it does not follow that it is forgotten. Rather it means that only people who experienced the original sculpture and those who incorporated it into new buildings knew about it and remembered it. Thus, hiding things and acts of secrecy may have added to the mythic power of objects and buildings. Some of the sculpture apparently needed to be both remembered and forgotten. Perhaps to be forgotten by the public and to be remembered by religious specialists?

As this example shows, memory and forgetting can apply to the same context. In other words: different memorial practices may be at work at any one time. Moreover, the same objects may have invoked different experiences and memories. In this respect, the ritual buildings at Nevali Çori had several ambiguous aspects. First, there was the merging of the old and the new in architecture as well as in sculpture. Then there was some sculpture that was of an ambiguous nature, both human and animal. Finally, some of the sculpture was present but invisible. These contradictory aspects, so typical of ritual practice, and especially their remembered history would have made the buildings special and powerful.

Bones

Apart from objects of stone, human and animal bones[7] were used in many different ways for symbolic and, very likely, ritual purposes. First of all, burials of humans and/ or animals should be mentioned as occasions for all kinds of ceremonies which were probably primarily related to ancestors. This need not be elaborated upon here.

Another, quite dramatic, example of the ritual use of bones is the wide-spread evidence for the manipulation of human skulls in the Pre-Pottery and occasionally the Pottery Neolithic, as a short-hand often termed the skull cult. The evidence consists of skull removal, skull caching, skull decoration and skull deformation. Perhaps most intriguing are the decorated skulls: by means of *e.g.* plaster, collagen, paint and cowrie shells as eyes these skulls were probably meant to portray and commemorate the deceased (Bienert 1991; Bonogofsky 2001). Skulls were probably especially honoured because of their vital powers or life force, something which has been documented in a host of ethnographic studies (Verhoeven 2002*a*). See for example what Smidt (1993, 21) writes on traditional initiation rituals of the Asmat, who live in the coastal swamp forests of southwest New Guinea:

> 'It was impossible for boys to become men without taking a head. A man's vital strength is said to be particularly present in the skull, and the life force of another provided the energy necessary for a boy to make the jump to manhood. Initiation traditionally took place not long after the boys head-hunting raid. At one stage in the group ceremony, each of the boys held a recently severed skull in front of his crotch, and meditated on it. At this stage, the young man was given the head-hunted enemy's name, and his vital strength assimilated into the group. To ensure the identification between initiate and victim was as close as possible, the boy mediated on the head for two or three days, and was also rubbed with the victim's blood and his burned hair. These acts were a tribute to the power of the enemy'.

There is actually no evidence for head-hunting in the Neolithic Near East; the example serves to illustrate the special significance which is often attached to human heads. In fact, in this period there was a preoccupation with heads, head removal and circulation ('headedness', *cf.* Meskell 2008, see also Hodder and Meskell 2011) of both humans and animals.

As to the heads of animals, the skulls and/or horns of cattle (*bucrania*) were often kept in Neolithic buildings. Especially Çatalhöyük is famous for this practice. Most of the cattle horns at the site come from large male wild animals, of which the postcranial remains were characteristic of special feasting deposits. This suggests that cattle horns were kept and displayed in commemoration of the hunting, slaughter and consumption of large and dangerous animals, which would have endowed hunters and feasters with considerable status (Twiss and Russell 2009, 30). Especially bull horns were displayed

---

7   'Bones' designate all skeletal parts, including skulls and horns.

Figure 6. Pillars with horn cores of wild bulls on the northeastern platform in building 77 in area 4040 at the East mound at Çatalhöyük, as excavated in 2010. Early Ceramic Neolithic, c. 7400-6000 cal BC. © Çatalhöyük Research Project, photo by Jason Quinlan.

on platforms and walls: see figure 6. However, it appears that many installed horns were invisibly integrated into the architecture as well. At other Neolithic sites[8] cattle horns were also concealed in or under walls, floors and benches (Russell 2009, 20). Thus, both display and concealment played a role. Perhaps display (commemoration) primarily focused on directly affecting people (promotion of status), while hiding (forgetting) and 'interiorization' aimed at the transmission of the power of heads and horns to the buildings and the production of secret knowledge of ritual specialists?[9] Cattle horns were particularly favoured for symbolic purposes, but horns of other animals were occasionally used as well. At Tell Sabi Abyad, for instance, the horns of wild sheep were included in a series of large oval objects of clay that surrounded two dead bodies on the roof of a building. These 'monsters' played a role in the already mentioned ritual conflagration of a settlement, apparently as part of a death and abandonment ritual.

Finally, I would like to mention the various associations between human and animal bones at the PPNB site of Kfar Hahoresh (8500-6750 cal BC) located in northern Israel. The site was probably a mortuary centre, given the fact that in all the areas of excavation quite unusual and spectacular remains of funeral ceremonies have been encountered. In the so-called *Bos* pit the bones of eight aurochs were deposited after their meat had been consumed, probably as part of a funerary feast. The pit was then covered by a human burial which was plastered over. After a while, the skull was removed. The aurochs skulls were also absent (Goring-Morris and

---

8   *E.g.* Mureybet, Halula, 'Abr 3, Dja'de in Syria and Ginnig in Iraq.
9   Cattle horns at Çatalhöyük and other sites were found in different contexts and deposits, probably indicating that they played symbolic key roles in a variety of rituals (Twiss and Russell 2009, 28; Hodder, ed. 2011).

Horwitz 2007). Apparently there was a special concern with establishing relations between humans and animals, as also indicated by a well-preserved human plastered skull, which was found just above a complete but headless gazelle carcass. Another such therianthropic context is represented by a pit in which mostly human long bones had been intentionally arranged in such a manner that when viewed from above they depicted an animal in profile, possibly a wild boar, an aurochs, or a lion (Goring-Morris 2000; 2008). These special associations of human and animal bones may appear very strange at first sight, and the precise meanings elude us, but in a general sense such use of both animal and human bones was one of the best ways to symbolize the links between the related domains of feasting, death, humans and animals. One category, bone, both typified and related these different processes and beings.

Heads and horns

Notwithstanding the multitude of symbolic expressions and meanings, I believe that there is a general reason for the symbolic, ritual and religious importance of bones. Bones are the material remains of once living beings. This is a very basic observation, but it makes us aware of the peculiar status of bones: they are part of both the living and the dead. The bones of animals, specifically mammals, refer to species that are both close to and different from humans. Bones are the durable and surviving remains of mortal bodies. Moreover, they refer to humans and animals that are no longer there, but with whom people might have had close and personal experiences. In other words, they play a major role in the construction of personal and collective memory.

As we have seen, some skeletal remains were especially favoured, *viz.* skulls and horns. While the objectives for and meanings of this preferential treatment may have been varied, the widespread use in different regions and at different times strongly suggests some underlying motive. I would argue that it had much to do with the fact that the head is the main means of perceiving the world and of communicating with the environment. It is also the location of the enigmatic brain. In fact, as we have seen, in many cultures the head is taken to be the locus of the vital power or life force of beings. The head is also the most personal aspect of a body and the main locus of identity. It is the first and most immediate element of encounter and recognition, in which especially the eyes play a pivotal role. Skulls, therefore, are powerful and dominant symbols; the face of death with large hollow 'eyes' and grinning teeth has inspired people all over the world, from prehistory to the present day. Likewise, animal horns are particularly compelling symbols (*e.g.* Rice1998). Well-developed horns signify the power of animals and to capture these horns, *e.g.* by hunting, is a sign of success and courage in many cultures. Moreover, as opposed to most other mammal bones, horns are very iconical and immediately signify particular animals (*e.g.* bulls, sheep, goats). For instance, the killing and communal consumption of large bulls in feasts and particularly the prestige of the feast giver(s) is most effectively symbolized by displaying the horns of the animals.

We have seen that the symbolic power of bones was actively used and manipulated in the Neolithic Near East. The transformations from (1) living beings to (2) dead bodies to (3) bones to (4) incorporation in the world of the living meant that bones could be parts of both life and death. Like the re-used stone objects, bones linked the past to the present. They were among the most direct and powerful materializations of history and of remembrance of relatives and other beings that shaped the world.

Conclusion

I hope to have shown that 'endings' like death, discard, abandonment, and so on, should in many cases not be perceived as terminations or failures, but as transformations, or beginnings of something new. Notions of enchainment, inscribed memorial practice, incorporated material practice, imagistic modes of ritual and the various examples of the 'cultural biographies' (Kopytoff 1986) of – ritual – objects of stone and bone have made it clear that things can have many life cycles and that they in fact can become extra meaningful after their 'first lives'. Their material presence, their history and the images and memories they evoke are all part of the complex web of past, present and future relations of beings and things. Rituals are among the most important mechanisms for getting a grip on this complexity, as they provide means for explaining, understanding and regulating society and cosmos (*e.g.* Guthrie 1993). In other words, they accompany the passage of time and the transformation of matter and thought. In a way, through ritual the past never ends.

Acknowledgements

I would like to thank Vasiliki Koutrafouri for inviting me to publish in this volume. Ans Bulles corrected the English text. Mikko Kriek made the drawing of the 'birdman'.

References

Alcock, S. 2002. *Archaeologies of the Greek past: landscape, monuments, and memories.* Cambridge: Cambridge University Press.

Bienert, H.D. 1991. Skull cult in the prehistoric Near East. *Journal of Prehistoric Religion* 5, 9-13.

Binford, L.R. 1983. *In pursuit of the past: decoding the archaeological record.* London: Thames and Hudson.

Bonogofsky, M. 2001. *An osteo-archaeological examination of the ancestor cult during the Pre-Pottery Neolithic B period in the Levant.* Ann Arbor: University Microfilms International.

Bradley, R. 1998. *The significance of monuments: on the shaping of human experience in Neolithic and Bronze Age Europe.* London: Routlege.

Bourdieu, P. 1977. *Outline of a theory of practice.* Cambridge: Cambridge University Press.

Butler, T. 1989 (ed). *Memory: history, culture and the mind.* Oxford: Blackwell.

Casey, E.S. 1987. *Remembering: a phenomenological study.* Bloomington: Indiana: University Press.

Chapman, J. 2000. *Fragmentation in archaeology: people, places and broken objects in the prehistory of South Eastern Europe.* London and New York: Routledge.

Coleman, J. 1992. *Ancient and medieval memories: studies in the reconstruction of the past.* Cambridge: Cambridge University Press.

Connerton, P. 1989. *How societies remember.* Cambridge: Cambridge University Press.

DeMarrais, E., C. Gosden, C. and Renfrew, C. 2004 (eds.). *Rethinking materiality: the engagement of mind with the material world.* Cambridge: McDonald Institute for Archaeological Research.

Garfinkel, Y. 1994. Ritual burial of cultic objects: the earliest evidence. *Cambridge Archaeological Journal* 4/2, 159-188.

Giddens, A. 1979. *Central problems in social theory: action, structure and contradiction in social analysis.* Berkeley: University of California Press.

Goldberg, P., Nash, D.T. and Petraglia, M.D. 1993 (eds.). *Formation processes in archaeological context.* Madison: Prehistory Press.

Goring-Morris, A.N. 2000. The quick and the dead: the social context of aceramic Neolithic mortuary practices as seen from Kfar Hahoresh, in: Kuijt, I. (ed.). *Life in Neolithic farming communities: social organization, identity, and differentiation.* New York: Kluwer Academic/Plenum Publishers, 103-135.

Goring-Morris, A.N. 2008. Kefar Ha-Horesh, in: Stern, E. (ed.). *The new encyclopedia of archaeological excavations in the Holy Land.* Vol. 5. Jerusalem: Israel Exploration Society and Biblical Archaeology Society, 1907-1909.

Goring-Morris, A.N. and Horwitz, L.K. 2007. Funerals and feasts during the Pre-Pottery Neolithic B of the Near East. *Antiquity* 81, 902-919.

Grinsell, L.V. 1960. The breaking of objects as a funeral rite. *Folklore* 71, 475-491.

Guthrie, S. 1993. *Faces in the clouds: a new theory of religion.* Oxford: Oxford University Press.

Hauptmann, H. 1993. Ein Kultgebäude in Nevali Çori, in: Frangipane, M., Hauptmann, H., Liverani, M., Matthiae, P. and Mellink, M. (eds.). *Between the rivers and over the mountains.* Rome: University of Rome, 37-69.

Hauptmann, H. 1999. The Urfa region, in: Özdoğan, M. and Başgelen, N. (eds.). *Neolithic in Turkey: the cradle of civilization: new discoveries.* Istanbul: Arkeoloji ve Sanat Yayinlari, 65-86.

Hauptmann, H. 2007. Nevali Çori, in: Lichter, C. (ed.). *Vor 12.000 Jahren in Anatolien: die ältesten Monumente der Menschheit.* Karlsruhe: Badisches Landesmuseum, 86-87.

Hauptmann, H. and Özdoğan, M. 2007. Die Neolitische Revolution in Anatolien, in Lichter, C. (ed.). *Vor 12.000 Jahren in Anatolien: Die ältesten Monumente der Menschheit.* Karlsruhe: Badisches Landesmuseum, 26-36.

Hodder, I. 1982. *Symbols in action.* Cambridge: Cambridge University Press.

Hodder, I. and Meskell, L. 2011. A "curious and sometimes a trifle macabre artistry": some aspects of symbolism in Neolithic Turkey. *Current Anthropology* 52/2, 235-263.

Hodder, I. 2011 (ed.). *Religion in the emergence of civilization: Çatalhöyük as a case study.* Cambridge: Cambridge University Press.

Ingold, T. 2000. *The perception of the environment: essays in livelihood, dwelling and skill.* London and New York: Routledge.

Jones, A. 2004. Matter and memory: colour, remembrance and the Neolithic/Bronze Age transition, in: DeMarrais, E., Gosden, C. and Renfrew, C. (eds.). *Rethinking materiality: the engagement of mind with the material world.* Cambridge: McDonald Institute for Archaeological Research, 167-179.

Jones, A. 2007. *Memory and material culture.* Cambridge: Cambridge University Press.

Kopytoff, I. 1986. The cultural biography of things: commoditization as process, in: Appadurai, A. (ed.). *The social life of things: commodities in cultural perspective.* Cambridge: Cambridge University Press, 64-91.

Le Goff, J. 1992. *History and memory.* New York: Columbia University Press.

Lichter, C. 2007 (ed.). *Vor 12.000 Jahren in Anatolien: die ältesten Monumente der Menschheit.* Karlsruhe: Badisches Landesmuseum.

Meskell, L. 2008. The nature of the beast: curating animals and ancestors at Çatalhöyük. *World Archaeology* 40/3, 373-389.

Meskell, L. 2005 (ed.). *Archaeologies of materiality.* Malden: Blackwell.

Miller, D. 1987. *Material culture and mass consumption.* Oxford: Blackwell.

Miller, D. 2005 (ed.). *Materiality.* Durham: Duke University Press.

Rathje, W. and Murphy, C. 1992. *Rubbish!: the archaeology of garbage.* New York: Harper Collins.

Rice, M. 1998. *The power of the bull.* London and New York: Routledge.

Schiffer, M.B. 1972. Archaeological context and systemic context. *American Antiquity* 37/2, 156-165.

Schiffer, M.B. 1987. *Formation processes of the archaeological record.* Albuquerque: University of New Mexico Press.

Simmons, A. 2007. *The Neolithic Revolution in the Near East: transforming the human landscape.* Tucson: The University of Arizona Press.

Smidt, D. 1993. The Asmat: life, death and the ancestors, in: Smidt, D. (ed.). *Asmat art: woodcarvings of southwest New Guinea.* Leiden: Periplus Editions.

Twiss, K.C. and Russell, N. 2009. Taking the bull by the horns: ideology, masculinity, and cattle horns at Çatalhöyük (Turkey). *Paléorient* 35/2, 19-32.

Van Dyke, R. and Alcock, S. 2003 (eds.). *Archaeologies of memory.* Oxford: Blackwell.

Verhoeven, M. 2002*a*. Ritual and ideology in the Pre-Pottery Neolithic B of the Levant and south-east Anatolia. *Cambridge Archaeological Journal* 12/2, 233-258.

Verhoeven, M. 2002*b*. Transformations of society: the changing role of ritual and symbolism in the Pre-Pottery Neolithic B and Pottery Neolithic periods in the Levant and south-east Anatolia. *Paléorient* 28/1, 5-14.

Verhoeven, M. 2007. Loosing one's head in the Neolithic: on the interpretation of headless figurines. *Levant* 39, 175-183.

Verhoeven, M. 2010. Igniting transformations: on the social impact of fire, with special reference to the Neolithic of the Near East, in: Hansen, S. (ed.). *Leben auf dem Tell als soziale Praxis. Beiträge des Internationalen Symposiums in Berlin vom 26.- 27. Februar 2007. Kolloquien zur Vor- und Frühgeschichte* 14, 25-43.

Verpoorte, A. 2001. *Places of art, traces of fire: a contextual approach to anthropomorphic figurines in the Pavlovian (Central Europe, 29-24 kyr BP).* Leiden: Archaeological Studies, Leiden University, No. 8.

Weiner, A. 1992. *Inalienable possessions: the paradox of keeping-while-giving.* Berkeley: University of California Press.

Whitehouse, H. 2004. *Modes of religiosity: a cognitive theory of religious transmission.* Walnut Creek: AltaMira press.

Willerslev, E. 2007. *Soul hunters: hunting, animism and personhood among the Siberian Yukaghirs.* Berkely: University of California Press.

Williams, H. 2003 (ed.). *Archaeologies of remembrance: death and memory in past societies.* New York: Kluwer Academic.

Chapter 2

The sky almost never falls on your head – why ritual rarely fails

Jeff Sanders[1]

Abstract

This paper explores the flexible nature of ritual practice, its ability to draw upon and incorporate elements of both local and much wider traditions. Although often considered to be conservative elements of society, ritual and religion are good at incorporating the new and novel, naturalising them within an established order. Identifying when rituals fail, however, is challenging, especially for the archaeological record of Scottish prehistory. These issues are explored in the context of the Ballachulish figure, an artefact found in the West of Scotland, created at some point between the Late Bronze and Iron Ages. This enigmatic object has been subject to a range of interpretation which serves to highlight the challenges of attempting to identify failure, or change generally, in ritual practice.

Keywords: *Scotland, ritual, Ballachulish figure.*

> *The Soothsayer: "By Borvo, God of the springs, and by Damona the heifer, and no matter what the skeptics think, I see that the sky will not fall on your heads, and that when the storm is over the weather will improve"* (Goscinny and Underzo 2004, 11).

Introduction

In archaeology it is generally the end of things that are most visible. As such, persistence and duration are often downplayed in favour of narratives based upon change. A recurring feature of prehistoric communities is that they are resilient, constantly developing mechanisms to cope with changing circumstances. The ultimate effects of this can only be seen over the long term, as decisions made

---

[1] 'Dig it! 2015', Society of Antiquaries of Scotland, National Museum of Scotland, Edinburgh EH1 1JF, jeff@socantscot.org.

generations previously are played out, often with unintended consequences. This is as true for ritual elements of society as it is for other aspects. Ritual is as intertwined in society as subsistence, culture or craft production, and as such, ritual success or otherwise is linked to society more broadly. Change therefore needs to be traced over a number of temporal and spatial scales to be fully grasped; otherwise sudden apparent 'breaks' or failures will continue to be identified, but not understood. It will be argued that narratives of 'success' or 'failure' based on archaeological remains are better considered over the Longue Durée and recast in terms of change more generally.

Ritual appears to form an integral element of human life: it is resilient and can adapt and incorporate new elements within an apparently timeless order (Bell, 1997, 145-150). How to measure 'success' or 'failure' in a ritual context is therefore challenging as it is both adaptive and actively masks failure. These challenges are accentuated when only archaeological data is available. However, archaeology can supply the time depth, and therefore the unfolding of unintended consequences, which might allow an exploration of ritual failure (as well as success) over a suitably long chronological scale. This also requires the wider social context to be fully understood; a context that stretches out into the landscape and operates on a number of scales, from the individual act, to wider contemporary social themes that may have an international element.

'Ritual' is of course a category imposed from an 'etic' perspective (Kyriakidis 2007*b*, 292-3) and caveats must be applied to any interpretation. If ritual is taken to be a fundamental element of human society however, there should be a reflex ritual empathy that if not providing a shared vocabulary, at least enables a basic foundation for understanding. Ritual practice has been theorized relatively intensively from an archaeological perspective (see Insoll, 2004). The reconstruction of other forms of past activity – subsistence strategies for example – appears far more confidently drawn, even though they are also an etic category, open to theoretical scrutiny. The difficulties of defining 'ritual' have led researchers to group together characteristics of ritual practice that often recur in various combinations, thus building an emergent view of ritual. Verhoeven (2011) outlines several of these, of which a number are particularly accessible and identifiable through archaeology. This paper will primarily look at 'religious ritual' *i.e.* that which appears to appeal to a supernatural or 'other' being, which may form a fundamental theme in ritual practice (McCauley and Lawson 2007). Notions of the 'sacred' and the 'profane', and their applicability in a prehistoric context, have been debated (Bradley 2005). This author takes the view that in past (as well as present) society it is better to view this as a continuum rather than a binary opposition, accepting the 'blurring' that this entails. However, there are contexts where primarily 'religious' rather than non-religious, ritual practice can be identified.

In this paper, ritual is viewed as constituted by repetitive action whereby the appearance of timelessness and subsequent naturalization of the current order ('traditionalism'; Bell 2007, 145-150), is either a central goal, or beneficial consequence, of ritual practice. The concept of 'ritualisation' (Bell 1992, 197-223) is also utilised as this places emphasis on the context of the ritual act, rather than a specific 'type' of material culture. The process of ritualisation involves the negotiation of norms and its success is contingent on the act of ritual – this serves to highlight the in-built flexibility of ritual as an arena where success or failure can be negotiated. Ritual is prefigured in that it is aimed toward an outcome, though there can be uncertainty both in the execution of the ritual and its end results. Failure or success of a ritual performance will therefore be based on agreed outcomes among those observing/participating (Bell 2007, 75). If a sacrifice to the gods is intended to ensure a rich harvest, the yardstick to measure the value of the harvest can be open to interpretation, and the degree to which, and causes of, a failure in the execution of a ritual similarly so (Hüsken 2007b, 352-3). Ritualisation also means that all categories of material culture contain potential ritual information, and not simply that considered 'odd' (Hodder 1982, 164). Thus ritualisation provides the bridge between the religious and non-religious rituals, meaning being dependent on context.

Ritual context is therefore essential in questions of failure, and this can be approached over a number of scales. Verhoeven's (2011, 126-7) idea of ritual context or 'framing' operates from individual to public scales, but how far that can extend into the landscape is not discussed. In the example of Ballachulish (see below), there are ritual elements that can be analysed in terms of the immediate environs of the site, whilst others are best understood within a local, regional or even international context. The chronological scale is also essential as aspects of ritual appear to be able to recur over long periods of time. Bradley (2002, 14) has noted that social memory in prehistoric societies has been estimated as potentially persisting for up to 200 hundred years unless 'special techniques' are employed. Ritual practice would certainly qualify as such a technique, with the potential to extend social memory considerably. Transitory or contingent elements can also be identified (even if these are intended to appear as 'timeless'), though the two categories can be separated over the deep view that archaeology affords – what is truly in for the Longue Durée can be uncovered.

The 'meaning' of ritual and the form that it takes has also been sought over different scales, from the structure of the mind (McCauley and Lawson 2007; Lévi-Strauss, 1968) to the functioning of society (Evans-Pritchard 1937; Radcliffe-Brown 1956; Rappaport 1999). Ritual practice serves as an effective medium for learning, for example, transforming the social role of individuals within a community through rites of passage (Bell 1997, 94-102) This is often effective through the deployment of danger (real or imagined), heightening the learning experience and subsequently making it easier to remember. McCauley and Lawson consider memory as the key to successful ritual (2007, 10) making the 'performance' of ritual the integral element. On a society-wide scale, religion has been characterised as socially conservative (*e.g.* Childe 1942). Ritual practised in such a context is highly effective as it attempts to mask time and change and thus acts as a 'brake' on social transformation. Ritualisation, however, opens up space for negotiation or contestation, although it does this within parameters that are pre-defined, so that although there may be the appearance of risk, or the possibility of change, this is a managed process (Hüsken 2007b, 341).

Superficially, this may appear to have the potential to subvert dominant practices or social organization, but may actually serve to increase the efficacy of the ritual by incorporating potentially harmful deviation within the ritual code (Turner 1969). Ritual performance may even exaggerate potential sources of conflict as a mechanism to release social tensions (Bell 1992, 71). Fundamental changes through ritual failure are therefore quite rare, as ritual is a mode of delivery designed to mask the more dynamic, subversive elements of a society. Ritual's association with repetition and an unchanging nature (Bell 1997) is part of why it works effectively as part of a masking process. Change appears most often during times of 'crises'external to the system that highlights the inner workings of the social order, free from the predefined parameters that ritual provides.

Ultimately, the very characteristics of ritual pre-figure it for survival, and the integral part ritualisation plays within a society, from an individual to group level, means that it is intimately bound up in a society's survival as a whole. Whether or not rituals and the form they take are selected from a pre-determined vocabulary in the mind (McCauley and Lawson 2007), fulfill a function in society (Evans-Pritchard 1937; Radcliffe-Brown 1956), or are a way of imposing some form of order on the effects of the external environment (Malinowski 1954; Tylor 1929), material culture has a lot to say as a constitutive element in each of the above (Donald 1991, Mithen1996 and McCauley and Lawson 2007). This paper will concentrate on one example from Scottish prehistory: a single ritual act at Ballachulish, in the West of Scotland, and from there look to explore wider themes in identifying ritual failure in prehistory.

Ritual in Scottish prehistory: Ballachulish

In the winter of 1880 workmen digging a drainage trench in Ballachulish Moss, Argyll, on the west coast of Scotland, uncovered a wooden statue. This came to be known as the 'Ballachulish figure' (Figure 7). It had been deliberately buried at the site and subsequently preserved by the boggy conditions. The figure was around 145 cm high, carved from a single piece of alder, and with two quartz peebles for eyes. It had been placed face down surrounded by twigs and branches probably indicating some form of basketry, while more substantial poles – possibly a framework for a 'wattled hut' – was laid on top of this (Stewart 1883, 22; Christison 1881). The figure has been radiocarbon dated to between c. 790-410 cal BC (HAR-6329; Ritchie 1997, 272), placing it around the transition from the Scottish Late Bronze Age to Iron Age.

Ballachulish Moss is found on the north side of a fast-flowing stretch of river that feeds into Loch Leven (Figure 8). The landscape is fjord-like, though the Moss forms a flat area of land separating otherwise mountainous terrain. The benefits of the area for travel combined with the flat elevation of the land would have ensured that the Moss would have been an attractive location for settlement. Broadly contemporary activity is suggested by finds at the nearby site at An Dunan, a potential fort site from which have been found iron fragments, a whetstone and crucibles for metal-working (PSAS 1970, 295). Other remains apparently from

Figure 7 (right). Photograph of the Ballachulish figure soon after discovery. The alder figure, 'rudely but boldly carved' (Stewart, 1883, 22), stood almost life-size with quartz pebbles inset into the eye sockets, with the right eye pebble larger than the left.
© National Museums Scotland. Licensor www.scran.ac.uk

Figure 8 (below). View of Ballachulish Moss, a flat area of land, forming a 'pocket' surrounded by a hilly landscape. The area would have been a fording point and provided the opportunity to control access to Loch Leven.
© British Geological Survey / NERC. All rights reserved.
Licensor www.scran.ac.uk

similar levels of the Moss include evidence of a substantial amount of flint-working (possibly associated with a circular wattled building) as well as wooden bowls and basins, ox and deer horns and a cask of 'bog butter' (Stewart 1883, 24), the latter considered a votive offering of the Iron Age and Medieval periods in Scotland and Ireland (Earwood 1997; see below).

There are parallels to both the figure and the mode of deposition that can be drawn over a number of scales, and which relate to the range of interpretations of what the Ballachulish figure represents. The main interpretations have included the figure being primarily used as: a) a shrine to ensure safe travel; b) a house god, c) a fertility symbol, d) a proxy for a ritually killed victim, and e) a boat prow/totem, and these will be considered in turn.

Ballachulish Moss is at a fording point for a dangerous stretch of water, it is also in an inlet from where people would have set out to sea, and would have gained access to inland waters from the coast (potentially controlled by sites such as An Dunan). There are dangers associated with all of these activities, as well as issues of control of rights of passage, and the Moss forms a liminal area (Brück 2011, 389) between the land and the sea, and the sea and inland waters. It is tempting then to interpret the Ballachulish figure as a traveller's shrine – possibly a god or other supernatural being to be placated or invoked to ensure safe passage. The location of the figure and the poles and wattling found in association with it might suggest an outdoor shrine (Christison 1881). Indeed, an early description referes to the figure (in a slightly tongue-in-cheek manner) as 'Our lady of the Ferry' (Stewart 1883, 24). The pedestal base had a carved recess that might provide the location for offerings, and gravel found still attached to the bottom of this suggests it was placed upright in the ground.

The interpretation of the figure as a house god draws on similar evidence to that of a traveller's shrine, though seeing the associated structural material as being reflective of a more 'domestic' arrangement (Armit 2005, 78-9; Piggott and Henderson 1958). The number of wooden and lithic artefacts found near to where the figure was found and the possible wattled hut (Stewart 1883, 24) might suggest a domestic craft production role. The fertility connection was drawn from the outset with the figure identified as a 'goddess (Stewart 1883, 21). A phallic symbol held in the figure's left hand was subsequently identified (Sheridan pers. comm.) and has served to reinforce this interpretation, along with broader parallels to fertility rites associated with deposition in bogs (Coles 1990; Bradley 1998, 170). A 'cross-sash' has also been identified carved into the figure's body, suggesting potential conceptual links to wealth as well as fertility (Coles and Coles 1996, 75).

The circumstances of the figure's deposition has also invited parallels with bog bodies, particularly the concept of ritual killing (*e.g.* Glob 1973, Chpt 1; Coles and Coles 1996, 60-62). The preservation of the figure's features suggests that it went into the bog as a one-off event and the presence of hurdling recalls the tradition of strapping down or covering bog bodies in other countries (Van der Sanden 1996, 95-99) often in association with wooden artefacts. Parallels have been drawn with interpretations of Irish figures made of alder and deposited in bogs, with the orange-red colour of cut alder used in folkloric connections with death (Stanley 2007, 190). Finally, the suggestion of the figure as a boat prow/totem reflects the initial interpretation of the artefact as of Norse origin (Christison 1881; Stewart 1883, 25-27). This saw the figure as a boat-based shrine discarded by sailors, although the Norse element was later disproven by radiocarbon dating. However, a maritime connection is seen in the presence of other figures associated with a boat at Roos Carr, Yorkshire and the Ballachulish area would have been an important location for maritime travel. Depictions in potentially contemporary rock art and bronze artefacts from Sweden (Coles 1990, 315-319, and 329-330; Coles and Coles 1996, 75-76) also provide parallels suggesting possible Scandinavian influence.

The role or meaning of the figure could of course have been something entirely different, or elements of several of these explanations combined: it is possible that the figure was used in a prow of a ship, converted to use in shrine as a god embodying both safe passage and fertility, before being 'ritually killed'. While no convincing parallel exists for the Ballachulish figure taken in its entirety, elements of its construction, use and deposition are reflected in other traditions (Coles 1990). The quartz used for the figure's eyes for example has long been associated with ritual usage in Scottish prehistory. Deposition in watery contexts is another recurring theme throughout later prehistory in Northern Europe. In Ireland, bog bodies may represent the 'decommissioning' of a king (Kelly 2012) and this may be a similar dismantling of a shrine to an old god. At this time in Scotland it is difficult to identify a norm in funerary rites: both due to lack of evidence, but also variety in what does survive, so it is difficult to identify 'special' treatment (Shapland and Armit 2012, 100). There are a number of Scottish bog bodies and although many are post-medieval in date (Turner 1995, 217-219), some remain undated (Coles and Coles 1996, 63) and could provide broader prehistoric parallels.

Coles (1990) draws comparisons to the Ballachulish figure with other wooden figures in Britain and Ireland, although it is the lack of direct parallels that she finds most striking. Nevertheless, she suggests a recurring pattern of intentional damage to the left side of the face, identified on the Ballachulish figure as well, and tentatively noting that this recurs in Scandinavian mythology (Coles 1990, 332). The phallic symbol and ambiguous sexual identity is another theme that can be traced through prehistory in other areas (Glob 1973, 182-185; Coles and Coles 1996, 75) and although the figure was confidently identified as a 'goddess' from the outset, the lack of breasts was noted (Stewart 1883, 23). The early accounts do not note the damage, but do consider the right eye pebble as being larger than the left (Stewart 1883, 23). The other artefacts, especially of flint, retrieved from the same area of bog have also led to the area being interpreted as a craft centre (Stewart 1883). There was also the discovery of 'bog butter' – the apparent sacrifice of a considerable amount of butter (a very important resource) – again finding parallels in Ireland and beyond, and relating to deposition in watery places. Bog butter is viewed as developing during the middle of the Iron Age, possibly reflecting a move to a more heavily pastoral economy (Earwood 1997, 34). The proximity of these finds hints at the importance of the Moss, potentially as both a centre for craft production and some form of sacral deposition. Finds of 2nd century

AD wooden 'pegs' from Pict's Knowe, an enclosure from Dumfries in south-west Scotland, provide an example of potentially 'functional' items that may have held a ritual significance (Crone, 2007) and may echo the ritualisation of 'functional' objects found near to the Ballachulish figure. Similarly, in many countries Late Bronze Age/ Iron Age hoarding appears to be more widely associated with fertility and food supply (Bradley 1998, 170), again hinting at the potential cross-over between subsistence activity and objects such as the Ballachulish figure. Survey of the Ballachulish Moss has investigated several potential Late Bronze Age features (Clarke *et al.* 1999; Clarke and Stoneman, 2001) and it seems likely that the area as a whole was a focus of activity in prehistory.

Was this therefore a successful ritual? This is difficult to answer in terms of archaeological remains generally. For ritual on its own terms it is tempting to view the Ballachulish figure as a failure – it seems likely that the figure references the supernatural, and all of the interpretations (bar the ritual killing) require some form of physical presence of the figure itself for repeated rites to take place. 'Decommissioning' this ritual resource highlights that something lost efficacy as it involved preventing access to a symbolic resource that would have likely been the focus of ritual activities. The location itself may have become a 'sacred place' as the result of this deposition, but there is no archaeological evidence for repeat activity or further ritual of this type. If a memory of sacredness was created, it was not maintained (and ritual is normally a good means to achieve this).

For the Ballachulish figure, the combination of ritual elements is unique in Scotland, while individual components fit within much broader scales of ritual traditions. Aspects of the figure are found recurring on a Scotland-wide and even international level. If Ballachulish is viewed as a local expression of a much wider ritual vocabulary it is harder to view as failure – it is a local expression, the meaning of which may or may not have had the desired effect in the real (or other) world. By the yardstick of repetition however, it seems that ritual (or perhaps rather the cosmological system behind this) failed: Ballachulish is unique. Perhaps it was intended as a beginning, but no subsequent tradition ensued. That no other Ballachulish figures are found suggests that this way of both coping with a crisis and the ritual expression of carving and using such a figure did not catch on. On one level, then, it is ritual failure.

Ritual failure or success in Argyll

How then to measure failure and success more broadly? And how to identify this in the archaeological record? Ritual activity, space for performance, activities and materials that could be considered 'odd' and appeal to a supernatural 'other' have all been identified in Scottish prehistory with varying confidence. How to pick up ritual failure within this however poses a challenge. Grimes (1988, 116) created a useful typology when considering 'infelicitous performance' under nine headings: misfire (misinvocation and misexecution), abuse, ineffectuality, violation, contagion, opacity, defeat, omission, and misframe. Of these, 'ineffectuality' is perhaps most readily identifiable if this can be equated with the closing down or decommissioning of previous ritual contexts. As at Ballachulish, 'closing' rites may in certain ritual frames be a category of ritual failure – a coping mechanism for when the ritual system breaks and needs corrective measures. However, this may not be the case in all instances and it is here that scale is important – if closure is a recurrent part of ritual at similar sites across a landscape, then this speaks to continuation (and therefore 'success'). Thus, closing activity and lack of parallel may be the best indicators (though the second category relies on being able to understand the broader context).

In Scottish prehistory other glimpses of ritual failure may be afforded. The Neolithic Temple Wood stone circle in Kilmartin Valley, Argyll for example appears to have had an abortive attempt to construct a wooden (or partially wooden) precursor monument (Scott 1989), before, literally, a change of plan. This site is interesting in that it is later 'closed' and converted into a funerary monument, a radically different form to the circle and its precursor and a major shift of the ritual 'framing'. Several other monuments in Kilmartin incorporate elements of earlier 'ritual' structures, with the re-use of a massive decorated standing stone as a cover slab for a cist at Nether Largie North (RCAHMS 1988, 68-70) or the reworking of early motifs on the slab of the cist burial at Ri Cruin (RCAHMS 1988, 72-74). Does this represent the drawing-on of earlier symbolic resources by a people with a different cosmology, or is there continuity? Do breaks in the ritual frame constitute failure, while repetition constitutes success? The reworking of earlier decorative forms could suggest an appropriation, or recognition of failure and a suitable corrective. There is a sense of symbolic resources being 'decommissioned', taken out of everyday access in a similar fashion to Ballachulish. Other monuments forms suggest a cumulative nature, such as the decorated rock shelves throughout Kilmartin Valley, with symbols added over time, both respecting and reworking earlier carvings (Stevenson 1997). Does such a simple formulation of repetition as a badge of ritual success, with the unique as failure, provide a way into the evidence? Can questions be formulated in such a way that they can be tested as hypotheses?

Asking the question: how to identify ritual failure in Scottish prehistory

How then to move forward with analysis of ritual failure in Scottish prehistory? Ultimately, this revolves around being able to connect changes in ritual practice to broader changes in society and the landscape. Datasets for this range of changes operate over different scales, and integrating them is challenging. However, three themes operating at different scales offer a potential route into the data: exploring links with changing climate and local environment; tracing the arrival and dispersal of new material; and examining change at the level of human cognition.

Linking any form of societal change to climatic data for prehistory is fraught with difficulty (Tipping *et al.* 2008), and can only operate within rich, localised data-sets that can reflect how wider-scale changes affect specific environments. Looking at the potential of, for example, linking the frequency and location of the deposition of metalwork, to environmental changes might prove fruitful (Cowie pers. comm.). This creates an approach that has a predictive element, and the types of deposition can be analysed to start creating an idea of what people felt 'worked' and what 'failed'. It might also allow a more detailed archaeological exploration of 'ritualisation' and how this is seen to work (or not), as different categories of material culture may have been deposited preferentially. If the concept of ritualisation is accepted, there is also a need to cast the net wider for ritual activity, in different categories of object, and their integration into ritual activity within wider landscapes of subsistence, movement and habitation – a fully 'cosmological' landscape (Brück 2011).

Tracing the arrival and spread of new material culture has a long pedigree in Scottish prehistory. For Ballachulish, the transition from bronze-working to the development of iron-working was a pertinent influence, evidenced by the finds of iron and iron production at An Dunan (PSAS 1970). Exploring similar transitions, and linking them to changes in ritual practice forms a promising area of research, whether those transitions are incoming peoples such as the Romans or Norse, material culture or new ways of organising society or obtaining food. Some earlier interpretations of the Ballachulish figure view its deposition as a reaction to incoming Christianity or a response to military defeat (Stewart 1883, 25). More broadly, processes such as the arrival of the Romans can be explored in reference to ritual activity such as hoarding (Hunter 1997, 122-3). Indeed, the 'closing' of Roman altars by burying them face down – the final acts of an inserted tradition that does not appear to have continued (at least not in the same form), recalls the Ballachulish figure itself. It may represent a relatively short-lived attempt at establishing a new tradition, or an unsuccessful response to a new crisis. A whole range of transitions and changes, both external and internal, provide the crises that society turns to ritual practice to deal with.

The workings of the individual mind offers another area of research. Cognitive science has potential in developing testable hypotheses out of the ritual of mind, beginning with the theory that human minds draw from a single vocabulary of potential ritual expressions (McCauley and Lawson 2007). This vocabulary is deemed more comprehensible when examining prehistoric communities, and is intimately connected to the broader social and natural environment. As such, the existence of parameters of religious thought and a probabilistic range of ritual ideas and material resources that can be drawn on by a community of people, can be tested against the archaeological evidence. The nature and form that those parameters take can also be explored. Models of the cosmology and ritual associated with a range of sites continue to be developed: these could be evaluated from a cognitive science perspective, and expectations from a cognitive point of view could be tested retrodictively against the archaeological evidence.

The Scottish prehistoric record provides a strong data-set of evidence for ritual behaviour within pre- and proto-historic societies over a range of spatial and chronological scales with which to explore a range of questions. Closure-like deposits, for example, are high-potential areas in which to study ritual failure as they often represent a moment of change identifiable through archaeology.

Whether or not they represent 'ritual failure' is a question to explore – lack of recurring similarities in the mode and manner of closure may be more likely to indicate failure. Similarly, persistence appears another important criterion when attempting to explore ritual failure. Some societal elements with a strong ritual element do seem to recur (or at least be identified at different periods), such as ancestor veneration or totemism. This can mask the relationship between events and longer processes, however, with connections emphasised and time compressed as a result. Categories of material that archaeologists would comfortably explain in terms of ritual behaviour traditionally include substantial things like chambered tombs. If ritualisation is accepted then this must be broadened to encompass 'everyday' material that can be incorporated within ritual. Material such as this, for example, animal bone or coarse stone tools, are attested at many 'ritual' contexts.

For Scottish prehistory, archaeologists have generally had to deal in chronological blocks, from which change is difficult to elucidate. Ideas of change and continuity are often muddied by this lack of precision– does later activity on an earlier site represent continuity, a hiatus, coincidence or an attempt to actively evoke the past? What lengths of timescale would actually differentiate between these? How long passes before people are attempting to evoke a past there is no surviving memory of? However, the application of dating techniques, sampling strategies, and contextual and statistical analysis can provide the level of data required to draw out this detailed picture. Recent work in Bayesian modeling, for example, is overturning modern notions of large Neolithic structures as monuments to the eternal (Bayliss and Whittle 2007), and is building a much more dynamic picture of prehistoric society. Developing work that can provide generational timescales will affect the scale of analysis that narratives can be built upon, in turn, allowing archaeology to better explore broader questions of change and continuity.

Conclusion

Whatever the meaning of the Ballachulish figure – fertility symbol, shrine to safe passage, house idol, boat totem, or proxy for ritual killing – its closure can be interpreted as ritual 'failure'. However, it is important to consider 'failure' within broader explanations of change – 'crises' might be a better term, as ritual is the mechanism by which failure is resolved as well as success achieved. Archaeology can provide fossilised ritual 'moments in time' when the inner workings of the ritual system can be glimpsed. Archaeology tends to recover these however, from societies that have 'failed' as a whole – the fossilised 'moment in time' is often a society's last. It is therefore difficult to separate ritual failure from societal failure. Ritual is also difficult to identify as a 'thing' – it is only possible to identify ritual activity through the context of performance (Verhoeven 2011, 126).

Ultimately, failure is an element of change, and it may be easier to view this along a continuum of change, rather than a binary system of 'success' or 'failure'. In any case, success or failure will be contingent on perspective – including modern perspectives where 'success' is often seen as continuance or persistence of a society. One danger is that archaeology often focuses on change rather than continuity, and by doing so may emphasise the elements where ritual systems creak or break, rather than the continued functioning which is more of a characteristic. In this sense, 'ritual failure' is more of an etic category than 'ritual'. Archaeological expectations of success and failure therefore need to be critically examined. If ritual is a fundamental aspect of human society, failure in this sphere could usefully be compared and contrasted to other types of 'failure' (*e.g.* market failure).

As the Soothsayer highlights at the beginning of this paper, ritual makes it difficult to question its own efficacy (Bloch 1989). The Asterix books are entertaining as individual publications as they take us on many different stories to many different places. However, they also entertain as a series – common themes are identified and their recurring appearance brings the reader enjoyment and value. The sky not falling on people's heads, even when it appears it must do so, is one such recurring theme.

References

Armit, I. 2005. *Celtic Scotland*, London: Batsford.

Bayliss, A. and Whittle, A. 2007 (eds.). Histories of the dead: building chronologies for five southern British long barrows. Journal supplement, *Cambridge Archaeological Journal* 17/1.

Bell, C. 1992. *Ritual Theory, Ritual Practice*, Oxford: Oxford University Press.

Bell, C. 1997. *Ritual: Perspectives and Dimensions*, Oxford: Oxford University Press.

Bloch, M. 1989. *Ritual, History and Power: Selected Papers in Anthropology*, London: Athlone Press.

Bradley, R. 1998. *The passage of Arms*, Oxford: Oxford University Press.

Bradley, R. 2002. *The Past in Prehistoric Societies*, London, Routledge.

Bradley, R. 2005. *Ritual and Domestic Life in Prehistoric Europe*, London: Routledge.

Brück, J. 1999. Ritual and rationality: some problems of interpretation in European archaeology, *Journal of European Archaeology* 2 (3), 313-344.

Brück, J. 2011. Fire, Earth, Water: An Elemental Cosmography of the European Bronze Age, in: Insoll, T. (ed.). *The Oxford Handbook of the Archaeology of Ritual and Religion*, Oxford: Oxford University Press, 387-404.

Childe, V.G. 1942. *What Happened in History*, Harmondsworth: Pengun.

Christison, R. 1881. On an ancient wooden image, found in November last at Ballachulish peat-moss. *Proceedings of the Society of Antiquaries of Scotland* 15, 158-178.

Clarke, C.M. and Stoneman, R. 2001. Archaeological and Palaeoenvironmental Investigation at North Ballachulish Moss, Highland, Scotland, in: Raftery, B. and Hickey, J. (eds.). *Recent Developments in Wetland Research* Dublin: Seandálaíocht Monograph 2 and WARP Occassional paper 14, 201-214.

Clarke, C.M., Utsi, E. and Utsi, V. 1999. Ground Penetrating Radar Investigations at North Ballachulish Moss, Highland, Scotland. *Archaeological Prospection* 6, 107-121.

Coles, B. 1990. Anthropomorphic wooden figurines from Britain and Ireland. *Proceedings of the Prehistoric Society* 56, 315-33.

Coles, J. and Coles, B. 1996. *Enlarging the Past: The Contribution of Wetland Archaeology*, Edinburgh: Society of Antiquaries of Scotland Monograph Series 11 and Wetland Archaeology Research Project Occasonal Paper 10.

Crone, A. 2007. God-dollies? An Assemblage of peg-like Objects from the Pict's Knowe, Dumfries, South-west Scotland, in: WARP (eds.). *Archaeology from the Wetlands: Recent Perspectives*, Edinburgh: Society of Antiquaries of Scotland, 339-342.

Earwood, C. 1997. Bog butter: a two thousand year history. *Journal of Irish Archaeology* 8, 25-42.

Evans-Pritchard, E. E. 1937. *Witchcraft, Oracles and Magic among the Azande*, Oxford: Oxford University Press.

Glob, P.V. 1973. *The Bog People Iron Age Man Preserved*. London: Faber and Faber.

Goscinny, R. and Underzo, A. 2004. *Asterix and the Soothsayer*. London: Orion Books.

Grimes, R.L. 1988. Infelicitous Performances and Ritual Criticism. *Semeia* 43: 103-122.

Hodder, I. 1982. *The Present Past*, London: Batsford.

Hunter, F. 1997. Iron Age Hoarding in Scotland and Northern England, in: Gwilt, A and Haselgrove, C. (eds.). *Reconstructing Iron Age Societies:* new approaches to the British Iron Age, Oxford: Oxbow Books, 108-133.

Hüsken, U. 2007a (ed.). *When Rituals go Wrong: Mistakes, Failure, and the Dynamics of Ritual*, Leiden: Brill.

Hüsken, U. 2007b. Ritual Dynamics and Ritual Failure, in: Hüsken, U (ed.). *When Rituals go Wrong: Mistakes, Failure, and the Dynamics of Ritual*, Leiden: Brill, 337-366.

Insoll, T. 2004. *Archaeology, Ritual, Religion,* London: Routledge.

Kelly, E.P. 2006. Secrets of the Bog Bodies: The Enigma of the Iron Age Explained, *Archaeology Ireland* 20/1, 26-30.

Kelly, E.P. 2012. Irish Iron Age Bog Bodies. *Society of Antiquaries of Scotland Lecture* delivered on 9th January 2012 http://www.socantscot.org/article.asp?aid=1786 <accessed on 10th May 2012>.

Kyriakidis, E. 2007a (ed.). *The Archaeology of Ritual* Los Angeles; University of California.

Kyriakidis, E. 2007b (ed.). Archaeologies of Ritual, in: Kyriakidis, E (ed.). *The Archaeology of Ritual* Los Angeles; University of California, 289-308.

Lévi-Strauss, C. 1968. *Structural Anthropology*, London: Allen Lane, The Penguin Presss.

McCauley, R.N. and Lawson, E.T. 2007. Cognition, Religious Ritual, and Archaeology, in: Kyriakidis, E. (ed). *The Archaeology of Ritual*. Los Angeles: Cotsen Institute of Archaeology Publications, 209-254.

Malinowski, B. 1954. *Magic, Science and Religion and Other Essays*, New York: Doubleday.

Piggott, S and Henderson, K 1958 *Scotland Before Prehistory*, Edinburgh: Nelson.

Society of Antiquaries of Scotland 1970. Donations to and purchases for the Museum and Library. *Proceedings of the Society of Antiquaries of Scotland* 102, 295-8.

Radcliffe-Brown, A. R. 1956. *Structure and Function in Primitive Society*, London: Cohen and West.

Rappaport, R. 1999. *Ritual and Religion in the Making of Humanity*, Cambridge: Cambridge University Press.

RCAHMS 1988. *The Royal Commission on the Ancient and Historical Monuments of Scotland. Argyll: an inventory of the monuments volume 6: Mid-Argyll and Cowal, prehistoric and early historic monuments*, Edinburgh: Stationery Office Books.

Ritchie, G. 1997. *The Archaeology of Argyll*, Edinburgh: Edinburgh University Press.

Scott, J.G. 1989. The Stone Circles at Temple Wood, Kilmartin, Argyll, *The Glasgow Archaeological Journal* 15, 53-124.

Shapland, F. and Armit, I. 2012. The Useful Dead: Bodies as Objects in Iron Age and Norse Atlantic Scotland, *European Journal of Archaeology* 15/1, 98-116.

Stanley, M. 2007. Anthropomorphic Wooden Figures: Recent Irish Discoveries, in: WARP (eds.). *Archaeology from the Wetlands: Recent Perspectives*, Edinburgh: Society of Antiquaries of Scotland, 183-190.

Stevenson, J.B. 1997. The prehistoric rock carvings of Argyll in: Ritchie, G. *The Archaeology of Argyll*, Edinburgh: Edinburgh University Press, 95-117.

Stewart, J. 1883. The Ballachulish Goddess, *Transactions of the Inverness Science Field Club* 2, 21-8.

Tipping, R., Davies, A., McCulloch, R. and Tisdall, E. 2008. Response to late Bronze Age climate change of farming communities in north east Scotland, *Journal of Archaeological Science* 35, 2379-2386.

Turner, V. 1969. *The Ritual Process. Structure and Anti-Structure*, New York: Aldine Publishing Company.

Turner, R.C. 1995. Gazeteer of Bog Bodies in the British Isles, in: Turner, R.C. and Scaife, R.G. (eds.). *Bog Bodies: New Discoveries and New Perspectives*, London: British Museem Press, 205-220.

Tylor, E.B. 1929. *Primitive Culture*, London: John Murray.

Van der Sanden, W. 1996. *Through Nature to Eternity: The Bog Bodies of Northwest Europe*, Amsterdam: Batavian Lion International.

Verhoeven, M. 2011. The Many Dimensions of Ritual, in: Insoll, T (ed.). *The Oxford Handbook of the Archaeology of Ritual and Religion*, Oxford: Oxford University Press, 115-132.

Chapter 3

Ritual failure in the business records of Mesopotamian temples[1]

Michael Kozuh[2]

Abstract

This paper aims to add to the understanding of Mesopotamian ritual failure by highlighting evidence from a type of cuneiform record that, although enjoying a renaissance of sorts since the 1990s, has been largely overlooked as source: the business records of Mesopotamian temples in the first millennium BC. Using these, one can reconstruct, often in great detail, the distinctive processes by which Babylonian temples managed the daily rituals that were fundamental to their existence – namely, the twice-a-day ritual of feeding of their gods. Dividing the process into supply, storage, and prebendal expenditure, I focus on ritual failure as it appears in those three steps. In the end, I argue that temple business records reveal the administrative weak points in the Mesopotamian ritual system, in effect presaging where and how rituals could fail.

Keywords: *Mesopotamia, ritual administration, temple ritual, daily ritual.*

The Mesopotamian cuneiform record of the first millennium BC provides ample evidence for the study of ritual failure. New editions of texts documenting a variety of Mesopotamia's ritual systems appear regularly, many of which include scholarly discussions that work to place various rituals in their socio-economic or –political context (Ambos 2004; Bidmead 2002; Linssen 2004; Maul 1994, 2011; Pongratz-Leisten 1994; Walker & Dick 2001). Mesopotamian commentary about rituals is also highly illuminating (Cole & Machinist 1998; Parpola 1993). Using these texts, Claus Ambos discusses three common types of ritual failure in Mesopotamia: the gods' outright refusal of the ritual; the divine interruption of a ritual; and human error in ritual execution (Ambos 2007, 25ff.). His list is certainly not

---

1 Cuneiform texts and publication series are cited with the system of abbreviations of The Assyrian Dictionary of the Oriental Institute of the University of Chicago (CAD), reproduced (with other abbreviations) at http://cdli.ucla.edu/wiki/doku.php/abbreviations_for_assyriology.
2 Auburn University (USA), mgkozuh@msn.com.

exhaustive. For example, at times the statue of a god went missing, either through outright "godnapping" or as a result of a calamity, which caused rituals to fail (Beaulieu 2001). Political instability, especially regime change, jeopardized temple rituals (Grayson 1970, 161ff.), as did famine, hardships, and basic ignorance of the proper rites (for these, see the edition of *BBst* 36 in (Woods 2004).

Temple business records show that ritual could fail for mundane reasons as well. Simply put, every Mesopotamian temple had a process, subject to local variation, by which it turned the products of its land and animals into ritual meals for its gods. In that process an administrative breakdown could occur at any point, leading to an "interruption" (Babylonian *baṭlu*) in the offerings. Three southern Mesopotamian temple archives in the first millennium BC provide ample – indeed, overabundant – information on this process: the Ebabbar temple of Sippar, the Ezida temple of Borsippa, and the Eanna temple of Uruk. Considering them together, and simplifying the process into supply, storage, and prebendal distribution, we can draw on the most edifying part of each archive to discern how Mesopotamians dealt with the threat of an administrative interruption in temple ritual. Although ritual interruption ultimately provoked theological contemplation, the business records reveal that, in the end, it was a distinctly human problem. In fact, by pinpointing weaknesses in the administration of temple ritual systems we can then link those vulnerabilities to the high-level contemplation of ritual in Mesopotamia.

In general, I aim to tread lightly over the textual material here. Assyriological literature can be intimidating and opaque to non-experts, but it is my hope that, seeing its potential, historians, anthropologists, and archaeologists specializing in ritual will turn their attention to the cuneiform record. It is particularly rich on this topic (Ambos 2007, 25f.) and has much to offer to outside specialists.

First, a few words on the terms "ritual" and "prebend/prebendary." Every Mesopotamian temple performed an indispensable two-part daily ritual – called either *sattukku* or *ginû* – in which it fed two meals to the statue(s) of its god(s) in the morning and another two meals at dusk (lit: at the "cool of the day"). (Oppenheim 1977, 183ff; Waerzeggers 2010, 111ff.) The basic meal consisted of bread, beer, and lamb meat, supplemented with fruits (like dates and pomegranates), dairy products, eggs, mice, raisins, honey, and confections. Meals varied not only from temple to temple but also within temples to meet an annual ritual calendar, of which we only have imperfect knowledge even for the best-documented temples (Waerzeggers 2010, 111f.). We do know that weekly, monthly, and annual festival days saw a significant uptick in the amount and frequency of food presented to the gods (Robbins 1996, 68ff.; Waerzeggers 2010, 119ff.). I assume the interruptions discussed below refer to the daily ritual, but it is possible that some texts refer to interruptions on festival days. Hence, the following uses the terms "ritual" and "temple ritual" without specification.

For "prebend/prebendary" I follow Caroline Waerzeggers' *The Ezida Temple of Borsippa*. Within the temple itself, the actual execution of ritual involved a variety of people. Waerzeggers puts them in two groups: for one there were the purveyors, to whom the temple gave the raw materials for them to manufacture into ritual foodstuffs, by "cutting, crushing, pressing, milling, churning, cooking, baking, brewing, or simply selecting – any type of activity that transformed ordinary raw products into special, sacrificial food." (Waerzeggers 2010, 302) The temple gave the other group a means of production, such as date-palm groves, fishponds, and oxherds (for milk), from which members of that group drew products for the ritual meal (in a ritualized way). (Waerzeggers 2010, 302, 289ff. [for oxherd service]). Members of each of these groups were prebendaries, in that they own a prebend (i.e., a share) in the execution of temple ritual, in the many functions listed above (and many others).[3] Ownership of a prebend was remunerative, both in terms of payment for ritual execution and a portion of the ritual meal itself. (Waerzeggers 2010, 303ff.)

Where this might cause confusion is in temple supply, considered next. The bulk of the supply in cereals and (lamb) meat for ritual came from outside temple contractors; prebendaries supplied other parts of the ritual meal, particularly prestige items and foodstuffs with short expiration windows (e.g. fish and dairy). While both technically supply, one differentiation between the two – as far as I can discern – is that the contractors paid into the temple's storehouses and stables, which were then put under the control of temple authorities, while the ritual task of some prebendaries involved both bringing food products to the temple and preparing those products for the meal of the gods. In general, contractors provided the raw material for the basic meal (cereals for bread and beer, lambs for meat) while prebendaries both provided and prepared supplemental foods of various sorts. Hence, I will discuss prebendal supply under prebendal distribution, as the two are inextricable from each other.

Temple Supply

Information on temple supply comes mainly from the Eanna temple of Uruk and the Ebabbar of Sippar. Both temples contracted out substantial parts of their land and animals to outsiders who, in turn, agreed to pay a stipulated amount of the yield to the temple each year (Cocquerillat 1968; Jursa 1995; 2004, 178ff.; Kozuh in press; van Driel 1999; Wunsch in press). As a simple observation, the large-scale scope of the contracts reveals that temples controlled significantly more productive capital than was needed to meet ritual requirements.[4] If nothing else, immense holdings certainly hedged against ritual failure from lack of supply. Perhaps for this reason direct connections between a temple's lands, gardens, or animal contractors and its ritual needs were rare – rather, contractors paid directly into the temple's storehouses or stables, from which temple administrators selected the products for divine meals.

---

3   I endorse the argument (Waerzeggers 2010, 3 and 34ff.) that "priest" is a more apt translation than "prebendary" for the people associated with this phenomenon. However, I use "prebendary" here in order to highlight the economic and administrative functions of the prebend-holders.
4   I estimate that the Eanna of Uruk controlled between 74,000 and 90,000 total sheep in any given year, with sacrifices requiring an annual total of 4,300 male lambs.

At times, however, economic stresses forced the temples to link suppliers directly to the perpetuation temple ritual. In 528 BC, the Eanna of Uruk, drawing from its suppliers, provisioned a royal banquet in a location within Uruk sphere of influence (Kleber 2008, 85ff.) For reasons I do not fully understand, this unusual event threw the temple's animal supplies and suppliers into disarray, from which the temple economy took over eighteen months to fully recover. (Kozuh in press) This disarray, in turn, threw temple ritual into potential jeopardy.

Leading up to the banquet, temple contracts begin to use language that reflects a fear of an interruption in the offerings. Two unpublished duplicate contracts (BM 114557 and NCBT 648) obligate a supervisor of the temple's sheep contractors to deliver 150 male lambs for sacrifices. The texts atypically link him directly to the offerings by stipulating that (following BM 114557: 10ff) *pu-ut* SÁ.DUG$_4$ *šá* ^{d}GAŠAN *šá* UNUG.KI *na-ši ⸢ki⸣-i la i-ta-ab-kam-ma la it-tan-nu* [*hi*]-*ṭu šá* ^{m}*gu-bar-ru* LÚ.NAM TIN.TIR.KI *u e-bir* I$_7$ *i-zab-bi-lu*, "[the herd supervisor] takes responsibility for the daily offerings of (the goddess) the Lady of Uruk; if he fails to bring (the lambs) in and give them (to the temple), he will be guilty of a crime against Gobyras, the governor of Babylon and the Transeuphratian region."

The fear of an interruption continued on after the banquet. We have a contract (YOS 7 127) for the same supplier to bring in another set of animals, indeterminate in number, for sacrifices later in the same year. The guarantee clause of this text states *pu-ut gi-ni-e šá* ^{d}GAŠAN *šá* UNUG.KI *na-ši ki-i hi-ṭu ina lìb-bi it-tab-ku hi-ṭu šá* ^{m}*gu-ba-ru* LÚ.NAM TIN.TIR.KI *u e-bir* I$_7$ *i-šad-da-ad*, "[the supervisor] takes responsibility for the daily offerings of (the goddess) the Lady of Uruk; if a mistake occurs therein, he will be guilty of a crime against Gobyras the governor of Babylon and the Transeuphratian region." Other texts from this stressful time are AnOr 8 67, BM 113415, GCCI 2 120, TCL 13 162, YOS 7 123, YOS 7 128, YOS 7 138, YOS 7 160, and YOS 7 163. The lattermost one ends adds the stipulation that *pu-ut baṭ-lu šá* UDU.NITÁ.ME SÀ.DUG$_4$ ... *na-ši*, "(the contractor) take responsibly for the (non-)interruption of the sacrificial lambs."

The point here is that, in times of economic stress, the temple shifted the ultimate responsibility for the continuation of the offerings onto its contractor class, adding a sense of urgency and importance to the deliveries. This also suggests that the temple's ultimate fail-safe of holding reserves that outstripped its ritual needs was only as effective as its administrators. In this case, ritual would have failed simply because the Eanna could not access its own reserve property, held under contract by outsiders, in a timely manner. In truth, though, we are only aware of these stresses because of the temple's requirement to draw up thorough contracts with outsiders. Were the temple to draw from its own dependents, it would involve a less explicit documentary regime (considered next) that might not make the threat of ritual interruption so evident.

Temple storage

Once collected and stocked in storerooms and stables, the temples tracked their goods through administrative texts, such as memoranda, short receipts, audits, and ledgers, which marked the movements of goods between temple departments. (Jursa 2005) Details in these texts vary widely. Often they name the supplier and/or the receiver of the goods, but they tend not to mention temple authorities involved in transactions, nor do they note the purpose of any transaction with regularity or with much supplementary detail (Kleber 2005; Kozuh 2011). If indeed temple authorities precipitously shifted goods around the temple in order to forestall an interruption in the offerings, it would not necessarily appear as such in these texts. Letters between temple authorities can be quite informative, but it is often impossible to identify the senders and receivers of the letters with precision. Moreover, given that the letters are undated and rarely contain chronological clues, it is difficult in our current state of knowledge to plug the actions and requests recorded in the letters into the temple economy in anything but a general way.[5]

We can, however, fit administrative texts and letters together in a way that sheds light on a recurring instance of ritual failure. The records of the Eanna temple of Uruk list goods sent to nearby temples – most commonly the temple of Shamash at Larsa and the temples of Nergal and Bēlet Eanna at Udannu – to forestall interruptions in their offerings. Paul-Alain Beaulieu, noting the many instances of such deliveries, argues that these temples were in a state of "administrative dependency" on the Eanna. (Beaulieu 1991, 1993; 2003, 73ff.) This administrative dependency, although imperfectly understood, enabled officials to draw from the (presumably) richer and better-endowed Eanna temple either to circumvent interruptions or to restart offerings after an interruption.

These texts can be uniquely informative. In one case, a letter (YOS 3 91) from two overseers of the Eanna, who were inspecting temple of Nergal at Udannu after a lightening strike, reported back to the Eanna's uppermost officials that the storm caused the perbendary personnel to flee (lines 17ff: LÚ.KU$_4$.É ... *gab-bi ih-te-liq-*). This left nobody to carry out the rituals, so the writers ask the uppermost temple authorities of the Eanna for instructions for what to do next (*kap-du ṭè-e-me šá* EN.MEŠ-*e-ni ni-iš-me*, "may we hear the instructions of our lords right away"). See the discussion in (Beaulieu 1991, 101ff.)

More often, officials from the dependent temples place the blame for interrupted offerings squarely on the negligence of the Eanna's officials. YOS 3 75: 8ff., for example, reads: *baṭ-la a-na* UDU.NITÁ.ME *šá-kin ki-i na-kut-ti ni-il-⸢tap⸣-ra*! 60(?) UDU.NITÁ.ME EN *liš-pur-an-na-a-šú ù* LÚ.SIPA-*ka it-ti-šú-nu lil-li-ku ia-a-nu-ú baṭ-la iš-šak-kan*, "there is an interruption in sheep, so we write out of concern. The lord should send 60(?) sheep to us and his (text: your) shepherd could come with them. If not, the interruption will continue." Some letters warn the Eanna's authorities that supplies in Larsa or Udannu are low (*maṭû*),[6] and

---

5   Michael Jursa's next project (http://imperiumofficium.univie.ac.at) will change much of this.
6   YOS 3 56: 15 UDU.NITÁ *a-na gi-ni-e ma-ṭu-ú* 20 30 UDU.NITÁ *a-na gi-ne-e šá* ^{d}UD PN *liš-pu-ru* (cf. YOS 3 99). YOS 3 92 (birds, wine), YOS 3 61 (barley) BIN 1 50 (cattle).

entries in ledger texts for supplies sent either to Udannu or Larsa *ana baṭli* "on account of an interruption" are numerous.[7]

Sandwiched between more informative supply and expenditure, the scant yet intriguing evidence for temple storage suggests that ritual failure was not a major concern at this level. It is difficult to judge if this is accurate. On the one hand, if the temple managed its suppliers well, then storage probably indeed generated little consternation. On the other hand, although administrative texts can lack crucial details, investigations that consider them in bunches or group them together in interesting ways can identify underlying issues in the temple's economy or administration, ones that are not evident in a plain reading of the texts. Letters indicate that fear of ritual failure lurked in the background – yet even this might reflect the hyperbole underlings often need to put goad superiors to act. More work is needed here to understand this level better.

Prebendal expenditure

The crux in the ritual system involves the transition from storage to expenditure; suppliers could fill the temple's stores, and the temple manage its reserves with steadfast accuracy, but it all came to naught with errors in execution at this final stage. Here, the direct connection between human action and ritual fulfilment became explicit. Failure or ineptitude at this stage caused unequivocal interruptions in ritual.

As a result, contracts between temples and their prebendaries stipulated against ritual failure.[8] For example, contracts between the Ezida temple and its prebendary brewers to produce high quality beer for temple ritual specify that, in exchange for income in performing the task, the brewer (or his deputy) *pu-ut qu-ur-ub nap-ta-nu baṭ-lu u mas-naq-tu$_4$ ... na-ši*, "takes responsibility for approaching the (divine) meal, (averting) interruptions, and punctuality."[9] In addition to these, a text from the Eanna temple of Uruk (YOS 7 90: 10ff.) stipulates that the fishermen prebendaries *pu-ut ... bu-un šá* KU$_6$.HI.A ... *na-šu-ú*, "take responsibility ... for the good quality of the fish."[10] Interestingly, this lattermost text records a penalty for failing to live up to the terms of the contract. It continues *ki-i* KU$_6$.HI.A *ina su-us-su-ul!-lu! in-da-ṭu-ú ù* KU$_6$.HI.A *bi-i-šú ina man-za-al-ti-šú-nu uq-tar-ri!-bi hi-ṭu šá* DINGIR *ù* LUGAL *i-šad-da-du*, "if there is a shortage of fish in the collection basket or if they bring low quality fish in their temple service, they will have committed an office against god and king." (K Kleber 2004, 142) This is one of the few texts that specifically attaches a penalty – ambiguous as it is – to ritual failure.

---

7   YOS 7 8: 18, YOS 7 74: 20, and see the references in Robbins 1996, 81).
8   The prebendaries, in turn, passed on those stipulations to their sub-contractors and agents, see Waerzeggers (2010, 177ff.).
9   On the variants to and discussions of this clause for the different prebendaries, see Waerzeggers (2010, 101, 174, 176ff., 293, 301ff., 304ff)
10 See Beaulieu (2003, 174f.).

In another interesting case (YOS 6 222), a prebendary gardener of the Eanna temple of Uruk failed to approach the divine meal on account of the bad quality of his dates and pomegranates. The text continues *baṭ-lu iš-ku-nu-ma*, "an interruption occurred," so the upperlevel temple authorities

> ZÚ.LUM.MA *ù lu-ri-in-du ul-tu* É.AN.NA *a-na* ᵈGAŠAN *šá* UNUG.KI *ú-qar-ri-bu* ᵐᵈ*a-num*-MU.SI.SÁ *si-mar-re-e ina* É.AN.NA *id-di ù* ZÚ.LUM.MA *ù lu-ri-in-du šá a-na nap-ta-nu ú-še-lam-ma ku-um bé-e'-e-šú la iq-ru-bu ina* É.AN.NA *ik-nu-uk*

> brought dates and pomegranates from the (the reserve stores of) the Eanna for the (goddess) The Lady of Uruk. They arrested (lit. threw in manacles) Anu-šuma-lišir and put under seal in the Eanna the dates and pomegranates that he brought for the meal but did not approach (the meal with) on account of the bad quality.[11]

Clearly the stoppage of offerings resulted in serious repercussions, even for the well-heeled prebendary class. In another text (TCL 13 221) nineteen prebendary bakers of various sorts are held responsible for the quality of the divine meal. The text continues *ki-i baṭ-lu il-ta-kan-[nu] ù nap-ta-nu bi-i-šú i-te-pu-ú mu-li-e ki-i* LÚ.TIL.LA.GÍD.DA.ME *šá* É.AN.NA *ṣi-bu-ú un-dal-lu-ú*, "if they cause an interruption (in the offerings) or cook a bad meal, they will pay whatever fine the officials of the Eanna desire."[12] Finally, in a text relating to the temples of Nippur, the prebendary brewers state (TuM 2/3, 211: 25ff.):

> *ba-aṭ-lu ina* ŠÀ-*bi la i-šak-ka-nu-u' u mim-ma šá ik-kaš-ši-du ana* GIŠ.ŠUB. BA LÚ.LUNGÀ-*ú-tú* MU.MEŠ *it-ti* LÚ.UN.ÍL.MEŠ-*šú-nu* LÚ.LUNGÀ. MEŠ DUMU.MEŠ *šá* PN *a-na u₄-mu* UL *i-na-áš-šu-ú pu-ut pa-lah* GIŠ. ŠUB.BA LÚ.LUNGÀ-*ú-tú* MU.MEŠ *u la šá-ka-nu ba-aṭ-lu ina* É.KUR.MEŠ MU.MEŠ ... *a-na u₄-mu* UL *na-šu-ú*

> They will not cause interruptions in (the offerings), and anything (else) that is obtained regarding that brewer prebend, they will carry (it) out forever with their collegial brewer prebendaries – (that is), the descendants of PN. They forever take responsibility for honoring that brewer's prebend and for not causing interruptions in those temples. (See Beaulieu 1995, 88f.)

Unfortunately, as interesting as these penalties and stipulations are, we simply do not know much about them. Bongenaar argues that prebendaries risked their private wealth in the event of a interruption, but this observation has not gained general approval (Bongenaar, 2000, 76). Moreover, the known penalties make no mention of it. As it stands now, only texts from Uruk have penalty clauses or mention penalties for ritual failure in other ways, despite the fact that the Ezida archive of Sippar contains many more prebendary contracts. This might reflect the fact that Uruk had a well developed "private sector." (van Driel 2002, 46) That said, the guarantee clauses and few references to fairly severe punishments for ineptitude attest to the fact that ritual failure at the last step was a grave concern.

---

11   For further discussion of this text see Beaulieu (2003, 175f.).
12   See TCL 13 187 as well.

Ritual failure and temple business records

The business records of Mesopotamian temples provide unique insights into ritual failure. Reflecting the mundane transactions of administrators and businessmen of various capacities and stations, the majority of texts stem from a time of relative prosperity and economic growth in Mesopotamia. (Jursa 2010, 783ff.) Indeed, in view of the thousands of texts that would appear to record steps in the successful completion of ritual, the limited references to ritual interruption appear aberrant and rare.

Their unusualness notwithstanding, business texts record multiple ways that ritual could fail before the actual ritual took place: suppliers fell behind in their deliveries or reneged on obligations; once the temple collected its supplies, delays and set-backs of various sorts affected the intra- and inter-temple processes, which seems particularly true for those temples that relied on other temples to subsidize their rituals; and the movement from supply to ritual expenditure appears to have been especially precarious. Discussing just one of the many prebendaries at Sippar's Ezida's temple, Caroline Waerzeggers makes the following astute observation:

> *The bakers spent more time on the job than a cursory reading of their prebend texts would suggest. Every single meal of Nabû was the result of a chain of activities that took several days to complete. From the first to the last step, these tasks were kept strictly separated: they consisted of small, identifiable work units that were assigned to identifiable persons stationed at different locations. This system provided visibility in the case of ritual failure, and the possibility for identifying cause and culprit. It also guaranteed that every cereal offering for Nabû was an unmixed product, the result of an interlocking chain of activities that transformed normal barley into selected, pure sacrificial food.* (Waerzeggers 2010, 236)

Indeed, this final stage of temple operations pit spheres of temple influence against each other in ways that we do not yet fully comprehend. The few references we have to punishments for ritual failure seem to suggest that temple officials – who themselves were a mix of local and royal interests (Bongenaar 1997, 11ff., 34ff.; Kleber 2008, 5ff.) – had authority over the prebendaries. On the other hand, the deep local roots and high social standing of the prebendaries certainly tempered any punitive actions against them.

The workaday purview of business texts and our stark ignorance of crucial information tempt one to downplay the significance of ritual failure, as though it concerned a few upper-crust members of a Mesopotamian city, intrigued only those experts in Mesopotamian religious arcana, or was simply an intermittent and inevitable administrative snafu. I think this is misguided. Failed ritual in Mesopotamia lent itself to deep theological and ideological contemplation. Although this contemplation paid little heed to issues of supply and storage, the temple business records make it clear that, if nothing else, ritual could fail at multiple levels and for multiple reasons. While any particular instance ritual failure might indeed have been unremarkable, such a failure helps us understand the process by which rituals might fail indefinitely, or at least fail in a way that it attracted the attention of Mesopotamian poets and scholars.

Claus Ambos presents evidence for common skepticism among Mesopotamians on the efficacy of rituals, casting doubt on their overall ideological or religious significance. (Ambos 2007, 42ff.) The evidence for skepticism is abundant and interesting, although much of it reflects individual, rather than collective, consciousness. Most commonly, Mesopotamians likened the eschewing of rituals to rustic, antisocial behaviour. In late legendary accounts of king Naram-Sin, the gods through extispacy deny the king's request to send his army out to conquer. After facetiously asking whether lions or wolves need rituals to condone their actions, the king proclaims: "I will go like a brigand according to my own inclination, and I will cast aside that (oracle) of the god(s); I will be in control of myself!" Like Naram-Sin, the skeptic in the Babylonian Theodicy balks at the "profitless servitude" of Mesopotamian rituals, adding that by abandoning rituals he will "forsake home... go on the road... roam about the far outdoors like a bandit... [and] prowl the streets, casting about, ravenous..." (Citations taken from Ambos 2007, 45ff.)

Ambos argues that this skepticism toward rituals never "developed into a coherent system and is only known through its opposite position. Both indifference and skepticism were expressed in the form of a general laxness toward the fulfilment of cultic duties." (Ambos 2007, 45) While perhaps true, I think this sidesteps the main issue. The literary texts contrast the participation in ritual with the repudiation of an orderly, urban life, ultimately equating eschewed rituals with the fear of banditry in the countryside, poverty, crime, disorder, and life without protection or patronage.

Indeed, Mesopotamians did not have to probe for long to contemplate a life free from temple ritual. Mesopotamian cities were surrounded by peoples, living nomadic or semi-sedentary lives, who "resisted the power of attraction of indigenous Babylonian culture with its prestigious network of beliefs and lore, ennobled by a great antiquity." (Fales 2003, 293) Mesopotamian history itself, punctuated with periods of ritual-less (or ritual-threatened) anarchy (Cole 1994, 234ff.), also made the alternatives quite clear. It was certainly with these in mind that Mesopotamians drew the connection between a life free from temple rituals and a life without the values of order, stability, sophistication, and prosperity. That the powerful took advantage of rituals to enrich themselves, or upstarts failed to understand how to work rituals to their advantage, meant only that rituals were corruptible, although certainly not replaceable; at best, the observations were a skeptic's Voltaire-like value judgement on the beneficiaries of rituals, not a repudiation of temple ritual itself.

Circling back to the temple business records, one might argue that the mentions of interruptions and failures in those are of a concern altogether different from ones that Ambos discusses. I think this is incorrect, at least in part. The business records give us piecemeal insight into of the processes of ritual failure – the weak points in any temple's economy and administration that, when put under pressure, would be the first to break down. Suppliers might abscond with temple capital and fail to make payments; smaller temples, overlooked in an administrative shuffle, might have to beg their patron temples to remit material for the offerings; and, finally, those charged with carrying out the ritual themselves might do so halfheartedly or not at all. In effect, failure at the weakest points of a complex ritual system, if not sufficiently attended to, might presage a larger collapse. And collapse was devastating. The condition of temple ritual worked as a handy reference – a barometer of sorts – for Mesopotamian economic heath. Good times were those in which offerings and rituals flourished or increased, bad times those in which offerings ceased. (Waerzeggers 2010, 236)

In short, the business records elucidate for us where the multistage and complex process of Mesopotamian ritual was most fragile and hence susceptible to breakdowns. The high-level contemplation of ritual failure, focusing only on whether rituals occurred or not, testifies to the fact that, in the end, getting various parts of this interlocking system to move together was indeed a prodigious accomplishment – an accomplishment, in fact, whose ultimate reasons invited speculation from poets and priests, not administrators and bureaucrats. Given this, one should not be surprised that the failure of ritual provoked fear of the collapse of what differentiated Mesopotamia from its rustic neighbours and occasional predecessors. Failure was ultimately equated to an abandonment of Mesopotamian values, and it is precisely in temple business texts that we see the complex mechanisms to which those values gave expression.

References

Ambos, C. 2004. *Mesopotamische Baurituale aus dem 1. Jahrtausend v. Chr.* Dresden: Islet.

Ambos, C. 2007. Types of Ritual Failure and Mistakes in Ritual in Cuneiform Sources, in: Hüsken, U (ed.). *When Rituals Go Wrong: Mistakes, Failure, and the Dynamics of Ritual.* Numen Book Series: Studies in the History of Religion, 115. Leiden, Brill, 25-47.

Beaulieu, P-A. 1991. UBARA (EZENxKASKAL)ki = Udannu. *Acta Sumerologica* 13, 97-109.

Beaulieu, P-A. 1993. Prébendiers d'Uruk à Larsa. *Revue d'Assyriologie* 87, 137-152.

Beaulieu, P-A. 1995. The Brewers of Nippur. *Journal of Cuneiform Studies* 47, 85-96.

Beaulieu, P-A. 2001. The Abduction of Ištar from the Eanna Temple: The Changing Memories of an Event, in: Abusch, T, Beaulieu, P-A. *et al., Proceedings of the XLVe Rencontre Assyriologique Internationale, Part I, Harvard University: Historiography in the Ancient World.* Bethesda: CDL Press, 29-40.

Beaulieu, P-A. 2003. *The Pantheon of Uruk during the Neo-Babylonian Period.* Leiden, Boston: Brill, Styx.

Bidmead, J. 2002. *The Akitu Festival: Religious Continuity and Royal Legitimation in Mesopotamia.* Piscataway, N.J.: Gorgias Press.

Bongenaar, A.C.V. M. 1997. *The Neo-Babylonian Ebabbar Temple at Sippar: Its Administration and its Prosopography.* Uitgaven van het Nederlands Historisch-Archeologisch Instituut te Istanbul, 80. Leiden: Nederlands Instituut voor het Nabije Oosten.

Bongenaar, A.C.V.M. 2000. Private Archives in Neo-Babylonian Sippar and their Institutional Connections, in: Bongenaar, A. (ed.). *Interdependency of Institutions and Private Entrepreneurs: Proceedings of the Second MOS Symposium (Leiden 1998)*. Uitgaven van het Nederlands Historisch-Archaeologisch Instituut te Istanbul, 87. Leiden: Nederlands Historisch-Archaeologisch Instituut, 73-94.

Cocquerillat, D. 1968. *Palmeraies et cultures de l'Eanna d'Uruk (559-520)*. Ausgrabungen der Deutschen Forschungsgemeinschaft in Uruk-Warka, Bd. 8. Berlin: Mann.

Cole, S. and P. Machinist 1998. *Letters from Priests to the King Esarhaddon and Assurbanipal*. State Archives of Assyria, 13. Helsinki: University of Helsinki Press.

Cole, S.W. 1994. The Crimes and Sacrileges of Nabû-šuma-iškun. *Zeitschrift für Assyriologie* 84: 220-252.

Driel, G. van. 1999. Agricultural Entrepreneurs in Mesopotamia, in: Klengel, H and Renger, J. (eds.). *Landwirtschaft im Alten Orient (CRRAI 41, 1994)*. Berliner Beiträge zum Vorderen Orient, 18. Berlin: Reimer, 213-223.

Driel, G. van. 2002. *Elusive Silver: In Search of a Role for a Market in an Agrarian Environment. Aspects of Mesopotamia's Society*. Uitgaven van het Nederlands Historisch-Archaeologisch Instituut te Istanbul, 95. Leiden: Nederlands Instituut voor het Nabije Oosten.

Fales, F.M. 2003. Arameans and Chaldeans: Environment and Society, in: Leick, G. (ed.). *The Babylonians: An Introduction*. London; New York, Routledge, 288-298.

Grayson, A.K. 1970. Chronicles and the Akitu Festival, in: Finet, A. (ed.). *Actes de la XVIIe Rencontre assyriologique internationale*. Ham-sur-Heure: Comité belge de recherches en Mésopotamie, 160-170.

Jursa, M. 1995. *Die Landwirtschaft in Sippar in neubabylonischer Zeit*. Archiv für Orientforschung, Beiheft 25. Vienna, Institut für Orientalistik der Universität Wien.

Jursa, M. 2004. Accounting in Neo-Babylonian Institutional Archives: Structure, Usage, and Implications, in: Hudson, M. and Wunsch, C. (eds.). *Creating Economic Order: Record-keeping, Standardization, and Development of Accounting in the Ancient Near East*. Bethesda: CDL Press, 145-198.

Jursa, M. 2005. *Neo-Babylonian Legal and Administrative Documents: Typology, Contents, and Archives*. Guides to the Mesopotamian Textual Record, 1. Munster: Ugarit-Verlag.

Jursa, M. 2010. *Aspects of the Economic History of Babylonia in the First Millennium BC: Economic Geography, Economic Mentalities, Agriculture, The Use of Money, and the Problem of Economic Growth*. Alter Orient und Altes Testament, 377. Munster: Ugarit-Verlag.

Kleber, K. 2004. Die Fischerei in spätbabylonische Zeit. *Wiener Zeitschrift für die Kunde des Morgenlandes* 94, 133-165.

Kleber, K. 2005. Von Bierproduzenten und Gefängnisaufsehern: dezentrale Güterverwaltung und Buchhaltung in Eanna, in: Baker, H. and Jursa, M. (eds.). *Approaching the Babylonian Economy: Proceedings of the START Project Symposium Held in Vienna, 1-3 July 2004*. Alter Orient und Altes Testament, 330. Munster: Ugarit-Verlag, 289-321.

Kleber, K. 2008. *Tempel und Palast: die Beziehungen zwischen dem König und dem Eanna-Tempel im spätbabylonischen Uruk*. Alter Orient und Altes Testament, 358. Munster: Ugarit-Verlag.

Kozuh, M. 2011. On the Generation of Administrative Texts at the Eanna of Uruk. *Canadian Society for Mesopotamian Studies* 5, 13-24.

Kozuh, M. (*in press*). *The Sacrificial Economy: Assessors, Contractors, and Thieves in the Management of Sacrificial Sheep at the Eanna Temple of Uruk (ca. 625-520 BC)* Winona Lake, Indiana: Eisenbrauns.

Linssen, M.J.H. 2004. *The Cults of Uruk and Babylon: The Temple Ritual Texts as Evidence for Hellenistic Cult Practises*. Cuneiform Monographs, 25. Boston: Brill.

Maul, S.M. 1994. *Zukunftsbewältigung: eine Untersuchung altorientalischen Denkens anhand der babylonisch-assyrischen Löserituale (Namburbi)*. Baghdader Forschungen, 18. Mainz am Rhein: Philipp von Zabern.

Maul, S.M. 2011. *Ritualbeschreibungen und Gebete*. Wissenschaftliche Veröffentlichungen der Deutschen Orient-Gesellschaft, 133. Wiesbaden: Harrassowitz.

Oppenheim, A.L. 1977. *Ancient Mesopotamia: Portrait of a Dead Civilization*. Chicago: University of Chicago Press.

Parpola, S. 1993. *Letters from Assyrian and Babylonian Scholars*. State Archives of Assyria, 10. Helsinki: Helsinki University Press.

Pongratz-Leisten, B. 1994. *Ina šulmi irub: die kulttopographische und ideologische Programmatik der akitu-Prozession in Babylonien und Assyrien im 1. Jahrtausend v. Chr.* Mainz am Rhein: von Zabern.

Robbins, E. 1996. Tabular Sacrifice Records and the Cultic Calendar of Neo-Babylonian Uruk. *Journal of Cuneiform Studies* 48, 61-87.

Waerzeggers, C. 2010. *The Ezida Temple of Borsippa: Priesthood, Cult, Archives*. Achaemenid History, 15. Leiden: Nederlands Insituut voor het Nabije Oosten.

Walker, C.B.F. and M. Dick 2001. *The Induction of the Cult Image in Ancient Mesopotamia: The Mesopotamian M`is Pî ritual*. State Archives of Assyria Literary Texts, 1. Helsinki: University of Helsinki Press.

Woods, C.E. 2004. The Sun-God Tablet of Nabû-apla-iddina Revisited. *Journal of Cuneiform Studies* 56, 23-103.

Wunsch, C. (*in press*). Neo-Babylonian Entrepreneurs, in: Baumol, W. and Mokyr, J. (eds.). *The Invention of Enterprise: Entrepreneurship from Ancient Mesopotamia to Modern Times*. Princeton: Princeton University Press.

Chapter 4

Ritual failure and the temple collapse of prehistoric Malta

Caroline Malone[1] *and Simon Stoddart*[2]

Abstract

The temple culture of Neolithic Malta is marked by impressive megalithic stone architecture, figurative art and collective burial hypogea. Sustained over nearly one and a half millennia, the distinctive culture apparently failed around 2400 BC without apparent cause. The paper questions whether ritual provided mechanisms that maintained cultural continuity in challenging island conditions, and how those mechanisms might have failed. The paper reviews theoretical approaches and suggests additional models for explaining culture change through ritual failure.

Keywords: *Malta, islands, prehistoric temples, ritual.*

Introduction

Three key elements characterise the case of prehistoric Malta: the centrality of ritual, the highly elaborate materialisation of that ritual for a prehistoric society that by definition lacked texts, and the potential fragility of the island environment in which this ritual developed.

The key question is how these three elements interacted in the failure of prehistoric Malta. By contrast to this case, most studies of collapse by archaeologists have concentrated on larger scale political collapse of explicitly hierarchical societies, in contexts where the setting was greater and where fragility was more easily buffered. In the Maltese case, political agency is embedded in ritual action and thus must receive our first focus. A detailed understanding of Maltese ritual gives situation to its eventual collapse.

---

1 School of Geography, Archaeology and Palaeoecology, Queen's University Belfast. c.malone@qub.ac.uk.
2 Division of Archaeology, Department of Archaeology and Anthropology, University of Cambridge and Magdalene College, Cambridge. ss16@cam.ac.uk.

Ritual activity in prehistoric society forms a line of inquiry that archaeologists and art historians find compelling and graphic. Monuments and their artistic embellishments ignite our interest and engage our imaginations by providing a window of sorts into an otherwise lost world of human activities, beliefs and creativity. Because ritual involves repeated actions and symbolism, the physical spaces and material objects involved with the related ceremonial activities are often structured and predictable. Repetition (or redundancy) is one key to archaeological recognition of an ancient ritual place, rich in predictable symbols, structural forms, locations, behaviour and content which might imply a cycle of ritual activity. Such assemblages can enrich and inform our speculation about the cosmological dimensions of prehistoric worlds, and the rituality of such "special" places. Most societies that earn the title of "semi-complex" or "complex" generally have distinctive cultural markers in artistic or architectural form associated with ritual-religious-ceremonial activities and identities. Temples, shrines, altars, monuments and burials are the very stuff of this evidence, often containing concentrations of revealing evidence marked by sacrificial and feasting materials, and a redundancy of symbols (Renfrew 1985).

The investigation of Ritual Failure – the subject of this paper, as an archaeological concept necessarily implies that evidence in these artefactual and structural forms combined with other, potentially compelling, archaeological evidence, supports the interpretation of the rejection or abandonment of a ritual tradition, an ideology or a ritual site. As we shall see below, reliable interpretation of archaeological evidence always remains problematic and open, and relies heavily on equally reliable excavated and recorded material – something that is more often than not, lacking in older, traditional archaeological work.

The great semi-literate and literate civilisations – the early states of Egypt, Mesopotamia, Maya and others not only developed highly recognisable art and architecture in association with complex ritual and religion, but also recorded their ideology through texts of various sorts. These texts often indicate how central the ritualised activities were in maintaining equally complex social and economic systems, together with ideological power that transcended all aspects of life. Frequently, the texts refer to centralised moral and ritual authority, to the supernatural, to the role of leaders and their legitimisation. Indeed, leaders, and the ceremonial ritual and religion that legitimised them are intimately bound up with a complex code of symbols and ideology (Earle 1991, 6-10). Scholarly knowledge of these literate "civilisations" presents a wealth of historical detail regarding their emergence, florescence and decline or collapse. In turn, this knowledge has been subjected to an evolution of theoretical thinking, most notably neo-evolutionary approaches (see Yoffee 2005) focused on the rise, florescence, fall and collapse of "civilisation". Neo-evolutionary thinking continues to characterise much recent discussion (Toynbee 1933-54; Bennett and Tumin 1949; Service and Sahlins 1960; Tainter 1988, 22-38).

Less explicitly hierarchical non-state societies such as prehistoric Malta in the IVth and IIIrd millennia BC or Chaco Canyon at the end of the first millennium AD, and indeed pretty well all 'prehistoric' societies produced no written texts to inform us about their belief or socio-political systems. Instead, archaeological evidence and data from the natural sciences must suffice. The emergence, florescence and decline or collapse of these less hierarchical societies is rarely a point of discussion in archaeological research, given that the remoteness of time or otherness of culture tend to restrict discussion. The fragile remnants preserved in monuments and their stratigraphy usually reveal the final moments of such a society's existence, documenting the evidence of collapse or failure of a system rather than its beginnings. This emphasis on the final moments may provide a connection with the broader body of theory on collapse in more hierarchical societies.

For Elman Service, whose work epitomises the Neo-Evolutionary approach to social-cultural collapse studies, the "Law of Evolutionary Potential" (1960) and his subsequent 1975 study of "State and Civilisation", described how a society may manage change by internally developed adaptation to a specific situation or environment (Service 1975, 321). Once that society however, ceased to adapt to ongoing change or threat, and became statically specialised and "over-adapted" and rigid (Yoffee 2005, 134), then collapse or failure of some kind became almost inevitable in the face of competition. Invariably, anthropological studies perceive such collapse as institutional in nature, affecting certain elements, rather than the whole social system. Archaeological approaches require physical evidence that imply collapse – evidence that may well be difficult to identify or interpret.

One recurring factor cited for the collapse of a society suggests that such a society is unable to adapt to diminishing returns from the environment, with population levels exceeding the ability of technology or nature to produce sufficient to sustain the expected standard of living or population levels. In addition to this, Tainter lists the following as significant factors in the collapse in complex societies (Tainter 1988, 42): the depletion of resources, catastrophes, economic and/or environmental change, invasions and influence from other societies, conflict, social breakdown and "mystical factors". The latter two reasons for collapse have been particularly popular and have seen extensive discussion over the decades (Tainter 1988, 72) in spite of the difficulty of tying down such moralising notions in archaeological evidence. However, the ideas of virtue, decadence, biological growth and decay, progress or the wrath of the gods, amongst several notions, persist and have been applied to debates on social development and social change, regardless that they fail to deal with tangible evidence. In neo-evolutionary models of collapse, (as discussed by Tainter 1988), "Ritual Collapse" or ritual failure is seen as only one component of the structural decline of a complex social organisation. Ritual as evidenced through the medium of monuments, symbols, ceremonies, religious practice and action may often signal the effectiveness of the "institutional" power in a society, capable of mobilising labour and investing resources in expensive and non-productive activity. In many senses, though, the shared actions and beliefs displayed through ritual, when formalised through institutions such as temples, churches or sects and their extrovert ceremonial, often form the glue that holds otherwise disparate groups and interests together. Ritual plays a vital role

– demonstrating the cohesiveness of shared values and identities, binding different levels of society together and mediating through times of hardship and stress.

Failing societies may additionally exhibit decline in economic life, and sometimes they appear to go to extreme measures to expand productivity, rather than to regulate themselves in response to diminishing resources. Sometimes, a society becomes disenchanted with the organisation that demands excess effort to maintain the status quo (Tainter 1988; Edgerton 1992, 170-78), resulting in various maladaptations, revolt and self-destructive behaviours. One extreme response (suggested from numerous archaeological examples) takes the form of hyperactive ritual activity and renewed episodes of monument building. Such activity signals unprecedented investment in the spiritual and religious dimension, presumably in an attempt to persuade "the numinous" power to deal with the problem of falling returns, intense social change, or as Rappaport calls it "disruption of the cybernetics of holiness" (Rappaport 1999, 448). As noted at the beginning of this section, archaeology has by accident or intent, often focused on the structures and paraphernalia of ritual activity, the monumental remnants that once embodied religious belief, the arenas of ritual practice, and their material furnishings. Often it is the smashed remnants and rubbish of these activities that provide the narrative interpretation of a failed civilisation or a failed ritual tradition, and archaeology is often best placed to identify the hints of failure, decline and collapse. Bones, burials, burning and destruction might seem obvious components, but so too would be enlargement, embellishment and decoration of existing facilities together with symbolic deposits and a lot of rubbish associated with sacrifice and offering. Perhaps, to explore archaeologically Service's proposal noted above – we can identify when a society became overly structured, rigid and hierarchical through analysis of ritual spaces and facilities. Restricted access and exclusivity to monuments could signal when ritual ceased to be a social activity and become a performance by the controlling elite. To cite Tainter (1988), control over belief, action and economic investment is time-limited and eventually fails.

Islands in prehistory – an unlikely scenario for the classic models of civilisation collapse

Islands provide a usefully defined context within which to examine the emergence, rise, decline and collapse of a social system. Island cultures can still be viewed as laboratories of culture change, to cite Evans (1973; 1977), and their response to internal and external conditions potentially identified from archaeological evidence. Indeed, their relative isolation, specificity and vulnerability make them excellent subjects to examine themes such as collapse and change, due to natural and man-induced perturbations. At the same time, island cultures have a tendency to develop extreme characteristics, as reported on numerous islands, such as Rapa Nui (Hunt *et al.* 2010), Marquesas (Kirch 1991) and across the Mediterranean. Repeated examples of very large monuments, innovative material culture, hoarding and food management, redistribution mechanisms and dense populations seem typical of several traditional island cultures, from Minoan Crete and many of the Cycladic-Aegean islands Hawaii, Iron Age Britain and Ireland. Malta's extraordinary later Neolithic temple culture may be an extreme example of what is perhaps a predictable island-focused trend – the development of a compelling ideology combined with elaborate ritual that involved monumental constructions, feasting and food.

Malta exhibits similar characteristics for the rise and fall of a ritualised social system. Malta and Gozo were first colonised and settled around 5000 BC, almost certainly from the island of Sicily, which in turn had been influenced by the cultures of southern Italy. For at least a millennium, the fully agricultural settlers maintained close cultural ties with Sicily – sharing economic strategies, pottery styles, building styles and basic raw materials sourced from similar places (Malone 2003; Leighton 1999; Trump 2002). From c.4000-3600 BC divergence between Malta and Sicily-southern Italy is evident in the increasingly formalised ritual of subterranean rock cut tombs and burial caves. From the end of the fifth millennium BC, the Maltese Zebbuġ phase represented an increasingly distinctive island identity asserted through distinct pottery and architectural structures which morphed from multi-chambered subterranean rock cut tombs (Xemxija) to ground level simple oval-lobed stone-built structures (Mġarr), and began an evolution of ritual buildings. By c.3600-3200 BC the construction of massive stone slab/rubble walls and elaborate lobed floor plan of the Ġgantija phase signals the full development of the megalithic temple of Malta. Over time structures became ever more complex, with a central corridor leading from a single entrance set within an impressive convex façade. The earliest buildings were two and three lobed (Trump 2002) (Figure 9) (Kordin III has two-lobed, and Skorba, Mnajdra and Ta Ħaġrat have three-lobed structures). Ġgantija's great west temple comprised 5 lobes, and later on, further elaboration at Ħaġar Qim saw multiple temple structures incorporated together within a single surrounding outer wall. Continuity in burial practice elaborated the distinction between the zone of the dead in subterranean structures, and the zone of the living in the temples on the ground surface.

In the centuries after c.3200 there appears to have been a flurry of ever more elaborate and extravagant monument building, adding larger apses, grand forecourts, corbelled roofs, carved panels, plastered and paved floors and many addition elements. These took the form of altars, hidden rooms, carved figures, stone bowls, painted decoration, libation holes and fire pits. With large forecourts, impressive entrances and hidden interiors the temple layout formed a stage for drama and performance. The potential for actors or ritual specialists to emerge from side areas or hidden rooms to perform to an assembled audience added to the mystique implied by the carefully designed ritual spaces (Anderson and Stoddart 2007). In parallel with the temple development, but with origins in the earlier rock cut tombs are the multi-spaced subterranean burial sites or hypogea, known from Hal Saflieni and the Brochtorff-Xaghra circle. Collective inhumation burial characterised the temple culture, but whilst hundreds, even thousands of burials were gathered in one place, separation of these spaces into compartments, chambers and pits enabled some distinction between one group of people and another. Architectural elaboration of these burial places echoed the built temples

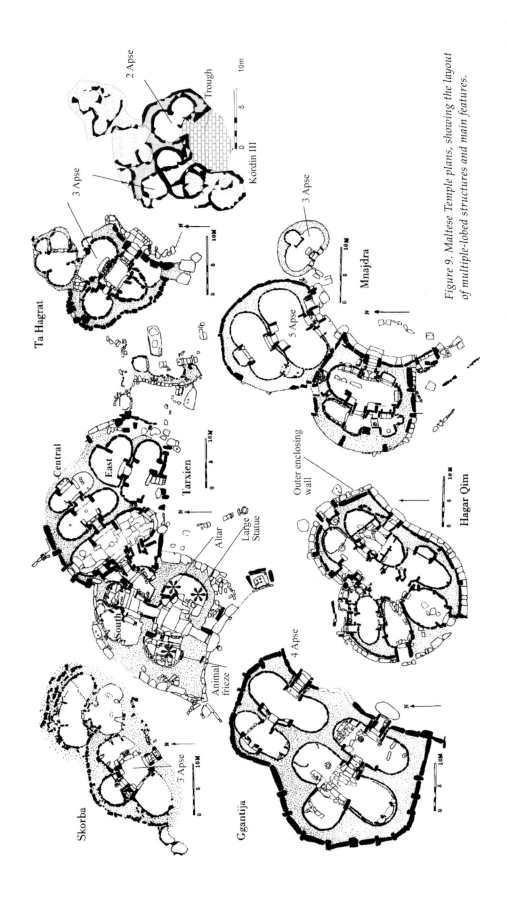

Figure 9. Maltese Temple plans, showing the layout of multiple-lobed structures and main features.

through elements of structural layout, megalithic additions, decoration and formality (Malone 2007).

Distinctive sculpture and decoration developed to embellish the temples. This comprised carved, pecked and drilled stone surfaces placed in significant areas of the temple interiors. Decorated panels of curvilinear patterns suggestive of vine-scroll-wave forms and figurative images of fish or domestic animals enhanced the compartmentalised interior spaces. Tactile as well as visually arresting, these panels enclosed central zones focused on fire pits, sacrifices and offerings, often visible from the main entrance and corridor of the temples. The panels seem to have been matched by figurative sculpture, perhaps placed together with objects or offerings on special shelves and altars. The possibility that these unusual buildings were intended for normal domestic, agricultural or industrial use is remote, given the intense focus on pattern, imagery and investment, and the repetition of form and decoration. Instead, the possibility that the buildings functioned as some type of ritual centre for feasting and food redistribution is supported by the large quantities of animal remains, burnt deposits and hundreds of ceramic offering bowls recovered. Elaboration of existing temples took place over at least half a millennium, with enlargements, such as at Tarxien where two individual lobed buildings (south and west temples) were combined by the insertion of an additional (central) temple to form a series of interconnected spaces (Cilia 2004, 52-62). At Hagar Qim, a complex arrangement of separate but adjacent buildings was enclosed by an outer wall and interlinked by corridors. The Hal Saflieni Hypogeum likewise was expanded, but downwards into the rock to form two additional levels beneath a larger upper burial area that connected the ground surface with burial cavities. The Brochtorff Xaghra Circle burial site also saw structural enlargement, modification, embellishment and destruction in its subterranean burial cave-hypogeum. This pattern of expansion, paired with new absolute dates, offers important insights into the final centuries and decades of the temple culture and its society (Malone *et al.*, 2009). The millennia of ritual and temple evolution reached a climax of decorative extravagance around 2700-2500 BC, before the structures (and perhaps the ideological tradition they encapsulated) were abandoned (Trump 1976). In several instances, the temple sites were reoccupied centuries later, in the Bronze Age or as revealed by current Italian excavation at Tas Silġ, buried beneath a Phoenician ritual complex.

Dating the megalithic stone structures remains problematic, given the lack of surviving stratigraphy or recent scientific excavation, but deposits below the floors of some buildings (Cilia 2004; Trump 2002) indicate prehistoric expansion and elaboration in places that had long sequences of occupation. Malta's prehistoric architectural distinctiveness was unparalleled in neighbouring areas of the central or western Mediterranean region, and much has been written about its cultural complexity and the type of society that engendered monumental building on such a scale (see for example Evans 1971; Malone *et al.*, 2009; Renfrew 1973; Trump 2002). Given the ruinous state of all the prehistoric sites, the identification of deliberate destruction or abandonment is contentious. At Brochtorff Circle and

Tarxien temple there are definite traces of destruction, removal, iconoclasm and desertion that confirm some type of ritual failure in prehistoric Malta.

The total land surface of the Maltese islands covers barely 315 square kilometres. The landscape, once tree covered and endowed with deeper soils than today, was always a dry, rocky limestone place, without perennial streams or bodies of fresh water, and further limited by suitable aquifers to retain humidity. Some valleys maintain relatively high soil fertility and moisture, but much of the small land area of the Maltese islands was, and remains, a challenging landscape for productive agriculture, with steep slopes and cliffs, rocky outcrops and clay badlands. In comparison to early Malta, most European Neolithic societies existed within relatively extensive landscapes, where boundaries were mainly marked by physical obstructions such as uplands or rivers, heavy soils, thick forests and perhaps the presence of aggressive neighbours. Technology, population levels, soil fertility, distance, seasonality and local resources in such situations would have been the controlling elements that determined population carrying capacity in a given zone. Within a restricted island environment, where the nearest human neighbours in Sicily were a perilous 80 kilometres across the unpredictable Mediterranean Sea, the economic picture for early Malta looks considerably more difficult than for comparable Neolithic communities within mainland landscapes.

Current environmental research on the ancient landscape of Malta remains unclear and more work is needed to understand the details of fluctuations in humidity and climate that may have affected the region during the period considered in this paper. Pollen data retrieved from a deep core taken from Marsa (Carroll al 2004) suggest that much of the Maltese landscape was cleared of its vegetation from the first settlement, and that by the Bronze Age in the second millennium BC, the native tree cover and vegetation was much as we find it today. Heavy autumn rain then, as now, can have a devastating effect on soil stability, washing topsoil from slopes into valleys or the sea. Terrace systems were developed, possibly as early as the second millennium BC and certainly in later prehistoric and Phoenician times, as a means to retain the precious soil that is the fundamental resource of a settled economic existence on a small island archipelago. Such soil management techniques or forward planning were absent in Neolithic Malta, and it may be that early farming and extensive clearance of the native vegetation wrought immense damage over a relatively short period of time on a landscapes that always would have been marginal because of its restricted size and fragile ecosystem. Of the farming in the Neolithic, we know that the first settlers and their successors employed the typical mixed agriculture of the region (Trump 2002). Cattle, sheep-goat, a few pigs, wheat, barley and probably pulses such as peas and beans made up the diet, although proportions and sub-species remain poorly known. Sheep-goat remains form the majority of the bone in samples from sites excavated in the twentieth century. These creatures are illustrated, together with images of cattle and pigs in friezes and carvings at Tarxien, and as incised designs or modelled handles on contemporary ceramic vessels. From the density of monuments and archaeological activity across the Maltese landscape, it is assumed that a large population was supported in the late Neolithic temple period. But what was the

Figure 10. Animals and Feasts: images from Tarxien and Buġgiba, showing friezes, altars and bowl. 1 & 2: Animal friezes from South Temple, Tarxien. Male sheep, pig, goat. 3: Female sheep. 4&5: Frieze showing fish from destroyed temple at Buġgiba. 6: Arichitectural Altar in South Temple, Tarxien, with curvilinear relief decoration and semi-circular panel below, enclosing flint knives and animal remains on discovery by Zammit. 7: Restored large stone bowl in Tarxien.

human carrying capacity for Malta in the later Neolithic? We can only speculate on the prehistoric population density, given the inconclusive and scant traces of houses beneath temples or fragmentary structures (Malone *et al.* 2009*b*, 41-52). If the population density was as much as 30 people per square kilometre (100 ha, or 247 acres), which seems a plausible level for intensive mixed farming in southern Europe, then the population could have reached 8,000-10,000 people at certain times. Periods of climatic instability affecting levels of rainfall and groundwater would well have had drastic impact on a dense and economically isolated population dependent on crops and grazing animals.

Analysis of the extensive human bone sample from Gozo indicates possible dietary and physical stress during the temple period, in comparison to earlier Zebbug phases (Stoddart *et al.* 2009, 325-30). Stable Isotope determinations from a small AMS dated sample of the human bone from the Brochtorff-Xaghra Circle on Gozo (Stoddart *et al.* 2009, 335-40) suggest that the human diet was largely terrestrially sourced, and possibly cereal rather than meat-based, in the final stages of that site's use. Marine foods seem, like so many other Neolithic populations, to have been insignificant in the Maltese diet, in spite of a surrounding sea rich in seafood. This sample – which is far from complete or conclusive, appears to show that animal protein was in short supply (c.2600-2400- BC). This final Tarxien phase conversely celebrated animals, as evidenced by decoration of spaces with zoomorphic friezes, carvings, models and altars devoted to their slaughter and the disposal of bone within altars (Figure 10) further testifies to this. Perhaps animals figured large in dietary aspiration during this late temple period for the very reason that they had become rare and especially valued. Why, when mixed farming was apparently a well established economy for early Malta, would stock animals become scarce and consequently celebrated in art?

The pollen sequence from Marsa (see above) might be one place to seek an interim answer to the problem of what happened to the agricultural base of late Neolithic Malta. The temple culture period is represented by slight, but distinct fluctuations in plant types, sometimes indicating cereals and grasses and at others, a proliferation of weeds (Hunt pers comm.) suggesting perhaps that grazing land is given over to more intensive cultivation of cereals and other plant foods (Figure 11). The weeds could indicate cultivation replaced grassland, perhaps because of overstocking or drought. This in turn could imply that the support of domestic animals may have been severely compromised if humans and stock were competing over a landscape affected by inadequate rainfall and water. Food supplies would soon fall and result in short-term economic pressure or even failure. Over the period of several years, such failure might spell catastrophe for an island culture and its very specific ritual system, based around an equally particular system of production in a restricted and physically isolated environment. Might the environment and the economy based on it, be one part of the story of ritual failure that is encountered in the wider culture of prehistoric Malta?

Some authors have suggested that the island nature of Neolithic Malta was more a state of mind (reviewed in Malone and Stoddart 2004) than a physical reality. We argue that the 80km were indeed significant, particularly for the supply of foodstuffs.

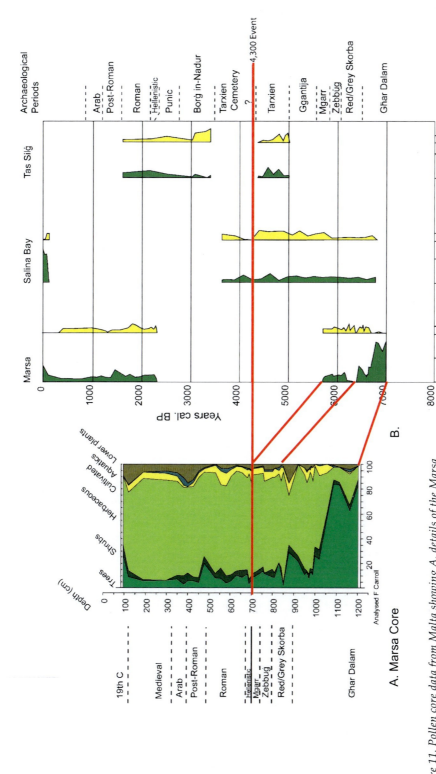

Figure 11. Pollen core data from Malta showing A. details of the Marsa core, and B. other cores from Malta. The horizontal line marks the episode of catastrophic vegetational clearance and decline c.4300 years BP at the end of the Temple Period and may be the response to a climatic change. The analysis was undertake by Frank Carroll (see Carroll et al 2012).

Crossing the 80km in a small, unmasted rowing boat involved unpredictability and risk that perhaps only the skilled would attempt on a regular basis. It is worth suggesting that knowledge and skill in ritual ran alongside knowledge and skill in marine travel. Interaction is difficult to assess, given the similar geology of south eastern Sicily to Malta, and even more difficult to date, given the potential for curation and residuality, but imports of exotic materials were relatively limited. Obsidian principally comprised small flakes and blades, which declined in quantity in the Tarxien period (Vella 2008, Charts 1-2; Trump *et al.* 2009, 251-252). Struck stone was substantially made up of local chert. Exotic greenstones were reduced and sacralised (often perforated for stringing on necklaces). Ochre from prehistoric deposits, originally considered an import, has been shown recently to be equally available from the Maltese island system (Attard-Montalto *et al.*, 2012). Imported pottery was very rare. All this evidence suggests that a substantial preoccupation with intra- rather than extra- island activity, setting the scene for the scenario we have outlined.

Structures, objects and archaeology

Whilst the interior spaces of the Maltese temples were focused on altars and hidden places that formalised a particular type of ceremonial activity, the buildings themselves looked out over a wider landscape and were orientated towards views of importance. In the case of Mnajdra this was the sunrise at the solstice, but at other sites orientation may have been certain constellations or solar-lunar movements, ancestral places in the heavens or the outer world of interaction. Internal installations such as altars and benches for sacrifice, offerings and participation were matched by facilities for cooking, burning, washing and storage. Hidden rooms that contained shelved niches for storage of goods and treasures were set deep within the buildings, covered by corbelled roofs, accessed through "porthole" doors and sealed with stone panels. Secrecy and control was a fundamental part of the practice of ritual, indicating perhaps paranoia towards egalitarian ceremony, instead signalling rites of passage and initiation for the elite. Entry for the privileged members of the community required procession over marked thresholds into restricted, perhaps dark interior space. At every stage of that procession, offerings could be made into libation holes on thresholds and at entrances, on altars and benches set along the main corridor, and in ever more hidden compartments inside the building, passing through barred doors at each stage, moving up through a hierarchy of controlled access (Anderson and Stoddart 2007).

The large temple forecourts seem to have been remodelled and enlarged (as at Ggantija), with entrance thresholds made ever more grandiose, formal and restricted. They presented stage-like settings for a contrived ritual performance that implies careful management and manipulation of the action. Such a level of sophistication and audience control has encouraged scholars to suggest Maltese society was hierarchically structured (Renfrew 1973; Zammit 1930), perhaps ritually managed by priests or ritual specialists. Much has been written about the arrangement and function of the temples (see Malone 2007; Malone *et al.*

forthcoming; Trump 2002; Cilia 2004), which may have housed ritual specialists (?priests or chiefs), their paraphernalia and tribute in the form of food offerings. It is tempting to see the temples as ritualised storage centres for theatrical sacrifice, feasting and food redistribution, where the local population would have gathered at certain times in the forecourt to observe the rituals and be fed by the hand of the controlling elite. However, more than food was on offer in these temple buildings. The imagery, theatre and privilege presumably granted to certain members of the community to enter inside the temple buildings and participate, might have added to the attraction and excitement of what must have been regular, cyclical events.

Ritual paraphernalia and interpretation of ritual failure

The semi-realistic statuettes and small figurines associated with the temple culture provide compelling visual aids in our exploration of the ritual world of early Malta. The human, animal and imagined figures may represent mythological characters from a cosmology that underpinned the temple culture, and may inform on social concerns. The anthropomorphic figures range from unclothed to semi-dressed, they include naturalistic to extreme monstrous images, and some figures stand whilst others are seated/squatting. Animal images range from terrestrial domestic creatures to birds and subterranean cold-blooded reptiles-fish, representing a layered world of different animal spirits. Large standing and skirted statuettes might suggest authority figures, wearing symbols of status such as headdresses, belts, necklaces and elaborate hair styles, and these details might suggest priestly or chiefly status. In contrast, obese and usually small seated/squatting figures imply a world of ample food and leisure, assembled to represent ideal conditions, perhaps of gods, ancestors or spirits. The larger of these figures are portrayed with skirts, and had removable heads that were operated like puppets with strings (Figure 12). Such "dynamic" puppet-icons may have been important components of ritual theatre in the temple spaces, on visible ledges for the reception of offerings, or in hidden rooms where "oracle holes" were used to impart special knowledge (Malone 2007; Barrowclough 2007). These statuettes were manipulated by an operator (a ritual specialist?), perhaps to provide predictions, to divine omens or for symbolic display to enact myths. The interchangeable heads perhaps portrayed different characters or symbolised components of the cosmology. Whatever the statuettes represented to the ancient Maltese, there is no doubt that they signalled powerful values and knowledge. They have been found hidden deep in temples, inserted into foundations, buried with human remains or placed in special prominent locations which give a graphic insight into parts of the ancient cosmological system of Neolithic Malta. The role and significance of these anthropomorphic images remains a topic of heated discussion and ongoing debate (Malone 2008; Vella Gregory 2005; Gimbutas 1982; 1991, Gimbutas and Dexter 1999).

The archaeological location of the statuettes may provide some understanding of their role. The findspots vary from intentional niches, pits, graves and other stores to rubbish heaps. From the scant information of old excavations, it seems some images retained special power and were carefully buried (for example, the

Figure 12. Large figurines from Ħaġar Qim temple, showing moving head mechanism. 1: Large stone figure from Ħaġar Qim temple, front view. 2, 3 & 4: Details of string holes and moveable head socket arrangement.

seven large stone figures from Ħaġar Qim), whilst other were casually thrown away in rubbish. Two fragile modelled terracotta standing skirted figures were retrieved from recesses at Tarxien (Figure 13). Certain authority figurines were intentionally broken into pieces or defaced. One life-size example built into the south temple of Tarxien was destroyed (ostensibly through agricultural activity) from the waist up, with only plinth, legs and skirted buttocks surviving (Figure 13). A recently discovered high relief figure was found buried under later construction at Tas Silg (Vella 1999). It represented a similar skirted figure on a plinth. In this case, the surface was badly damaged and probably intentionally defaced by a frenzied attack on the features of the image (Figure 14). Intentional iconoclasm of large authority figures also seems to be a strong likelihood in the case of a prestigious figure found scattered across the burial deposits of the Brochtorff Xaghra Circle on Gozo (Malone *et al.* 2009c, 283-89). The very finely carved stone figure stood about 60-70 cm high, and represented a skirted obese individual, with arms crossed, the legs rising from an oblong base, following the canon for the figures described above. The surface had been painted in yellow ochre, carefully smoothed, polished and decorated with fine drilled dots. The statuette had been smashed into more than thirty fragments and spread across and crushed into the burials in a pattern that could not have occurred naturally, and far beyond the place of breakage (Figure 14) suggesting pieces were intentionally thrown into various burial compartments.

Importantly, the burial site seems to have been abandoned at the same time as the vandalism, and perhaps the broken fragments represent an act of closure. This apparently ritual closure was accompanied by the physical collapse of the cave roof, which in spite of large stone props placed to support the thin cave roof, fell in and closed the caves to further access. The stone structures (shelves, interior walls) of the easternmost cave had already been partially dismantled and the burials left buried in falling debris (Stoddart *et al.* 2009, 195), abandoned along with remainder of the burial caves. The temple complexes across Malta and Gozo, likewise, seem to have suffered a variety of destructive collapse, of stone removal, of reuse, and of abandonment over time. The chronology implied from recent AMS dates from Gozo suggests that burial activity ceased along with structural collapse and abandonment after 2450 BC. The archaeological sequence remains mute on what happened next. Whether the decline and abandonment of the temple culture was slow or rapid is unclear, and evidence is lacking on any human activity on Malta until sometime after 2000 BC when a Bronze Age society was settled on the islands. The Tarxien Cemetery levels discovered by Zammit (1930) imply a very different cultural ideology expressed through cremation burial rites together with metals and pottery of very different tradition. An entirely different sensuality (Malone and Stoddart 2009, 376-380) and new social context focused on the individual rather than the community (Stoddart and Malone 2008, 26). Currently no secure archaeological sequence with dated remains has been identified to testify to any occupation at all on Malta for the intervening centuries.

If we accept the criteria suggested by Tainter, the failure of one component within a social-economic-ritual system seems unlikely to have precipitated so complete a decline that it resulted in abandonment of the islands, or a decline

Figure 13. Standing and skirted figures from Tarxien and Tas Silġ, showing vandalism. 1 & 2: Vandalised remains of stone statue from Tas Silġ – original in the National Museum of Archaeology, Malta, 97cm high. 3 & 4: Terracotta skirted figure from Tarxien: dissembled parts and former reconstruction. 5: c. 60cm high. 6: Life-sized stone statue at Tarxien (replica) in-situ in Tarxien South Temple. 7: Original statue fragment in National Museum of Archaeology, Malta and scale drawing.

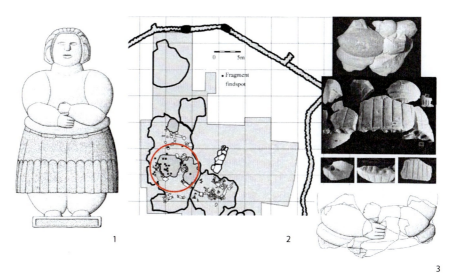

Figure 14. Distribution of broken figure fragments from Brochtorff Circle, Xaghra, Gozo and reconstruction of figure. 1: Reconstruction. 2: Brochtorff Circle, Xaghra, Gozo, excavation plan showing distribution of large figure fragments, within marked red circle. 3: Drawing and photographs of selected fragments of large stone figure, Gozo.

in cultural life that no recognisable occupation evidence formed. The role of the environment is often treated with caution by archaeologists, aware that over reliance on such determinism is unacceptable, but Malta may be one case where the environment may have been a major determining element and have influenced the development of the unusual ritual organisation. Myths and gods (such as Egyptian Ra and Osiris) from ancient Egypt, and others from Mesopotamia, India and China expose deeply felt concerns about the climate, the environment and the uncertainty of economic success or even survival. Such concerns were often formalised into elaborate seasonal ritual and ceremonial that symbolised death and rebirth in particular. In Chinese Han myth the uncertainties of rain, drought and the dangers of climate change were incorporated into cosmology, and articulated as notions of pendulum-like yin-yang dualism or a rotating sequence of elements (Hsu 2000, 212). More than likely, prehistoric people on Malta similarly referenced a mythology that engaged their concerns of seasonal change, perhaps expressed in some of the snake, lizard, fish and bird images that celebrated the mass migration of birds in spring, the survival of reptiles in drought or the shoals of fish in early autumn. The symbolic use and ritual manipulation by the temple elite of the elements water and fire, of colour, of mythological figures, may have made demands for offerings such as food and gifts, much as relics of Medieval saints were employed to demand alms from pilgrims.

There are parallels between the archaeological characteristics of the Maltese islands and the ethnography of the Polynesian Marquesa islands. There, hereditary chiefs had both ritual and economic power wrested from them by "inspirational" priests (tau'a) (Kirch1991, 121) who induced an inversion of the established social order. In the Marquesas the priests cared for the remains of the dead, controlled ceremonials "and learning and giving utterance to the will of god" (Handy quoted by Kirch 1991, 125). Drought and ecological pressure had significant impact on the local subsistence, but elite storage by chiefs ensured such groups survived when others perished through famine. These elites also had control of the means of production, of fishing, land, storage and labour, and a yearly cycle of rituals that assured good harvests, and provided the priest-chief's source of power. Feasting too played a significant and competitive role in the society, reflected in settlement, monuments, warfare and cults. Distanced by geography and millennia, this comparative example can only suggest ideas for understanding Malta. However, the relatively rapid escalation in temple enlargement and elaboration that occurred in the late stages of the temple culture surely implies a change in social hierarchy, where power over ritual, subsistence and labour was increasingly in the hands of ritual specialists. Coupled with control of ceremonial and ritual, these elites may have controlled access to the burial sites of ancestors and spirits, adding power to their role. The architecture asserts notions of power and control, whilst the archaeological evidence suggests a populous and stressed environment, where overproduction and exploitation was reflected in poor diet, failed crops and grazing land and weed growth, coupled with extravagant feasting rubbish. Sooner or later the system ceased to be seductive or believable. Perhaps the priest-chiefs in their skirted finery were toppled, just as the statues were destroyed. Scattered in pieces over the remains of ancestors, perhaps the smashed Brochtorff statuette showed how a society rejected its spiritual masters. The closure of the burial sites and the rejection of those ancestral places might also imply that the population no longer felt their ancestors had influence over economic productivity. If the stable isotope readings are reinforced by yet more samples, indicating a marked economic downturn in the middle of the IIIrd millennium BC, these may, in turn, confirm indications from the environmental pollen data that a combination of social, economic, technological and environmental conditions led to the collapse of the temple culture and the ritual failure that this demise implies. The rise and fall of prehistoric Malta were characterised by ideology supported by an intra-island economy rather than the economics vested in portable wealth and cross Mediterranean connectivity which permeated the Bronze Age that followed.[3]

Acknowledgements

Caroline Malone took the lead role in this article. Thanks to the following for their contributions to the illustrations: Steven Ashley, Jason Gibbons, Simon Stoddart, Ben Plumridge and Caroline Malone.

---

3   These ideas are shortly to be investigated further (http://www.qub.ac.uk/sites/FRAGSUS/ through the support of an Advance ERC Researchers Grant). Greater detail of many of the assumptions made here about settlement density, environmental degradation, human diet and stress and extra insular connectivity will be rigorously examined.

References

Anderson, M. and. Stoddart, S. K. F 2007. Mapping Cult Context: GIS applications in Maltese temples, in: Barrowclough, D. and. Malone C.A.T (eds.). *Cult in Context.* Oxford: Oxbow, 41-4.

Attard-Montalto, N., Shortland, A. and Rogers, K. 2012. The provenancing of ochres from the Neolithic Temple Period in Malta. *Journal of Archaeological Science* (39/4, 1094-1102).

Barrowclough, D. 2007. Putting cult in context, in: Barrowclough, D. and Malone, C. (eds.). *Cult in Context.* Oxford: Oxbow Books, 45-53.

Bennett, J.W. and Tumin, M.M. 1949. *Social life, structure and function: an introductory general sociology.* New York: A. A. Knopf.

Carroll, F.A., Fenech, K., Hunt, C.O., Jones, A. and Schembri, P.J. 2004. The past environment of the Maltese Islands: the Marsa cores, in: *Exploring the Maltese Prehistoric Temple Culture 2003, Conference in Malta.* CD-Rom. Ed Eneuk, Sarasota: Fl. EMPTC.

Carroll, F.A., Hunt, C.O., Schembri, P.J. and Bonanno, A. 2012. Holocene climate change, vegetation history and human impact on the Central Mediterranean: evidence from the Maltese Islands. *Quaternary Science Reviews* 52, 24-40.

Cilia, D. 2004. *Malta before history. The world's oldest freestanding architecture.* Sliema: Miranda Publishers.

Earle, T. 1991. The Evolution of Chiefdoms, in: Earle, T. (ed.). *Chiefdoms, Power, Economy and ideology.* Cambridge: Cambridge University Press.1-15.

Edgerton, R.B. 1992. *Sick Societies: challenging the myth of primitive harmony.* New York: The Free Press, MacMillan.

Evans. J.D. 1971. *The Prehistoric Antiquities of the Maltese Islands.* London, Athlone Press.

Evans. J.D. 1973. Islands as laboratories for the study of culture process, in: Renfrew, A.C. (ed.). *The Explanation of Culture Change.* London: Duckworth, 517-20.

Evans. J.D. 1977. Island archaeology in the Mediterranean: problems and opportunities. *World Archaeology* 9, 12-26.

Gimbutas, M. 1982. *The Goddesses and Gods of Old Europe 6500- 3500 BC.* Myths, Cults and Images. London: Thames and Hudson.

Gimbutas, M. 1991. *The civilisation of the Goddess: the world of Old Europe.* New York: Harper Collins.

Gimbutas, M. and Dexter, M.R. 1999. *The Living Goddess.* Berkeley (CA): University of California Press.

Hsu, C-Y. 2000. Chinese attitudes toward climate, in: McIntoch, R.J., Tainter, J.A., and Keech McIntosh, S. (eds.). *The way the wind blows: Climate, History, and Human Action*. New York: Columbia University Press. 209-219.

Hunt, T.L. and Lipo, C.P. 2010. Ecological catastrophe, Collapse, and the Myth of "Ecocide" on Rapa Nui (Easter island), in: McAnny, P.A. and Yoffee, N. (eds.). *Questioning Collapse: Human resilience, Ecological Vulnerability, and the aftermath of Empire*. Cambridge: Cambridge University Press, 21-44.

Kirch, P.V. 1991. Chiefship and competitive involution: the Marquesa Islands of eastern Polynesia, in: Earle, T. (ed.). *Chiefdoms, Power, Economy and ideology*. Cambridge: Cambridge University Press, 119-145.

Kristiansen, K. 1991. Chiefdoms, States and Systems of social evolution, in: Earle, T. (ed.). *Chiefdoms, Power, Economy and ideology*. Cambridge: Cambridge University Press, 16-43.

Leighton, R. 1999. *Sicily before History: an archaeological survey from the Palaeolithic to the Iron Age*. London: Duckworth.

Malone, C. 2003. The Italian Neolithic: a synthesis of research. *Journal of World Prehistory* 17/3, 235-310.

Malone, C. 2007. Ritual, Space and Structure – the context of cult in Malta and Gozo, in: Barrowclough, D. and Malone, C. (eds.). *Cult in Context*. Oxford: Oxbow Books, 23-34.

Malone, C. 2008. Metaphor and Maltese Art: explorations in the Temple Period. *Journal of Mediterranean Archaeology* 21/1, 81-109.

Malone, C. and Stoddart, S. 2004. Towards an island of mind? , in: Cherry, J., Scarre, C. and Shennan, S. (eds.). *Explaining social change: studies in honour of Colin Renfrew*. Cambridge: McDonald Institute, 93-102.

Malone, C., Stoddart, S., Trump, D., Bonanno, A., Gouder, T., and Pace, A. 2009 (eds.). *Mortuary Customs in Prehistoric Malta: excavations at the Brochtorff Circle Gozo 1987-94*. Cambridge: McDonald Institute Monographs.

Malone, C., Grima, R., Magro-Conti, J., Trump, D., Stoddart, S. and Hardisty, H. 2009. The domestic environment, in: Malone, C. Stoddart, S., Trump, D., Bonanno, A., Gouder, T., and Pace. A. (eds.). *Mortuary Customs in Prehistoric Malta: excavations at the Brochtorff Circle Gozo 1987-94*. Cambridge: McDonald Institute Monographs, 41-56.

Malone, C, Bonanno, A., Trump, D., Dixon, J., Leighton, R., Pedley, M., Stoddart, S. and Schembri, P.J. 2009. Material culture, in: Malone, C. Stoddart, S. ,Trump, D, Bonanno, A., Gouder, T., and Pace. A. (eds.). *Mortuary Customs in Prehistoric Malta: excavations at the Brochtorff Circle Gozo 1987-94*. Cambridge: McDonald Institute Monographs, 219-313.

Malone, C. and Stoddart, S. (eds.). forthcoming. *The Art of Ritual in Prehistoric Malta*. Cambridge: Cambridge University Press.

McAnny, P.A. and Yoffee, N. 2010 (eds.). *Questioning Collapse: Human resilience, Ecological Vulnerability, and the aftermath of Empire.* Cambridge: Cambridge University Press.

Rappaport, R.A. 1999. *Ritual and religion in the making of Humanity.* Cambridge: Cambridge University Press.

Renfrew, A.C. 1973. *Before Civilisation.* Harmonsworth: Penguin Books.

Renfrew, A.C. 1985. *The Archaeology of Cult.* London: Thames and Hudson.

Sahlins, M.D. and Service, E.R. 1960 (eds.). *Evolution and Culture.* Ann Arbor: Michigan University Press.

Service, E.R. 1960. The Law of Evolutionary Potential, in: Sahlins, M.D. and Service, E.R. (eds.). *Evolution and Culture.* Ann Arbor: Michigan University Press, 93-122.

Service, E.R. 1975. *The Origins of the State and Civilisation: the process of cultural evolution.* New York: Random House.

Stoddart, S. and Malone, C. 2008. Changing beliefs in the human body in prehistoric Malta 5000-1500 BC, in: Boric, D. and Robb, J. (eds.). *Past Bodies. Body-Centred Research in Archaeology*, Oxford: Oxbow Books, 19-28.

Stoddart, S., Malone, C., Mason, S., Trump, B. and Trump, D. 2009. The Tarxien Phase Levels, in: Malone, C., Stoddart, S., Trump, D., Bonanno, A., Gouder, T., and Pace. A. 2009 (eds.). *Mortuary Customs in Prehistoric Malta: excavations at the Brochtorff Circle Gozo 1987-94.* Cambridge: MacDonald Institute Monographs, 109-205.

Stoddart, S., Barber, G., Duhig, C., Mann, G., O'Connell, T., Lai, L., Redhouse, D., Tykot, R., and Malone, C. 2009. The Human and Animal remains, in: Malone Stoddart, S. Trump, D, Bonanno, A. Gouder, T, and Pace. A. (eds.). *Mortuary Customs in Prehistoric Malta: excavations at the Brochtorff Circle Gozo 1987-94.* Cambridge: McDonald Institute Monographs, 315-340.

Tainter, J.A. 1988. *The Collapse of Complex Societies.* Cambridge: Cambridge University Press.

Toynbee, A.J. 1962 (1933-54). *A study of History.* Oxford: Oxford University Press.

Trump, D. 1976. The collapse of the Maltese temples, in: Sieveking, G., Longworth, I. and Wilson, K.E. (eds.). *Problems in Economic and Social Archaeology.* London: Duckworth, 605-9.

Trump, D. 2002. *Malta: Prehistory and Temples.* Malta: Midsea Books Ltd.

Trump, D., Malone, C. and Bonanno, A. 2009. Obsidian, in: Malone, C., Stoddart, S., Trump, D., Bonanno, A., Gouder, T. and Pace. A. 2009 (eds.). *Mortuary Customs in Prehistoric Malta: excavations at the Brochtorff Circle Gozo 1987-94.* Cambridge: MacDonald Institute Monographs, 250-3.

Vella, N.C. 1999. Trunkless legs of stone: debating ritual continuity at Tas-Silġ, Malta, in: Mifsud, A. and Savona-Ventura, C. (eds.). *Facets of Maltese Prehistory.* Malta, The prehistoric Society of Malta, 225-39.

Vella, C. 2008. Report on the lithic tools of Sicilian origin from the prehistoric site of Skorba, Malta, in: Bonanno, A. (ed.). *Malta and Sicily: Miscellaneous Research Projects*, Palermo: Officina di Studi Medievale, University of Malta, no pagination.

Vella Gregory, I. 2005. *The human form in Neolithic Malta*. Malta, Midsea Books Ltd.

Yoffee, N. 2005. *Myth of the Archaic State: evolution of the Earliest Cities, States and Civilisations.* Cambridge: Cambridge University Press.

Yoffee, N. and Cowgill, G.L. 1988 (eds.). *The Collapse of Ancient States and Civilisations.* Tucson: University of Arizona Press.

Zammit, T. 1930. *Prehistoric Malta: the Tarxien Temples.* Oxford: Oxford University Press.

Chapter 5

From wells to pillars, and from pillars to…?

Ritual systems transformation and collapse in the early prehistory of Cyprus

Vasiliki G. Koutrafouri[1]

Abstract

The formation of a fluid but distinct ritual system can be identified in the first part of the early prehistory of Cyprus. This is followed by a period of excessive and conservative ritual practices on the one hand, and of new and highly variable practices on the other. This coexistence possibly mirrors the conservative character of a social reality that dies, while a new perceptual and social world emerges. The gradual transformation of the ritual system guaranteed a great degree of continuity of symbolism and was finally replaced by a rigid, well defined, stable and clearly structured system of beliefs, expressed practices and social realities. This system characterized a long lived and prosperous community on the island, which then suddenly collapsed. People dispersed and disappeared from the archaeological record. When they reappeared, only scattered segments of their ritual past can be traced in their new world. What is it that allows communities to go through transitional phases and survive, while others prove unable to adapt to change and ultimately fail? Does social survival presuppose gradual transformation of a community's perceptual world? Focusing on two transitional phases of Cypriot early prehistory, this paper posits that the first signs of radical change in a community's worldview, values, cosmological and social order are evident in their ritual practices.

Keywords: *Cyprus, prehistory, wells, pillars, ritual, collapse.*

---

1   Society of Antiquaries of Scotland, National Museum of Scotland, Edinburgh EH1 1JF, vasiliki@socantscot.org.

Introduction

Ritual failure is a theme which has been extensively explored in anthropology. Clifford Geertz' (1957) *Javanese Example* and Ronald Grimes' (1988) *Infelicitous performances* have especially influenced current anthropological research on ritual shortcomings the most (Kreinath *et al.* 2004; Ute Husken *et al.* 2007). Geertz (1957) saw fundamental incongruity in the performance of a Javanese burial ritual after the local society had shifted in the ways in which it 'interacted with itself'. Culture had not quite caught up; its symbolic systems remaining unchanged could not serve to order the changing social interaction (Wyllie 1968, 30). Grimes (1988, 110-116), enriching Austin's (1965) observations and with emphasis on performance, ordered ritual failure in the ways in which it may occur, constructing a typology. Kreinath's (2004) and Husken's (2007) collections provide a wide range of anthropological approaches to ritual failure through practice, performance, speech and text, and socio-cultural communication theories. The examples of ritual failure range from shifts and variations, to transformations of ritual practices, and complete failures, in terms of unrecognised or unaccepted practices in comparison to a set of recognised ritual actions (Köping 2004, 97-114). These collections also include examples of revivals of old traditional practices or incorporations of innovations in existing practices because of specific kinds of dynamic cultural and social interactions of socio-political groups or agents. The dynamics of emerging motifs incorporated in the process of ritual change are often shown to mirror concurrent socio-cultural negotiations; at other times to conform to those or confirm them, or often to initiate or ignite socio-cultural changes with regard to cultural symbols and social forms.

Anthropology provides evidence for a wide range of variations of ritual failure, not all of which could be traced through archaeology. Particularly, prehistoric archaeology misses the testimonies of speech (Grimes 1988), of sound / music, colours, smells; the performance (Whyllie 1968), the ambience, and the emotions (Geertz 1957). It also misses the degree of involvement of the practitioners and various other agents; their agendas and concerns and the processes of regeneration and renegotiation (Bell 1992,196); the float of communication of the society with itself (Bloch 1974; 1977, 279, 285; 1989, 38-45); all of which are so often described by anthropologists. We miss the "insight" view (-in contrast to the extent to which this may be possible even in anthropology). Trying to reconstruct ritual performances from the residues of patterned practices, (namely from the remains of actions, which produced patterns and have altered the physical world (Renfrew 1985, 12; Leach 1976) in ways traceable by the methodologies of our discipline,) archaeology, however, can provide a long-term overview of ritual practices within a given sociocultural system. In this endeavour, current anthropology seems to be supportive: *[…] it is the durable (long-lasting) representation which shapes our notion of rituals (and other actions and events) rather than its performance* (Hüsken 2007, 362; Hoffmeister 2007, 223-240). The long-lasting representations of ritual practices to which prehistoric archaeology has access, can therefore provide insightful information, especially in terms of change.

Although having passed the archaeology of snapshots, and investigating the process, we nevertheless usually explore ritual practices in their crystallized form at their peak, when they are usually most easily recognisable. We identify patterns of past ritual behaviour and we analyse how these interrelate with other socio-cultural realities at a specific time-period. The manifesting changing dynamics in a performance, the shifts in the typology or the decay process of practices seem to have been lost in time. Ritual is a multidimensional phenomenon, of which all of its dimensions are worth studying (Verhoeven 2002*a*). It is also a dynamic structure of which all of the internal components are interlinked in a complex manner, but are also linked with external components of other socio-cultural structures in a multiple and complex web (Preucel 2006). Both phenomenological and (post-)structural approaches, although exceptionally helpful in the analysis of ritual practices in archaeology, offer a static view which cannot adequately account for the emergence of change (Wylie 1968). In contrast, viewed as systems over a long-term perspective, ritual practices offer the possibility for the archaeological identification of variations, gradual shifts, and also sharp distinct changes. Thus, my analytical category for the exploration of ritual failure will be the 'ritual system'. A system has dimensions, structural elements, purposes and functions. When systems fail, they fail in one or many of the goals and purposes of their functions. This may or may not lead to structural change and/or collapse. Ritual systems studied over a long-term archaeological perspective can be identified as undergoing severe structural changes, to the extent of disappearance and/or complete transformation. From a systems perspective such profound changes would constitute "system failure". It is the latter I will seek to explore and explain, as when this regards the particularities of a ritual system, this constitutes a paradox.

Ritual practices have a property of self preservation: anthropological research shows that if a ritual practice fails, it would be the practitioners, or other agents, equally important for the success of the ritual, who would be blamed for not permitting the ritual performance to take place successfully, in the prescribed form or order. The purpose and goal of the ritual is hardly ever questioned since this is deeply rooted in the belief system and therefore the core of the ritual system (Evans-Pritchard 1937; Morris 1987): *The divine is divine exactly because it does not make mistakes* (Polit 2007, 200). If the goal for which the ritual had been practised was not achieved, and the outcome was not the one for which the ritual was practised, there would most probably be additional rituals to protect or prevent an even worse outcome (Wylie 1968). All of this is an emic view of the function of rituals. Ritual systems incorporate practices which feed back into the validity and perpetuation of the functions of the system.

From an etic perspective, one of the most important functions of ritual practices would be bringing and keeping a society together: one of the widely accepted 'purposes' of ritual practices is promoting social cohesion and the community's longevity and prosperity (Durkheim 1912; Evans-Pritchard 1937; Malinowski 1954; Radcliffe-Brown 1956). By bringing and keeping the society together, the ritual system also reassures socio-political and socio-cultural perpetuity. Again though, the ritual system itself needs the social, political and cultural systems to be functioning in specific accordance – not necessarily entirely harmonious – but benefiting the ritual system for it to remain in place; to be able to revalidate, preserve and perpetuate itself, through necessary practices. It is a complex web of interdependencies of systems and subsystems feeding into each other, so that the communal connecting social web remains intact, despite the risks and challenges of ritual practices (Wylie 1968). When a part of these systems changes, minor changes or shifts in the ritual system are acceptable and usually easily incorporated (Odenthal 2004:218); the system is adjusted and continues to function with minor incongruities. There are transformation rituals and there are rituals which are there to keep the status quo in place (Stausberg 2004, 233). Both types though would belong to the same system and would be there to foster sociocultural expressions with the goal of successful practice of all types of rituals as integral parts of a given system. Then, the ritual system also feeds back to the other social systems by producing opportunities of re-affirmation of social, political and cosmic order, offering the prospect for the society to come together and meaningfully express itself, its ideals, ideas and emotions, and re-affirm its raison-d'etre, as a society first and foremost. Ritual systems are as strict and as fluid as the practices, of which they are comprised, and the societies, who practise them. Their intrinsic properties of regeneration and self-preservation are there to reassure their success.

How is it possible then that ritual systems do fail? How does it happen that a series of practices that we testify archaeologically to have taken place for millennia, suddenly disappears from the archaeological record or changes to such an extent that is no longer recognisable? With regard to other aspects of social life, such as the economy or the choice of architecture and the material culture in general, stages of change can easily be identified and explanations for change are relatively easily justified. On the basis of archaeological evidence we are also able to describe what these changes mean for a society under study; how their lives would have been changing in terms of socio-economic organisation and how they would have moved to the following stage of their organisation. We do not seem though to have achieved this to a similar extent with regard to ritual practices. What would constitute the beginning of the end in a ritual system? Can we trace the beginnings of the end archaeologically? Can we trace the first appearances of change, or are we only able to testify the aftermath? When does a ritual system fail, and is this traceable in the archaeological record? How does a well organised system which incorporates integral parts with transformative powers to reassure its preservation and perpetuity, ever fail?

How and why this happens, and how the failing of a ritual system affects the web of interrelated systems is a central point of this study. Anthropologists who have explored problems of ritual failure have also confronted the problem of under which criteria 'ritual failure' is identified, and by whom this can be assessed (Grimes 1990, 207). This is a general problem for anthropology, the distinction between participants and observers, but an assessment can be delivered and described from either group's perspective. In archaeological investigation though, the failure of a ritual practice may be unrecognisable unless a ritual stops being practised and/or a completely different practice replaces it. The clearest indication certainly would be the disappearance of specific ritual practices from the archaeological record; such an indication would obviously denote that a given ritual system failed. Then it would be the archaeological record which would certify the failure. However, variations or shifts in the practice – if they are traceable- could also constitute (minor?) failure, indicating some sort of change in the system. Is it possible to trace elements which would signify that such a change was approaching and analyse the emerging social changes to which such a system failure would lead to?

I will attempt to provide answers to these questions by describing two ritual practices in their crystallized form. These practices took place consistently and extensively at two different time-periods in early prehistoric Cyprus. Subsequently to the description of the practices, I will focus on the two succeeding transitional periods and examine possible explanations for the change which occurred in the ritual system of that society. A ritual practice – 'the well ritual' (Koutrafouri 2009, 169-234) – was identified for the Cypriot Pre-Pottery Neolithic B (C-PPNB, hereafter). Structural ritual elements of this practice have also been identified for 'the pillar ritual' (Koutrafouri 2009, 235-347) which took place in the Cypriot Aceramic Neolithic – otherwise known as 'Khirokitian', from the name of the main settlement in this era of Cypriot prehistory. There are important identified shifts, which will be highlighted, but the core of the practices seems to have been very similar and linkages between the two practices will be demonstrated. Elements of the earlier practice, 'the well ritual', were absorbed gradually into the new socioeconomic conditions of the Cypriot Aceramic Neolithic, giving its place to a new ritual practice, 'the pillar ritual'. At the end of the Aceramic Neolithic though, the ritual system failed; along with it, the Khirokitian society collapsed. 'The pillar ritual' was suddenly, briefly and unsuccessfully replaced, and then disappeared from the archaeological record along with the people who practised it, creating the first lacuna in Cypriot Prehistory. The social collapse at a central site for the practice of 'the pillar ritual' constituted a tremendous and dramatic change which must have shaken the whole island (Peltenburg 2004, 75-77). After having described the two practices identified for the C-PPNB and Aceramic Neolithic, I will aim to show how in the first phase the focal point of the practice shifted gradually enabling societal development and smooth transition, while during the subsequent transitional phase it simply failed to do so. I will explore and suggest elements which revealed the forthcoming system collapse, and attempt to explain how these functioned in a way which did not manage to maintain the Khirokitian society together or safeguard its passage to the following stage of social organisation.

The Practices

'The Well Ritual'

Based on the evidence from seven wells excavated in Kissonerga-Mylouthkia (Peltenburg 2003, 2012; Flourentzos 2011; Koutrafouri 2009, 2011*a*), a well shaft would be opened for water to be obtained. All of the Mylouthkia wells successfully targeted underground running water streams. The well shafts could be described

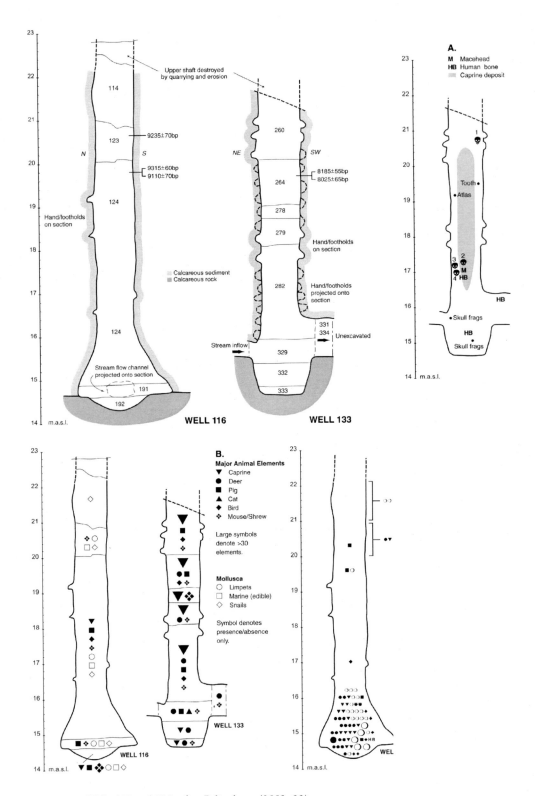

Figure 15. Wells 116 and 133, after Peltenburg (2003, 88).

as mostly vertical tubes of diameters ranging from 90cm to 1.20m. It is construed that the successful targeting of underground water would be accomplished through the use of dowsing rods. While there is no clear material evidence, it can be speculated that some sort of ritual practice would have been associated with this process. Ritual actions possibly also took place during the digging of the well shaft, which could surpass a depth of 10m. This laborious process would likely have involved diggers alternating places and sharing shifts, ascending and re-descending the well shaft at frequent intervals, carrying with them some form of portable light source (*e.g.* fat or oil lamps or torches) to illuminate their work (Koutrafouri 2009, 140). It can be hypothesised that the successful targeting of water would also have triggered some sort of ritual response. It is notable that all of the known Mylouthkia wells produced water with the exception of Well 110. Well 110 also targeted an underground water stream but part of its shaft collapsed shortly after it was opened (Croft 2003*a*, 2-4; Koutrafouri 2009, 210-212). If divination sticks were used and ritual performances took place during the digging of the shaft and at the point when water was targeted, the soon-to collapse shaft of Well 110 could have been perceived as failure of the practised rituals.

All of the Mylouthkia wells were found close to old creek beds suggesting that ancient running water sources would not have been located too far away. This adds a cultural perspective to well digging and obtaining water from underground streams, instead of or in addition to water taken from above-ground water sources. Water taken from the wells could also have been necessary, amongst other uses, for ritual practices (Miller 1985, 129; Koutrafouri 2009, 201). Several thoughts have been put forward on this matter: (a) wells could have been supporting the rich stone vessel production, as water would soften the limestone and would make vessels easier to work. It is notable in this regard that many stone vessel fragments were thrown into the well shafts after the wells had dried up (Peltenburg 2003*a*, 92; 2003*b*, 24); (b) the wells could reflect hitherto underestimated conflict during the Neolithic period over water sources. An exquisite macehead of pink conglomerate was found in the interior of Well 133, suggesting the possible existence of 'chiefs' and therefore several competing communities (Peltenburg 2003*a*, 92,95); (c) well digging could have constituted an integral part of a cultural tradition which also necessitated well water use in ritual practices (Koutrafouri 2009, 169-234). However, all of these possible reasons are not necessarily mutually exclusive.

Evidence for ritual practices is apparent during the backfilling of all the well shafts through identified patterned actions and the selected artefact and ecofacts, which formed the content of the backfill. In all instances this appears to have taken place after the wells had dried up and/or ceased to function as a viable water source. Variations in ritual practice are also apparent, which seem to relate to the time period when the ritual was practised: *i.e.* whether or not it was the outset of the practice, the practice at its peak, at a development or late stage. Additionally, the backfilling and the content of the shaft of the collapsed well (Well 110) present different properties from the rest of the wells, showing an aspect of "synchronic" variation in the practice, in contrast to the variation seen diachronically. It can be hypothesised that Well 110 was treated differently in this regard since it represented a failed attempt at the construction of a productive well. It may also be the case, however, that the variations in the content of the rest of the wells, along with the variations in the process of backfilling, may have also been influenced by other or additional factors not apparent in the archaeological record. These could include natural or cultural events such as the death of a significant chief (?) or other agent, an eclipse, or a (non) fertile season *etc*.

Selected artefacts and ecofacts were deposited in all of the well shafts. These deposits exhibit varying structures and degrees of fragmentation from well to well. The depositions in the collapsed Well 110 show the least variation of artefacts and ecofacts, limited structure, and complete lack of human bones. Deliberate depositions in Well 110 were predominantly head animal parts showing distinct selection (Croft 2003*b*, 56). With the exception of Well 110, which is clearly an atypical case, the following pattern can be identified for all remaining six wells: Large numbers of fragments of limestone/chalk vessels were thrown into the well shaft as soon as the well would have been identified to have dried (Koutrafouri 2009, 205); Limestone/chalk vessel fragments were deposited throughout the cultural episodes of backfilling, but a distinct large concentration was always closer to the bottom of the well (Koutrafouri 2009, 205). This can be clearly seen in the sections and figures of Wells 2030, 2070 and 2100 (Peltenburg 2012, *in press*). Food processing equipment (querns and rubbers) were generally absent, along with scraps of groundstone (Jackson 2003, 40). Complete stone vessels which can be reconstructed from fragments were extremely rare and restricted to the content of only two well shafts (Well 2030 and Well 2400). By way of example Well 133 produced an extremely high number of limestone vessel fragments (400), of which none presented joints. Along with or right after the vessel fragments, specific animal parts were also deposited in the well shafts during the course of this practice. Whole animal carcasses were also frequently deposited. The richest evidence comes again from Well 133 which counts 23 whole caprine carcasses amongst other animal bone fragments (Croft 2003, 51-52). Human body parts were then deposited after or concurrently with animal remains. An exception to this pattern is Well 116, where the human bone was deposited at the bottom of the shaft, at the beginning of the series of deposition events along with the vessel fragments followed by the faunal remains. The human remains are all secondary depositions. It can be speculated that those backfilling the wells would have needed to visit primary burial sites, in order to retrieve limbs and skulls which would then have been redeposited in the well shafts (Koutrafouri 2009, 191-196). Only one well (Well 2400) presented adequate evidence to suggest that a complete individual may have been placed in the well shaft. However, the unusual articulation and poor preservation of this skeleton (Gamble 2011) could indicate that it also represents a secondary interment, transported to the mouth of the well and thrown into the shaft (Koutrafouri 2011*a*). All the remaining wells present evidence for selected parts of several individuals and/or human bone scraps[2], some of which

---

2   168 human bone fragments were found in Well 133 representing a minimum of four individuals (Fox 2003, 44).

were charred prior to being thrown or deposited in the well shaft along with other fragmentary depositions. In addition to the instances of fragmentary artefactual, faunal and human remains outlined above, selected chunks of non-worked stone of similar size and colour were deliberately deposited in the wells (Croft 2003a, 3-7, 8; Peltenburg 2003a, 92). An upstanding stone construction of cobbles of similar size, connected with mud mortar, was constructed inside the shaft of Well 2030, 40cm above the bottom of the shaft (Koutrafouri 2009, 189-190). Two distinct layers of large boulders and cobbles were found in Well 2400 (Koutrafouri 2011a). A small number of prestige artefacts, such as the pink conglomerate macehead, fine obsidian blades and stone beads were also deposited in the well shafts.

Subsequent to single or multiple episode(s) of concentrated ritual depositions, the well shafts were left unattended. Soil coming down the well shaft, transported by rain water and bringing tiny pieces of overlying ecofacts and artefacts with it, naturally backfilled the well shafts over time. After a considerable amount of time had passed, practices of ritual deposition were then repeated, albeit usually on a smaller scale. The clearest example of this is found in Well 2400 where the entire length of the shaft is preserved. After a series of very well structured and defined depositions (first vessel fragments, then animal bone, followed by two layers of stone, and the possibly complete inhumation), the well was left to be backfilled naturally, until almost to the very top. After this prolonged interval, a limestone vessel fragment was then wedged with the support of a small pebble against the north edge of the shaft, along with a hammer stone placed next to it, about a metre down from the mouth of the well. This staged deposition was then covered by three large pieces of havara stone. Although absolute dates for Well 2400 are currently expected, it presents characteristics which may indicate that it dates to a mature phase of the practice of 'the well ritual'. Well 2400 exhibits the clearest depositional structure from all of the wells, with distinct layers of grouped artefacts and ecofacts of the same kind, rather than them being mixed as in the other wells, and much lower degrees of fragmentation (Koutrafouri 2009, 222-223; 2011) especially in comparison to Well 133, which exhibited the highest degrees of fragmentation of all of the wells.

The series of ritual practices relating to the wells can be summarised as staged and structured depositions: human corpse dismemberment, transport and final deposition in the well shafts; accumulation of fragmented artefacts and final deposition in the interior of the wells; animal parts and wholes deposited possibly in a votive manner; non-worked stone boulders selected, transported and structurally deposited. All of these elements constituted 'culturally controlled deposition-able categories of artefacts and ecofacts' (Koutrafouri 2009, 233) exhibiting excessive degrees of fragmentation (Chapman 2000), and properties of permanency and durability (Cooney 2007). These elements, transported to the mouth of a well and thrown or deposited in its interior, were the *symbolic force* which fulfilled the well shaft and transformed it into a *symbolic container* (Gable 2004, 119-124). After the water production phase was over, the wells became autonomous ritual locales (Hamilakis 2004, 146) where de facto refuse (Schiffer 1995, 29) took place.

Chapman's (2000) *fragmentation* and *enchainment process* are evident in the assemblages coming from all of the wells. The majority of the depositions were in the very last stage of fragmentation and discard chain (Chapman 2000, 24) and were selected through a 'mytho-logically' bounded categorization process (Leach 1976, 69-70; Koutrafouri 2009, 49, 67, 95, 99, 101), on the basis of their natural and culturally ascribed qualities, which rendered them appropriate for the building up of the desirable content within the wells. The secondary burials of dismembered humans were also a part of a series of culturally controlled deposition-able categories. These were symbolic burials, included only for the completion of a meaningful content for the container. The enchainment of meaningful relations between animals, humans, plants, stone and artefacts was emphasised by the high degrees of their fragmentation and their mixture in the wells. Ethnographical examples (Bloch 1982) suggest that parts of a whole not only represent all the chain of meaningful relations and processes, which the whole and parts of it partook and underwent until they became *fractals* (Chapman 2000), but also have symbolic force (Gable 2004, 88), both metaphorical and metonymical value (Jones and Richards 2003, 46) and expressed social and ideological relationships and a sense of affinity and of shared identity (Helms 2004, 120, 122). Hence a part of a whole would have represented the whole, but also referred to specific attributes that the whole was considered to have (Bloch 1982; Chapman 2000, 49-104; Gable 2004, 86-89; Jones and Richards 2003, 46; Miller 1985). The most durable animal parts: shells, skulls, teeth, horn and antler, and the most materially enduring human portions: skulls and long bones, the most durable natural elements (non worked stone) were usually selected for structured deposition, especially due to their quality of *permanency, durability and stability* (Helms 2004, 120, 124; Cooney 2007). This choice can be explained as a systemic ritual function expressing the eternal human struggle to create and maintain stability, order and durability in the environment and to control natural and cosmic forces (Helms 2004, 120).

A web of social and culturally meaningful relations can be identified in the process of the selection of elements and their final deposition in the wells. Artefactual biography entails involvement of an artefact in the life of its maker/user and therefore in the social life of its maker, user, donor, borrower, re-user, gift-giver, gift-taker, inheritor and agent who finally deposits the object in a selected closed context; from liquid bearing vessel, to solid bearing vessel, then to tool, and finally to culturally appropriate deposition-able artefact. Excessive numbers of *fractals* (Chapman and Gaydarska 2007) suggest strong group interrelations, production and reproduction of social practices and structures (Meredith 2007; Williams 2004). With the passage of time, as the *inalienable* artefact (Chapman 2000, 23-48; Chapman and Gaydarska 2007; Earle 2004; Hodder 1982*a*, 1982*b*; Weiner 1992) became fragmented, it was reused and recycled and became even more fragmented, it gradually accumulated a culturally specific value, or possibly lost an aspect of this, while other values and meanings were ascribed to it. As a water producing agent in the framework of possible symbolism, personhood and agency of all that partook the early Neolithic world (Cooney 2007; Dorbes 2000; Helms 2004; Renfrew 2004; Verhoeven 2002*b*; 2004; Watkins 2004; 2005), wells must also have been seen as taking part in the formation of sociocultural perceptions and relations regarding water production. The productive and non productive seasons/periods of a well could not have been attributed to environmental reasons or explained by the laws of physics. It should be hypothesised that it was 'the well' or some other related 'mytho-logically' understood entity who offered the water to the community being the first and most important link in a chain of water transfer, offering, sharing (?) and use, with corresponding sociocultural importance. Therefore, the 'well' participated in the social relations linked with the production and use of the water, as a social agent and must have acted upon and interacted with the community as central agent of 'the well ritual'. 'The well ritual' as instances in the continuum of symbolic communication (Bloch 1974; 1989, 38-45) was central to the reproduction of social relations between human and non-human agents (Chapman and Gaydarska 2007, 69).

'The well ritual' was collective, communal and possibly public, using symbols of a common identity, shared worldview and knowledge. 'The well ritual' transformed the wells into liminal containers with symbolic force from agents represented mainly by their most enduring fragmented parts. A life-giver (well producing water) was also transformed into a life-receiver. Dead humans, animals and artefacts were used for the ritual to be practised. Dead were buried, exhumed (or collected), disembodied (Taylor 2002) and re-buried. Concerns relating to ancestors (who built the well?), appropriate descendants' actions, the meaning of life and death and natural and cultural regeneration must have been central to the significance and metaphorical value of the human remains. Their exhumation (or collection), their transport and their secondary burial through their deposition in the interior of previously functioning wells, along with their association with other categories of material inside the wells (*e.g.* stone, specific animal remains, specific classes and conditions of artefacts) show a certain preoccupation with death; dead humans, dead animals, dead artefacts inside a dead well. The series of structured depositions of dead enduring fractals relate to possibly death ritual, regeneration ritual, votive and/or sacrificial ritual. 'The well ritual' exhibits concerns strongly related to death-associated ritual also through the encounter and confirmation of the "death" of the well at the end of the water-production phase; recognition of the breakage of a socio-cultural chain of relations; confirmation of an end and the 'ritual reaction' to the event with the symbolic depositions of other dead (*fractals*: human, animal and objects); the cultural empowerment of the container with *symbolic force*, and finally ritual closure and abandonment. Amongst the dimensions that this ritual practice presents, it is worth emphasising its functions: creation of a long-lasting tradition on the island of pit digging; structured deposition in underground structures; re-affirmation of cosmological and social order; fulfilment of obligations towards disembodied souls (Taylor 2000); creation, establishment and re-establishment of mytho-logical categories; appropriation of cultural categories; reaffirmation of sociocultural links and production of social cohesion. Emotional functions could entail reassurance that world order would be maintained (despite the end of the productive phase of a well) and the society would continue to prosper through the structured backfilling of a deceased well and the construction of a new well nearby.

Figure 16. Kalavasos-Tenta: Circular Pillar Building, Structure 42 (after Todd 1987, Plate X).

'The Pillar Ritual'

The society which practised 'the well ritual' continued to find ways to maintain strong bonds and prosperity through the communication of similar ideational concerns, the negotiation and renegotiation of their values, and the material expressions of these in new structures and associated practices. Within the walls of the Cypriot mega-sites of the Aceramic Neolithic, 'the well ritual' was irrelevant and had given its place to 'the pillar ritual', practised now by well settled communities, with well founded sociocultural links and tight social order and cohesion.

'The pillar ritual' took place at Kalavasos-Tenta periods 4-3 and throughout the life-time of Khirokitia. It was conducted inside the Circular Pillar Buildings (henceforth 'CPBs', after Peltenburg 2004). CPBs contained one, two, or three non-structural and free standing pillars in their interior (Peltenburg 2004, 75-77; Koutrafouri 2009, 262-264). Kalavasos-Tenta had eleven CPBs: seven dating to a time period (4-3) when 'the pillar ritual' was practised. The remaining four, dating to period 2, were built as satellites to a new 'Circular Radial-Pillar' building-type, which was central to the settlement at Kalavasos-Tenta. The most representative site for the function of CPBs and 'the pillar ritual' is Khirokitia, but evidence from Kalavasos-Tenta is crucial for the understanding of the emerging change and the forthcoming Khirokitian-society collapse. Eleven CPBs were also found at Khirokitia and date from the earliest occupation levels to the most recent (Dikaios 1953; Le Brun 1984; 1985; 19899; 1994; Stanley Price and Christou 1973, Koutrafouri 2009, 262-309). When a CPB was built, it was carefully maintained and remained in use for a very long time. The extensive longevity during which CPBs were in use at Khirokitia is incomparable to any other structure in Cypriot prehistory (Koutrafouri 2009, 265-266). At Khirokitia, CPBs were spread in the settlement at distinct neighbourhoods (Koutrafouri 2009, 264-265, 268-269, 344-346). They were also distinct in space with corridors and uncovered spaces around them at an otherwise extremely densely inhabited town. Communal decision making, sustained commitment and general social agreement would need to have been in place for these buildings to be constructed at selected spaces and regularly maintained (or in a limited number of cases reconstructed) over such a long period.

At Khirokitia, CPBs accumulated 1/3 of the burials which took place within the settlement walls (Koutrafouri 2009, 252-253, 257-258, 268-269). Half of the buildings at Khirokitia were abandoned without any burial having ever been deposited under their floors; but there was no CPB without a burial in its interior (Koutrafouri 2009, 333). Especially at Khirokitia, it can be noticed that customarily the burials were placed both in association with the construction and the existence of the pillars in a staged manner within the CPBs. A selected burial would be deposited at the one opening of the pillars, further off it, towards the doorway (CPBs Th. IA, Th. XLVII, Th. XX, S 122). A second burial would be usually deposited in the opposite opening of the pillars closer to the circular wall in the interior, in the back, or in between the pillars. If more burials were deposited, they would usually be placed along the interior of the circular walls. More burials then would be placed close to the pillars, at one of their edges or sides. Examining this evidence floor after floor within a CPB, it becomes evident that intentionality charged the burial placement in relation to the pillar(s). The sequence of the following appropriate depositional place of a burial was directed by the previous burial placements. A shallow pit would be opened in a floor for a primary burial or burials to be interred, and a new floor would be constructed to cover that burial or burials (Niklasson 1991, 230; Koutrafouri 2009, 284). Burials which show some sort of post-mortem manipulation or were found in extremely badly preserved condition may suggest secondary burial use in a minority of cases (Koutrafouri 2009, 329). The selection of the dead to be buried in CPBs does not seem to have been based on gender, age or status and affirms patterns identified for broadly contemporary neighbourhood buildings for Çatal Höyük (Düring 2007).

CPBs were generally heavily furnished. Burials were found inside platforms and elaborately paved areas. Burned substances and occupational surfaces together with small hoards of pebbles, shells, or bone and installed basins furnished the CPBs and seemed to have been present in association with the pillars and the burials. Fire remains were found over platforms above burials, in areas of the floor as a marker and within burial fills. It can be speculated that burning was repeatedly practised in CPBs, for purification, ritualization and/or creation of a mystifying ambiance (?) or as a marker. Elaborate platforms and seats were also a reoccurring type of construction within CPBs. The great majority of platforms were constructed in order to cover dead human bodies and fire was sometimes lit on top. A few of these platforms were monumentally constructed and restricted the space in CPBs covering a considerable area. Installed, embedded and built-in stone basins were found in the interior of many CPBs at Khirokitia (S 35, S 105, S 116, S 117, S 122), suggesting use of liquid (water? blood? other?). A large built-in plastered basin was found next to the pillars in CPB S 11 at Kalavasos-Tenta (Todd 1987, 76-77; Koutrafouri 2009, 311-315). Pits containing only ashes, pebbles and/or small sized selected stone were found repeatedly in association with the pillars in several CPBs (Khirokitia Th. XLV (I), Th. XLVII, S 116). Pebbles were also used to surround a burial pit and areas or platforms for burning substances. Sea shells were transported and deposited within burials, over burials or deposited in small hoards (Khirokitia CPBs Th. XLVII, and Th. XX enclosure). Next-to-the-doorway symbolic depositions of animal remains took place in CPBs (Khirokitia: CPBs Th.VII and Th. XLVII). Semicircular enclosures were found outside a few CPBs (Khirokitia: Th. XX, S 131), stone "tables" (altars?) were found outside others (Khirokitia: Th. XX and Th. IA), surrounded by small pits with animal bone depositions and others with ash and animal bone. Inside the CPBs benches or seats placed close to the wall provided the seated with full surveillance of the entire interior circular space of pillar building and control over the entrance. All actions within the circle could be clearly observed and nobody could enter without being noticed. In addition to where seats were placed within the CPBs, the permanency and elaboration that characterised their construction transformed them into a kind of privileged seating setting and the interior of the CPB into a *stage* (Tambiah 1979). Seats, hearths, basins, tables, were all instruments for ritualized actions such as burning substances, using liquids, burying or re-burying the dead in a stage for ritual performance practised around the pillars inside the CPBs. Ritual closure and ritual sealing was attested within most and for most of the CPBs. Striking examples are CPBs Th. XLVII, S 116, S 117, S 122, at Khirokitia, where not only the practice of ritual-sealing of burials was particularly evident, with the construction of a new floor above them, but also these CPBs were buried by deposits, sealing and transforming them into *containers* with symbolic content (Gable 2004).

It would not be safe to describe 'the pillar ritual' sequence and structure within CPBs and associated buildings, in the same way as for 'the well ritual' based on the available contextual accounts. The sequence of actions from information obtained from a horizontal space – same level – cannot be reconstructed as safely as for a vertical cylindrical space such as a well, where the sequence of depositions is inherently clearer. Broadly 'the pillar ritual' would entail the following actions: a place for a CPB to be erected and maintained would have to be chosen within the settlement; construction of the CPB and the pillars; construction of seats for the performance would possibly happen concurrently or right after; as soon as the pillars would have been erected, a burial or burials would be transported and would be interred within the CPB, in some association with the pillars. Concurrently with the burials, or afterwards, burning substances, depositing hoards structurally in relation to the burials, closure, cleaning, and sealing of the floor, which was subsequently followed by the construction of a new floor. 'The pillar ritual' involved the use of dead bodies for it to be practised. The event of the burial does not though seem to have been the focus of the ritual activity. Burials were used for ritualization, symbolic empowerment of the space, for creation of liminality, for 'the pillar ritual' to be practised, and for the CPB to be transformed into a container. The burial as symbol of previously well-established ritual practices and of the same socio-cultural system was introduced into the upstanding structures, and into the 'habitat' / the 'domus' (Bourdieu 1972; Hodder 1987), which was the new ritual locale (Hamilakis 2004). Pillars became the materialization (Watkins 2004) of ideas and beliefs, and burials were possibly the symbol of the liminal or the unknown / the natural that had to be controlled. Death was used and manipulated, and introduced into the habitat and the domus, and therefore was tamed and "domesticated".

Transition and Collapse

'The pillar ritual' inside the limited space of CPBs could not have been public, in the same way as 'the well ritual' would have been, but both can certainly be characterised as communal. It was most probably practised by social groups in neighbourhoods at Khirokitia, and served to reinforce the community's bonds and social cohesion over a long period. Both wells and pillars expressed their communities' shared concerns and social bonds; they were both subterranean and free standing structures of shared identity. The shift in the practice is evident: from wells to pillars; from the outside to the inside; from the natural and uncontrolled to the constructed and controlled; from liminality constructed through a natural medium to liminality developed through constructed space. However, internal structural categories of actions show a continuation in the core of the ritual expressions. Stone and pebbles maintained the significance, which they had culturally and ritually accumulated in the previous period (C-PPNB) and were repeatedly deposited in pits close to burials, in the context of the burial pit, embedded around platforms and grave-pits, and in hoards. Water or other liquids must have been used in the ritual sequence, since built and installed basins were identified in the ritual context. The use of fire, only minimally evidenced on charred human and animal bones at Kissonerga-Mylouthkia wells, became a necessary link in the ritual sequence at Khirokitia and Kalavasos-Tenta. Fire, tamed and domesticated, may have symbolised control over the natural and a hope for the supernatural and death (?) also to be tamed. Dead bodies were used for a ritual different from that of the burial per se to be performed for both practices. Taming, controlling and domesticating, which must have been central notions to the psychology and identity both of the first colonists and the first settlers in general, was expressed in the ritual practices both in the Cypriot PPNB and Aceramic Neolithic. Practices at Kissonerga-Mylouthkia exhibited excessive familiarity with the dead and the focal aspect of this tradition continued at Khirokitia and Kalavasos-Tenta. The performative aspect of the practice (Tombiah 1979) must have been central both to 'the well ritual' and 'the pillar ritual'. Symbolic and structured depositions took place repeatedly in formally organised areas, while the CPBs themselves also became *containers* of structured depositions (Gable 2004) loaded with sacrality.

The transition from the C-PPNB to the Aceramic Neolithic happened smoothly; the ritual practice shifted efficiently along with the shifting priorities and concerns of the settling communities. Commonly shared concerns were expressed in similar ways within walls and above wells (Koutrafouri 2009, 343-345). Key evidence to this shift comes from Kalavasos-Tenta period 5 to 4. A settled community, while conforming to the ritual system of the previous period, where dead bodies were not interred at the settlement (C-PPNB, Kalavasos-Tenta period 5, McCartney 2005), followed the emerging shift in the ritual practices, which appropriated burial within the settlement walls, in relation to specific sacral symbols and structures; they started constructing those in the outset of period 4, when they also fortified their settlement (Aceramic Neolithic). At Kalavasos-Tenta (periods 4-3) burials were used as symbols for the foundation of the new world order of a society, which had to function within walls, and had to establish its identity and a tradition upon which it could be based and flourish. The neighbouring newly founded village, Khirokitia, practised the same ritual. Those settlers and settling colonists brought their cultural categories of understanding of their world (Helms 2004) to the societies they organised within the walls of their newly founded villages. At Khirokitia, the society succeeded in establishing this tradition and flourishing, basing its socio-ritual organisation in discrete neighbourhoods on the basis of ritual buildings. Khirokitia securely founded this tradition, which was firstly introduced at Kalavasos-Tenta (period 4). At Khirokitia the established ritual brought people closer together and allowed them to live peacefully in this way. It emphasised the meaningful things that held their society together. It took conscious social decision to maintain these buildings with their pillars, to customarily bury selected dead inside them, to forbid any other construction nearby them and thus to maintain open spaces and distinguish these buildings in space and time. Generation after generation implemented those rules and tradition was created; the same ritual was practised for almost 2,000 years. It would appear that ritual held successive generations at Khirokitia together for longer than any other identified settlement in the prehistory of Cyprus.

In extreme contrast the transition from the Aceramic Neolithic to the Ceramic Neolithic signalled downfall, disperse, and almost disappearance of prehistoric Cypriots from the archaeological record. A lacuna, which until recently was thought to be of a thousand years was formed (Clarke 2007). Recent reconsideration of the evidence (Lehavy 1974, 1989; Clarke 2007) and newly excavated evidence (McCarthy 2009, Koutrafouri 2011b) indicates now a shorter lacuna of 400-300 years. This evidence, coming from permanent, but short lived installations of seasonal use and hunting bases, shows movement of dispersed groups inland and highland. When the prehistoric Cypriots appeared again settled in organised permanent villages, a thousand years after the Khirokitian collapse (Dikaios 1961; Peltenburg 1982), the profound changes in their architecture, the introduction of pottery, the minimalistic expressions of their rituals and the privatisation of their practices, allow hardly anything to remind of the glory and excess of the ritual practices of the C-PPNB, or Aceramic Neolithic.

What had happened to that well regulated, excellently organised Khirokitian society with its cultural-ritual roots coming from far in the past? How did a well founded ritual system, in place to perpetuate that society's longevity and ancestral rules and values, come to collapse and disappear? Why did it not hold them together through the new transition? The answer seems to come again better formulated from the developments at Kalavasos-Tenta. While Khirokitians continued using the death-related 'pillar ritual' to express their beliefs and ideology, to manage their fears and fertilise their ever-lasting flourishing societal prosperity, at Kalavasos-Tenta, period 2, death was exiled from the village walls. Concurrently, a new building symbol appeared on the top of the hill, centrally in the settlement. It was the largest building in the whole village: the Circular Radial-Pillar Building (CRB hereafter, after Peltenburg 2004), Structure 14; a type of architecture appearing in Cyprus for the first time. New CBPs were constructed around the CRB, but if a ritual was practised in their interior, no dead were used in its performance. If ritual was practised within the satellite CPBs of the CRB complex S 14, it was not related to the re-establishment of ancestral traditions associated with birth, death and rebirth of a perpetual socio-cultural ritual system. The absence of burial from the settlement must have been linked with a new ideology, which did not appropriate burial use for the ritual practice. This new ideology was expressed by the adoption of this new (for the island) architectural trend, in a single building: the CRB, larger than any other seen on the island until that point, with elaborate, spectacular decoration and strategically positioned on the top of the settlement hill. The new ritual principals and the new architectural trend were most probably associated with the rise of a particular group in power. The particular concentration of CPBs around CRB S 14 possibly expressed the exploitation of popular and previously well-functioning ritual symbols by a particular group in order to establish their authority. The satellite CPBs do confirm a continuity of ritual-cultural symbols. However, a fundamental part of their ritual association, the dead, was suddenly and strikingly missing. Such crucial ritual traditions could not have simply disappeared. It would seem most probable that some form of political influence was involved.

At Kalavasos-Tenta the concentration of CPBs with burials in period 4 in the southern slope of the hill, and the subsequent concentration of CPBs without burials around the large CRB complex S 14 on the top of the hill in period 2, may mirror a particular social group empowerment. While burials were no longer interred at Kalavasos-Tenta during period 2 the significance, symbolism and status of ritual buildings such as CPBs would very likely have been used to enhance the authority that this new building-type held in Cyprus. New authorities often use older and already established symbols in order to secure their legitimacy (Douglas 1970, 54-81). While the CRB type appeared in Cyprus suddenly at Kalavasos-Tenta in period 2, at Khirokitia it appeared at the very top level of the settlement (Ic), shortly prior to the site abandonment. At Khirokitia, the CRB was extremely short-lived, never well established, and potentially reflects a new trend in the island that a particular group may have decided to adopt. At Kalavasos-Tenta, it seemed to have succeeded in strongly founding this new trend for the very last period of the settlement. At Khirokitia, where the CPBs seemed to gather all the communal attention and the tradition they represented was better founded and supported until the very end, the CRB appeared briefly in the West side of the settlement at a very top level and shortly after, it disappeared with the rest of the society and societal ties that had held Khirokitia together for so long (Peltenburg 2004, 85).

These radical changes at Kalavasos-Tenta must have taken place without major social disruption and most probably happened gradually within the questionable horizon of period 3 (late). It should be noted, however, that no major destructions or indications of violence have been evidenced for this juncture at Kalavasos-Tenta. At their very end, both Khirokitia and Kalavasos-Tenta appear to have been peacefully abandoned. With the continual presence of CPBs with burials at the very last levels of Khirokitia, and therefore the perpetual practice of 'the pillar ritual', it would be difficult to encapsulate the emerging change. Indeed, signs of change were arguably already apparent, with uncertainty and social tension leading a group at Khirokitia to experiment unsuccessfully with a different cosmotheory, expressed through the CRB type of building. This could have represented a clumsy, groundless attempt to save Khirokitia from declining. The hopelessness of this attempt was evidenced by the introduction of burials into the CRB at Khirokitia and its extreme short occupation thereafter. This shows a society trying to shift in ways which are not supported by their structural cultural symbols and psychosyntheses (Geertz 1957). The rite may have been performed but it stopped producing the "goods" for which the society performed the rite; thus the rite had become ineffectual (Grimes 1988, 113). Other means were sought which incorporated new symbols, and possibly demanding different rites. The life-giving, nurturing properties of 'the pillar ritual' at Khirokitia must have started no longer adequately expressing the Khirokitians themselves or explaining the world around them.

Peltenburg (2004, 85) posited the decline of Khirokitia as a result of its excessive size not permitting socio-economic management in a traditionally egalitarian Neolithic way. The ritual evidence reviewed above affirms that hypothesis. Despite the fact that social organisation at Khirokitia was likely based on groups in neighbourhoods which surrounded ritual buildings, these must have functioned on a group-egalitarian basis, since significant differences in symbols, size or architecture are not apparent. The organisational foundation of ritual with its theoretical "pillars" functioned perfectly and provided an explanation for the world on the basis of neighbourhoods. When this base was shaken by its inability to regenerate itself in a larger size, ritual failed to explain and support the cohesion of such a world. The perception of the world had started changing and a new ritual language was required to explain and express the new world and the emerging social order and cultural reality. The old practices failed to incorporate and host the necessary equivalent shifts for them to securely lead the society to a new stage of socio-ritual oragnisation.

'The well ritual' permitted long term variations incorporating shifts in the practice. It absorbed social tensions and successfully renegotiated and expressed social realities in the ritual. In contrast 'the pillar ritual' allowed internal variation only within the limits of the ritual performance, and was practised strictly through millennia, eventually offering only a superficial permission for re-negotiation of societal values and beliefs. 'The pillar ritual' seemingly more fluid than 'the well ritual', in fact was more rigid, stricter and much less flexible. It was a group-based communal ritual of co-inhabiting egalitarian groups confined behind settlement walls, with their expansion highly inconvenient and their membership fluidity highly questionable. 'The pillar-ritual' suffocated an expanding and shifting Khirokitian society. Political intervention not justified or supported by the ritual system failed to save Kalavasos-Tenta also. Khirokitians with their inflexible persistence in their traditions, beliefs, ideology and cosmic order did not manage to comprehend and organise their changing world in a different way that would have guaranteed their societal survival; the structure of Khirokitian society fell apart completely.

> [...] *the social group is anchored, not just by political power, but by some of the deepest emotions, beliefs and fears of people everywhere. Society is made both emotionally and intellectually unassailable by means of that alchemy which transforms death into fertility.* (Bloch and Parry 1982, 41)

When ritual systems fail to nurture and allow expressions of those emotions, then symbols and practices are *de-ritualized* (Koutrafouri 2009, 57-59), lose meaning, become inefficacious, fail to have dimensions, functions and achievable purposes; and societies simply fail.

Acknowledgements

I am grateful to Eddie J. Peltenburg and Ian Todd for their permissions to use illustrations of wells and pillars; to Jeff Sanders, Michael Brown and Ben Clarkson for their proof-reading and insightful comments. All errors and omissions remain mine. I'm further grateful to Jeff Sanders for keeping morale high, throughout the publication process and Karsten Wentink for his precious support and advice.

References

Austin, J.L. 1965. *How to do Things with Words.* New York: Oxford.

Bell, C. 1992. *Ritual Theory Ritual Practice.* Oxford: Oxford University Press.

Bloch, M. 1974. Symbol, song and dance and features of articulation: Is religion an extreme form of traditional authority? *European Journal of Sociology,* Vol. 15, No. 1, 55-81.

Bloch, M. 1977. The Past and the Present in the Present. *Man, New Series,* Vol. 12, No. 2, 278-292.

Bloch, M. 1989. *Ritual History and Power: Selected Papers in Anthropology.* London School of Economics. Monographs on Social Anthropology No 58. London and Atlantic Highlands: The Athlone Press.

Bloch, M. and Parry, J. 1982 [1999] (eds.). *Death and the regeneration of life.* Cambridge: Cambridge University Press.

Bourdieu, P. 1972 [2007]. *Outline of a Theory of Practice.* Cambridge: Cambridge University Press.

Chapman, J. 2000. *Fragmentation in archaeology: people, places and broken objects in the prehistory of South-eastern Europe.* London: Routledge.

Chapman, J. and Gaydarska, B. 2007. *Parts and Wholes. Fragmentation in prehistoric context.* Oxford: Oxbow Books

Clarke, J. with McCartney, C. and Wasse, A. 2007. *On the Margins of Southwest Asia. Cyprus during the 6th to 4th Millennia BC.* Oxford: Oxbow Books.

Cooney, G. 2007. *Living in an Age of Stone. Neolithic People and their Worlds.* Rhind Lectures, 27-29 April 2007, Society of Antiquaries of Scotland, National Museum of Scotland, Edinburgh.

Croft, P. 2003*a*. The Wells and Other Vestiges, in Peltenburg E.J. *et al. The colonisation and settlement of Cyprus: investigations at Kissonerga-Mylouthkia, 1976-1996,* Lemba Archaeological Project Cyprus, Vol. III. 1. Studies in Mediterranean Archaeology Vol. LXX:4. Sävedalen: P. Åströms, 3-9.

Croft, P. 2003*b*. The Animal Bones, in Peltenburg E.J. *et al. The colonisation and settlement of Cyprus: investigations at Kissonerga-Mylouthkia, 1976-1996,* Lemba Archaeological Project Cyprus, Vol. III. 1. Studies in Mediterranean Archaeology Vol. LXX:4. Sävedalen: P. Åströms, 49-58.

Dikaios, P. 1953. *Khirokitia. Final report on the excavation of a Neolithic Settlement in Cyprus on behalf of the Department of Antiquities 1936-1946.* Published for the government of Cyprus by Geoffrey Cumberlege. Oxford: Oxford University Press.

Dikaios, P. 1961. *Sotira.* Museum Monographs. The University Museum. Philadelphia: University of Pennsylvania.

Dorbes, A.M. and Robb, J. 2000 [2005]. *Agency in Archaeology.* London and New York: Routledge.

Douglas, M. 1970. *Natural Symbols: Explorations of Cosmology.* New York: Random House.

Durkheim, E. 1912 [2001]. *The Elementary Forms of Religious Life.* A new translation by Carol Cosman. Oxford World's classics. Oxford: Oxford University Press.

Düring, B.S. 2007. Reconsidering the Çatalhöyük Community: From Households to Settlement Systems. *Journal of Mediterranean Archaeology Vol. 20, No. 2: 155-182.*

Earle, T. 2004. Culture matters: Why Symbolic Objects Change, in: DeMarrais, E. *et al.* (eds.). *Rethinking materiality. The engagement of mind with the material world.* McDonald Institute Monographs. Oxford: Oxbow Books, 153-165.

Evans-Pritchard, E.E. 1937. *Witchcraft, Oracles and Magic among the Azande,* Oxford: Oxford University Press.

Flourentzos, P. *et al.* 2011. The Neolithic Well 2400 in Kissonerga. *Reports of the Department of Antiquities of Cyprus* 2011, *in press.*

Gable, C. 2004. Materiality and Symbolic Force: a Palaeolithic View of Sedentism, in DeMarrais, E. *et al.* (eds.). *Rethinking materiality. The engagement of mind with the material world.* McDonald Institute Monographs. Oxford: Oxbow Books, 85-95.

Gamble, M. 2011. *The Human Remains,* in The Neolithic Well 2400 in Kissonerga, in P. Flourentzos, P. *et al. Reports of the Department of Antiquities of Cyprus 2011, in press.*

Geertz, C. 1957. Ritual and Social Change: A Javanese Example. *American Anthropologist, New Series,* Vol. 59, No. 1, 32-54.

Grimes, R.L. 1988. Infelicitous Performances and Ritual Criticism. *Semeia* 43, 103-122.

Grimes, R.L. 1990. *Ritual Criticism: Case Studies in its Practice, Essays on its Theory.* Columbia: University of South Carolina Press.

Hamilakis, Y. 2004. Pigs for the Gods: Burnt animal sacrifices as embodied rituals at a Mycenaean sanctuary. *Oxford Journal of Archaeology* 23/2, 135-151.

Helms, M.W. 2004. Tangible Materiality and Cosmological Others in the Development of Sedentism, in DeMarrais, E. *et al.*(eds.). *Rethinking Materiality. The engagement of mind with the material world.* McDonald Institute Monographs. Oxford: Oxbow Books, 117-127.

Hüsken, U. 2007 (ed.). *When Rituals Go Wrong: Mistakes, Failure, and the Dynamics of Ritual.* Leiden, Boston: Brill.

Hodder, I. 1982*a. The Present Past.* London: Batsford.

Hodder, I. 1982*b. Symbols in Action. Ethnoarchaeological Studies of Material Culture.* Cambridge: Cambridge University Press.

Hodder, I. 1982*c* (ed.). *Symbolic and Structural Archaeology.* The Cambridge Seminar on Symbolic and Structural Archaeology. Cambridge: Cambridge University Press.

Hodder, I. 1987 [1990]. *The Domestication of Europe: structure and contingency in Neolithic Societies.* Oxford: Blackwell.

Hoffmeister, M. 2007. Change of View: the Ritual Side of Serial Killing and the Conditions for Fortunate Failure, in Ute Hüsken (ed.). *When Rituals Go Wrong: Mistakes, Failure, and the Dynamics of Ritual.* Leiden, Boston: Brill, 223-240.

Hüsken, U. 2007. Ritual Dynamics and Ritual Failure, in Hüsken, U. (ed.). *When Rituals Go Wrong: Mistakes, Failure, and the Dynamics of Ritual.* Leiden, Boston: Brill, 337-366.

Jackson, A. 2003. The Ground Stone Industry, in Peltenburg E.J. *et al. The colonisation and settlement of Cyprus: investigations at Kissonerga-Mylouthkia, 1976-1996,* Lemba Archaeological Project Cyprus, Vol. III. 1. Studies in Mediterranean Archaeology Vol. LXX:4. Sävedalen: P. Åströms, 35-40.

Jones, A. and Richards, C. 2003. Animals into ancestors: domestication, food and identity in Late Neolithic Orkney, in Parker Pearson M. (ed.). *Food, Culture and Identity in the Neolithic and Early Bronze Age,* edited by. BAR International Series 1117. Oxford: Hadrian Books, 45-51.

Köpping, K-P. 2004. *Failure of Performance or Passage to Acting Self? Mishima's Suicide between Ritual and Theatre,* in: Kreinath, J., Hartung, C. and Deschner, A. (eds.). *The Dynamics of Changing Rituals. The Transformation of Religious Rituals within Their Social and Cultural Context,* Toronto Studies in Religion 29. New York: Peter Lang Publishing, 97-114.

Köpping, K-P. *et al.* 2006. *Ritual and Identity. Performance Practices as Effective Transformations of Social Reality.* Performances Volume 8. Berlin: Lit Verlag.

Koutrafouri, V.G. 2009. *Ritual in Prehistory; Definition and Identification. Religious Insights in Early Prehistoric Cyprus.* Unpublished PhD Thesis, University of Edinburgh, also accessible from the Edinburgh Research Archive: http://www.era.lib.ed.ac.uk/handle/1842/3288.

Koutrafouri, V.G. 2011*a*. Lithology and Contextual Analysis, in Flourentzos, P. *et al.* The Neolithic Well 2400 in Kissonerga, *Reports of the Department of Antiquities of Cyprus 2011, in press.*

Koutrafouri, V.G. 2011*b*. Narrowing the Gap? The Aceramic and Ceramic Neolithic of Prastio-Mesorotsos, Cyprus, Paper presented at the American Schools of Oriental Research Annual Meeting, 16-19 November 2011, San Francisco.

Kreinath, J., Hartung, C. and Deschner, A. 2004 (eds.). *The Dynamics of Changing Rituals. The Transformation of Religious Rituals within Their Social and Cultural Context.* Toronto Studies in Religion 29, New York: Lang Publishing.

Leach, E. 1976. *Culture and communication: the logic by which symbols are connected.* Cambridge: Cambridge University Press.

Le Brun, A. *et al.* 1984. *Fouilles Recents à Khirokitia, Chypre,* 1977-1981. Etudes Néolithiques. Editions Recherches sur les Civilisations. Memoir no 41. Paris.

Le Brun, A. *et al.* 1985. *Les fouilles recentes de Khirokitia. Quelque Resultas.* 1-3 in *Practica International Congress of Cypriot Studies.* Society of Cypriot Studies, 1. Nicosia: Zavallis Press.

Le Brun, A. *et al.* 1989. *Fouilles Recents à Khirokitia, Chypre, 1983-1986.* Etudes Néolithiques. Editions Recherches sur les Civilisations. Paris.

Le Brun A. *et al.* 1994. *Fouilles Recents à Khirokitia, Chypre, 1988-1991.* Etudes Néolithiques. Editions Recherches sur les Civilisations. Paris.

Le Brun A. *et al.* 2003. Idéologie et symboles à Khirokitia: La "fermeture" d'un bâtiment et sa mise en scene, in Guilaine, J. and Le Brun, A. *Le Néolithique de Chypre. Act du coloque International organise par le Départment des Antiquités de Chypre et l'école Française d'Athènes.* Nicosie 17-19 Mai 2001, Bulletin de correspondence Hellénique, Supplement 43. École Française d' Athènes, 341-349.

Lehavy, A.J. 1974. Excavations at Neolithic Dhali-Agridhi, Part 1: excavation report, in Stager, L. E., Walker, A. and Wrights G.E. (eds.). *American Expedition to Idalion, Cyprus: First Preliminary Report: Seasons of 1971 and 1972,* Cambridge, Massachusetts: American School of Oriental Research, 95-102.

Lehavy, A.J. 1989. Excavations at Neolithic Dhali-Agridhi, 1972, 1974, 1976, in Stager L. E. and Walker, A. (eds.). *American Expedition to Idalion, Cyprus:1973-1980,* Chicago, Oriental Institute, 203-232.

Lowe, J.W.G. and Barth, R.J. 1980. Systems in Archaeology: A Comment on Salmon. *American Antiquity,* Vol. 45, No 3, 568-575.

McCarthy, A.P. *et al.* 2009. The Prastio-Mesorotsos Archaeological Expedition: First Preliminary Report of the 2008 Survey. *Reports of the Department of Antiquities of Cyprus 2009,* 60-88.

McCartney, C. and Todd, I. 2005. Chipped stone, in Todd, I. (ed.). *Excavations at Kalavasos-Tenta. Vol II,* Studies in the Mediterranean Archaeology Vol.LXXI:7. Sävedalen: P. Åströms, 177-264.

Malinowski, B. 1954. *Magic, Science and Religion and Other Essays*, New York: Doubleday.

Meredith, S.C. 2007. Remembering and Forgetting in Early Bronze Age Mortuary Practices on the Southeastern Dead Sea plain, Jordan, in Laneri, N. *Performing Death. Social Analyses of Funerary Traditions in the Ancient Near East and Mediterranean.* The Oriental Institute of the University of Chicago. Oriental Institute Seminars. Number 3. Chicago: Illinois, 109-123.

Miller, D. 1985. *Artefacts as categories. A study of ceramic variability in Central India.* Cambridge: Cambridge University Press.

Morris, B. 1987. *Anthropological Studies of Religion: An Introductory Text.* Cambridge: Cambridge University Press.

Niklasson, K. 1991. *Early Prehistoric Burials in Cyprus.* Studies in Mediterranean Archaeology Vol. XCVI. Paul Åströms Förlag. Jonsered.

Odenthal, A. 2004. Ritual between Tradition and Change: The Paradigm Shift of the Second Vatican Council's Liturgical Reform, in: Kreinath, J., Hartung, C. and Deschner, A. (eds.). *The Dynamics of Changing Rituals. The Transformation of Religious Rituals within Their Social and Cultural Context*, Toronto Studies in Religion 29, New York: Peter Lang Publishing, 211-219.

Peltenburg, E.J. 1982. *Vrysi. A subterranean Settlement in Cyprus. Excavations at Prehistoric Ayios Epiktitos Vrysi 1969-1973.* England: Aris and Philips Ltd. Warminster.

Peltenburg, E.J. *et al.* 2003*a. The colonisation and settlement of Cyprus: investigations at Kissonerga-Mylouthkia, 1976-1996.* Lemba Archaeological Project Cyprus, Vol. III. 1. Studies in Mediterranean Archaeology Vol. LXX:4. Sävedalen: P. Åströms.

Peltenburg, E.J. 2003*b*. Identifying Settlement of the Xth-IXth millennium BP in Cyprus from the contents of Kissonerga-Mylouthkia wells, in: Guilaine, J. and Le Brun A. (eds.) *Le Néolithique de Chypre. Act du coloque International organise par le Départment des Antiquités de Chypre et l'école Française d'Athènes.* Nicosie 17-19 Mai 2001, Bulletin de correspondence Hellénique, Supplement 43. École Française d' Athènes, 15-33.

Peltenburg, E.J. 2004. Social Space in early sedentary communities of Southwest Asia and Cyprus, in: Peltenburg E.J. and Wasse, A. *Neolithic Revolution. New Perspectives on Southwest Asia, in light of recent discoveries on Cyprus.* Levant Supplementary Series Volume 1. Oxford: Oxbow Books, 71-89.

Peltenburg, E.J. *et al.* 2012. Excavations of Neolithic Kissonerga-Mylouthkia, 2000-2006: Interim Report. *Reports of the Department of Antiquities Cyprus 2012, in press.*

Polit, K. 2007. Social Consequences of Ritual Failure: a Garhwali Case Study, in: Hüsken, U. (ed.). *When Rituals Go Wrong: Mistakes, Failure, and the Dynamics of Ritual.* Leiden, Boston: Brill, 199-207.

Preucel, R.W. 2006. *Archaeological Semiotics.* Oxford: Blackwell Publishing.

Radcliffe-Brown, A.R. 1956. *Structure and Function in Primitive Society*, London: Cohen and West.

Stanley Price N.E. and Christou D. 1973 Excavations at Khirokitia, 1972. *RDAC* 1973, 1-33.

Renfrew, C. 1985. *The archaeology of cult: the sanctuary at Phylacopi*. London: British School of Archaeology at Athens.

Renfrew, C. 2004. Towards a theory of material engagement, in: DeMarrais, E. *et al. Rethinking materiality. The engagement of mind with the material world*, McDonald Institute Monographs. Oxford: Oxbow Books, 23-31.

Schiffer, M.B. 1995. *Behavioral Archaeology. First Principles*. Foundations of Archaeological Enquiry. Salt Lake City: University of Utah Press.

Stausberg, M. 2004. Patterns of Ritual Change among Parsi-Zoroastrians in Recent Times, in: Kreinath, J., Hartung, C. and Deschner, A. (eds.). *The Dynamics of Changing Rituals. The Transformation of Religious Rituals within Their Social and Cultural Context*. Toronto Studies in Religion 29, New York: Peter Lang Publishing, 233-242.

Tambiah, S.J. 1979. *A performative approach to ritual*. Oxford: Oxford University Press.

Taylor, T. 2002. *The Buried Soul: How Humans Invented Death*. Great Britain: Fourth Estate.

Todd, I. 1987. *Excavations at Kalavassos- Tenta. Vol.I.* Studies in the Mediterranean Archaeology Vol. LXXI: 6. Götenborg: Paul Åströms Förlag.

Verhoeven, M. 2002*a*. Ritual and its Investigation in Prehistory. in: Gebel, H.G.K. *et al. Magic Practices and Ritual in the Near Eastern Neolithic,* Proceedings of a Workshop held at the 2nd International Congress on the Archaeology of the Ancient Near East (ICAANE), Copenhagen University, May 2000. Studies in Early Near Eastern Production, Subsistence, and Environment 8. Berlin: Berlin *ex oriente*, 5-40.

Verhoeven, M. 2002*b*. Ritual and Ideology in the Pre-pottery Neolithic B of the Levant and Southeast Anatolia. *Cambridge Archaeological Journal 12:2, 233-258*.

Verhoeven, M. 2004. Beyond Boundaries: Nature, Culture and a Holistic Approach to Domestication in the Levant. *Journal of World Prehistory, Vol.18, No.3, 179-282*.

Watkins, T. 2004. Architecture and "Theatres of Memory" in the Neolithic of Southwest Asia, in: DeMarrais, E. *et al. Rethinking materiality. The engagement of mind with the material world.* McDonald Institute Monographs. Oxbow Books. Oxford, 97-106.

Watkins, T. 2005. The Neolithic revolution and the emergence of humanity: a cognitive approach to the first comprehensive world-view, in: Clarke, J. *Archaeological Perspectives on the transmission and transformation of culture in the eastern Mediterranean*, Levant Supplementary Series 2. Oxford: Oxbow books, 84-88.

Weiner, A. 1992. *Inalienable Possessions. The paradox of Keeping-While-Giving*. Berkley: University of California Press.

Williams, H. 2003. *Archaeologies of Remembrance. Death and Memory in Past Societies*. New York: Kluwer Academic/ Plenum Publishers.

Wylie, R.W. 1968. Ritual and Social Change: A Ghanaian Example. *American Anthropologist, New Series,* Vol. 70, No.1, 21-33.

Chapter 6

When ancestors become Gods

The transformation of Cypriote ritual and religion in the Late Bronze Age

David Collard[1]

Abstract

During the course of the Late Bronze Age (*c.*1700-1050 BCE), the primary expression of Cypriote ritual practice changed from tomb-centred mortuary rituals to larger scale ceremonies conducted within monumental public buildings. These changes appear in concert with a number of significant socio-economic changes in Cypriote society, exhibited by large-scale population movement and settlement expansion, the introduction of craft specialisation, the establishment of coastal trading emporia and the construction of monumental architecture. At the same time, however, certain aspects of Cypriote ritual behaviour appear to remain constant, particularly the practice of feasting and the consumption of psychoactives, such as alcohol and opium. This suggests that earlier ritual practices, and the religious beliefs that motivated them, were somehow appropriated and adapted to suit more institution-directed roles.

Using this Cypriote context as a case study, this paper explores theoretical questions relating to the observation of changes in ritual practice and the possibility of interpreting corresponding religious beliefs. In particular, this paper discusses the way apparent changes in ritual may have related to wider socio-political changes and whether it is possible to infer any corresponding changes in metaphysical beliefs, if it is indeed possible to infer these in the first place.

Keywords: *late Cypriote period, ritual Crange, socio-economic change, psychoactive consumption, metaphysical beliefs.*

---

1 Department of Archaeology, University of Nottingham, University Park, NG7 2RD, UK, acxdc1@nottingham.ac.uk.

Introduction

Over half a century ago Christopher Hawkes (1954) argued that one of the most difficult interpretive challenges in archaeology is to infer religious beliefs from the remnants of rituals which may or may not have been the physical expression of a particular aspect of those beliefs. Unfortunately, this notion has lead to significant pessimism over whether ritual and particularly religious beliefs are viable topics of archaeological research (*e.g.* Wasilewaska 1994). Furthermore, a lack of explicit theoretical concern for these topics has often led to over-imaginative interpretations of ritual practice or religious beliefs, discouraging their study by other scholars (Kyriakidis 2007, 2; for examples see Insoll 2004, 53-59). Metaphorically, archaeologists often climbed too high up Hawkes' 'Ladder of Inference' without an adequate footing.

Given that ritual and religion are ubiquitous and integral components of human social life (Glazier 1997, 3), however, disregarding these topics surely limits our ability to develop plausible understandings of past societies. Furthermore ritual and religion are increasingly being accorded a central role in the development of complex societies throughout the ancient world, particularly in relation to our understanding of how social and political authority were established and legitimised (Aldenderfer 1993; Hayden 2003, 347-379; Marcus and Flannery 2004; Schachner 2001; Trigger 2003, 79-91). Fortunately, interest in the archaeology of ritual and religion appears to be experiencing somewhat of a revival (Hodder (ed.) 2010; Fogelin (ed.) 2008; Insoll 2004; Kyriakidis (ed.) 2007; Whitley and Hays-Gilpin (eds.) 2008), thanks partly to the introduction of more explicit theoretical frameworks primarily derived from anthropology.

This paper considers religious ritual in the context of Late Bronze Age Cyprus (*c.* 1700-1050 BCE) and attempts to demonstrate that it is possible to make nuanced inferences about ritual behaviour and religious beliefs when sufficient contextual archaeological evidence is available. Of particular relevance to the theme of this volume, significant changes in Cypriote cult practice are exhibited during this period and appear to parallel major developments in many other aspects of Cypriote society. As such, this context also presents an ideal opportunity to examine the possible relationships between ritual and social transformation.

Theoretical Concerns

Before considering the Cypriote data, it is first necessary to discuss certain theoretical concepts which may assist in developing an understanding the way in which ritual and religion can be transformed, beginning with a definition of the two terms.

At a very general level, religion can be defined as, *'an institution consisting of culturally patterned interactions with culturally postulated superhuman beings'* (Spiro 1987, 197).

Ritual, on the other hand, has proven particularly difficult for both archaeologists and scholars from other disciplines to define. While it is often described as action characterised by formalism, traditionalism, invariance, rule-governance and performance (Bell 1997, 138-169), some scholars consider ritual to only pertain to practices with an overt religious motivation, distinguishing them from everyday, 'secular' practices (Haviland 2002, 363; Hill 1995, 98; Webb 1999, 11). In this case, ritual can thus be defined as physical attempts to interact somehow with the supernatural forces described in a particular religion; to interpret, manipulate or appeal to them (Haviland 2002, 363). Other scholars, however, also define prescribed 'secular' practices, such as the installations of the office of a civic dignitary, as rituals, preferring to use the expression 'cult' for overtly religious ritual (Renfrew 2007, 110). As the Cypriote evidence considered in this paper was almost certainly associated with overtly religious ritual, however, further discussion of the somewhat debatable concept of pre-enlightenment secular rituals in unnecessary here (for further discussion, see Bell 1997, 198; Bradley 2005; Hill 1995, 97; Insoll 2004, 12-18).

Within archaeology, ritual action is generally privileged over religious thought, as might be expected given that the latter is far less likely to leave physical traces. This trend, however, seems to have created a simplistic dichotomy within the discipline between ritual action and religious belief (Fogelin 2007, 56; Insoll 2004, 78), downplaying the strong dialectic relationship between the two. Anthropology, on the other hand, has long recognised this relationship and, as a result, commonly considers both topics together. Archaeological treatments of ritual, therefore, need to similarly recognise that the range of cognitive processes that guide and give meaning to ritual action are integral elements of this behaviour, regardless of our ability to elucidate them.

Early, explicitly theoretical approaches to an archaeology of ritual can broadly be defined as structuralist (*e.g.* Fritz 1978; Renfrew 1985) or neo-Marxist (*e.g.* Knapp 1986; Shanks and Tilley 1982). Such approaches view religion and ritual as a form of communication, often an ideology linked to political authority. They emphasised the relationship between the ideas, values, theologies and symbols expressed in ritual and the social organisation of the groups conducting them (Bell 1997, 45-46). Such approaches often focus upon the social 'functions' of ritual, such as: forming and maintaining social bonds; socialising individuals via the unconscious appropriation of community values and categories of knowledge and experience and channelling and resolving conflict (Bell 1997, 59). Structuralist approaches, however, often view religion as a particularly stable, long-lasting and static cultural phenomenon (Fogelin 2007, 57), making them ill-suited to the consideration of diachronic change. They have similarly been criticised for being ahistorical and assuming a relatively passive role for ritual participants, overlooking their ability to effect change (Bell 1997, 76; Morris 2006, 4).

Symbolic and, in particular, practice-based approaches to ritual and religion, on the other hand, see these as more dynamic social phenomena; creative strategies by which human beings continually reproduce and reshape their social and cultural environments (Bell 1997, 76-83; *cf.* Geertz 1973). While practice theories retain a focus upon the political dimensions of social relationships, these are considered in relation to the way in which positions of dominance and subordination are variously constituted, manipulated and resisted. Rather than merely being a passive expression of authority, ritual is seen as an active part of a historical process in which past patterns are reproduced, but also reinterpreted or transformed. Bell (1997, 81-82) encapsulates this 'ritual agency' under the term ritualisation, which describes the way in which agents associate certain actions with forces seen to derive from beyond the immediate (the supernatural) as part of the negotiation of ritual authority.

Given that practice approaches view ritual as deeply embedded within human society, it follows that ritual should be analysed in its cultural context, not just as a category of action unrelated to other forms of behaviour (Bell 1997, 81). As Bell (1997, 171) remarks, *'for each and every ritual, there is a thick context of social customs, historical practices and day-to-day routines that ... influence whether and how a ritual action is performed.'*

These associations are commonly reflected in replicated symbols and gestures that create homologies or structural resonances between different ritual contexts. For example, symbols of birth can mark not only rites for a newborn, but can also be seen in other rites of passage and even in ancestral ceremonies that link the dead to the fertility of successive generations (Bell 1997, 173-174). As these systematic linkages are of central importance for understanding the significance of a single ritual act (Bell 1997, 174), it is vital to consider the wider socio-cultural context when seeking to interpret archaeological evidence for a specific ritual context. This focus upon context also suggests that practice approaches to the study of ritual are well suited for use in combination with contextual approaches to archaeological interpretation.

Consideration of the wider socio-cultural context also appears to be of significant importance in understanding changes in ritual practice and religious belief. Bell (1997, 190) also argues that when a society passes through social and historical changes, affecting its worldview, organisation or economy, or introduces it to competing ideas, it will probably witness concomitant changes in its ritual system. Not only can the structure of certain rituals change, but more often the meaning associated with them is also altered as people look to them with different concerns and questions (Bell 1997, 223). At the same time, however, the formalism, traditionalism and invariance that commonly characterise ritual are also particularly resistant to change and often do so more effectively than other forms of social custom (Bell 1997, 211). This therefore suggests that ritual is a particularly effective means of mediating tradition and change, as a way of appropriating some changes while maintaining a sense of cultural continuity (Bell 1997, 251).

Given these theoretical observations, the wider socio-cultural context of Late Bronze Age Cyprus will now be briefly reviewed before considering evidence suggesting transformations in religious belief and ritual practice in this period.

The Late Cypriote Context

During the Late Bronze Age, Cyprus experienced significant social, cultural and political transformations which seem to have primarily been driven by increasing exploitation of the island's abundant copper resources in order to meet a burgeoning international market (Knapp 1988; 1990; 1996; Muhly 1989; Peltenburg 1996).

The need to organise the administration of copper production and trade appears to have resulted in significant increases in social complexity on Cyprus, including the establishment of a settlement hierarchy aimed at accessing, controlling and supporting copper production (Peltenburg 1996, 29-37).

These changes resulted in significant disturbance to the relatively unstratified, kin-based agricultural communities that characterised Cyprus during the Early and Middle Bronze Ages. Early in the Late Cypriote period (*c.* 1700-1400 BCE) there was a substantial increase in population and expansion of settlement, with new settlements incorporating monumental architecture developing in coastal regions in order to engage in international trade (Catling 1962; Knapp 1988; 1996; Merrillees 1971; Negbi 1986; Peltenburg 1996). Changes to mortuary patterns suggest the partial fragmentation of traditional kin-based communities and the development of new social groups, with wealthy burials containing gold, jewellery and imported Levantine and Egyptian exotica suggesting elite competition through conspicuous consumption and funerary ritual (Keswani 1989, 66-69; 2004, 119-126, 157-159; Webb 1992, 90-91). New Cypriote pottery styles such as Base-ring, White Slip and Plain White Wheel-made wares, also appear during this period and suggest a change to specialised and standardised production (Crewe 2004; 2007; Kling 1987; 1989; Steel 2010).

During the 14th and 13th centuries BCE, Cyprus became pivotal in the dissemination of Aegean pottery throughout the East Mediterranean (Steel 1998). This expansion of Cyprus' international trading networks led to further development of the island's copper producing industry, to its apparent peak in the 13th and 12th centuries, with corresponding developments in urbanisation. There was a further increase in population and expansion of settlement, particularly along the coast, culminating with the rise of a number of urban centres along the south coast in the 13th century BCE (Catling 1962; Keswani 1996; Knapp 1996; Negbi 1986). Construction episodes at a number of sites reflect a programme of town planning and site-wide restructuring which suggest increasing socio-political organisation (Crewe 2004, 159).

Despite a number of disruptions to Late Cypriote society around 1200 BCE[2] the majority of these urban centres flourished for around another century, at which point most were abandoned prior to the establishment of the city kingdoms of the Cypriote Iron Age (Catling 1994; Iacovou 1989; 1994).

Mortuary Ritual

For the majority of the Bronze Age (*c.* 2500-1050 BCE) the primary expression of ritual behaviour on Cyprus appears to have been mortuary ritual.[3] These mortuary practices generally consisted of the use of rock-cut chamber tombs

---

2   Including the widespread adoption of Aegean-style pottery in place of indigenous ware types.
3   Although it is possible that Early Cypriote 'shrine' models such as those from Vounous and Kotchati (Frankel and Tamvaki 1973) may depict sites of non-mortuary ritual, there is a complete absence of corresponding architectural evidence, with the possible exception of a potential Middle Cypriote ritual structure from Sotira-*Kaminoudhia* (Swiny 2008).

located within formalised extramural cemeteries; multiple burial and the elaborate and protracted treatment of bodies, possibly involving primary inhumation, exhumation, secondary treatment and reburial; the reuse of tombs over long periods of time and the deposit of a steadily increasing wealth of grave goods, primarily metalwork (including large amounts of gold jewellery in the LCA) and pottery (Keswani 2004, 37-82). At newly established Late Cypriote sites, however, tombs were incorporated into the settlement, often beneath open spaces adjacent to buildings, such as streets or squares, instead of collectively located within the extramural communal spaces favoured in the preceding periods (Keswani 1989, 51; Manning 1998, 47). This suggests that those moving from their ancestral villages into these new localities chose to bury their dead in a new setting. Keswani (2004, 87) suggests that within communities composed of disparate kin-groups, closely related individuals and/or descent groups would have maintained their own burials near their houses and workshops, separated from those of more distant or unrelated groups within the community. This change may reflect the renegotiation of social status following population movement, with smaller competing groups trying to assert their position and economic rights through highly visible funerary ritual within the limits of new settlements (Steel 2004a, 172). The proximity of one's ancestors and continued use of these tombs would have helped to affirm kin group identity, whilst also providing an important symbolic validation of rights of ownership or control over surrounding residential and productive complexes (Keswani 2004, 88, 107; Manning 1998, 47).

With regard to the ceramic assemblages of these tombs, it seems that most vessels are actually residues of mortuary feasting by the living rather than grave offerings or the possessions of the deceased (Herscher 1997, 31-35; Manning 1998, 47; Steel 1998, 290; 2002, 109-110; 2004b, 168; Webb and Frankel 2008, 288).[4] As bowls, jugs and juglets account for over 75 per cent of the pottery assemblage of all tombs for most of the Bronze Age (Webb 1992, 89), it appears that the consumption of liquids, particularly alcohol, was a significant component of the activities conducted in or around the tombs. In Late Cypriote tombs, bowls found inside craters suggest a common Cypriote practice of serving wine from these craters (South 2008, 313; Steel 2004a, 174). As the Late Bronze Age progressed, the increased elaboration of drinking and serving vessels, including the replacement of drinking sets in indigenous wares by more exotic Mycenaean-style sets, suggests that ritual alcohol consumption was an important element of the Late Bronze Age practice of mortuary display (Steel 1998, 290-291). Frequent animal bone further implies that the sacrifice and consumption of adult cattle was another common component of Cypriote mortuary feasting (Keswani 2004, 67-68).

Such feasting activities were likely to have been used to express status and negotiate access to resources within Bronze Age Cypriote society, with their incorporation into mortuary ritual further suggesting that ancestral relationships were central to the formation and legitimisation of individual and sub-group

---

4   Calculations by the present author based on data from intact Late Cypriote chamber tombs conservatively estimates 7.1 vessels per burial, providing further support to this hypothesis.

Figure 17. Comparison of an opium poppy capsule and a BRI juglet (Merrillees 1962, Pl.XLII).

identity (Steel 2002, 113; Webb and Frankel 2008, 292). Cypriote mortuary feasting has also been likened to the *marzēah* (Herscher 1997, 32; Steel 2002, 109), an elite ancestor veneration ritual involving the excess consumption of alcohol, described within Late Bronze Age texts from nearby Ugarit (Armstrong 1998, 92-93; McLaughlin 2001, 66; Pope 1972, 190-193).

Significantly, it appears that opium was also consumed in association with Late Cypriote mortuary ritual. Base Ring juglets have long been associated with opium by Merrillees 1962) who argues that the shape and decoration of these juglets mimicked an opium poppy capsule (*papaver somniferum*) incised to retrieve the psychoactive latex (Figure 17), thereby advertising the vessel's contents as a liquid solution containing opium. This interpretation has recently been confirmed through the identification of opium alkaloid residues within both early and late examples (Koschel 1996; Stacey 2008). Poppy-shaped Base Ring juglets occur within Late Cypriote chamber tombs in significant numbers. They are found within around 53 per cent of intact, currently published tombs, with certain tombs containing dozens or even hundreds of examples.[5] It therefore appears that significant quantities of opium were consumed, or at least deposited, during the ceremonies conducted in association with many Late Cypriote tombs.

Given the evidence for the consumption of at least two different psychoactive substances during Late Cypriote mortuary ritual, it seems likely that it was in fact the psychoactive nature of such substances, or more precisely, their ability to induce altered states of consciousness (ASCs), that prompted their consumption

---

5   Tomb 2 at Kazaphani-*Ayios Andronikos* contained 218 examples between two tomb chambers.

in this context. As pointed out by Bourguignon 1973, 3, 9-11), the experiential characteristics of ASCs commonly accord these phenomena an important role in the ritual practices of a wide range of ethnographically and historically documented cultures. These include feelings of intense emotion; changes in body image; dissolution of boundaries between self and others, often interpreted as an experience of cosmic 'oneness'; perceptual distortions and hallucinations and the ascription of increased meaning or significance to such experiences. It has also been observed that the worldviews of many cultures often involve a dualistic metaphysic, whereby a distinction is made between an 'everyday' world and a 'spirit' or 'other world', where spiritual beings reside (Morris 2006, 313). In this context, entering an ASC is commonly seen as a way to enter or interact with the supernatural world and its inhabitants (Bourguignon 1973, 3). This may particularly be the case in pre-modern contexts, where neuro-psychological explanations for ASCs were unavailable. Given that the beliefs behind mortuary practices commonly concern the soul and its journey to the world where ancestral spirits are thought to reside (Parker Pearson 1999, 31), such metaphysical beliefs are clearly relevant to any consideration of mortuary ritual.

While uncritically applying such cross-cultural generalisations is extremely problematic (Wylie 1985), evidence for the consumption of psychoactive substances does provide a relatively rare opportunity to archaeologically investigate ancient cognitive processes. Indeed, as all humans share an identical nervous system, the neuro-physiological aspects of ASCs experienced by ancient people, induced via the consumption of a specific substance, for instance, were closely analogous to those described in modern sources (*Cf.* Lewis-Williams 1999). Furthermore, Late Bronze Age textual references to mortuary beliefs from nearby Ugarit provides evidence from which extremely close relational analogies (Wylie 1985) can be derived. Combined with a rich corpus of tomb assemblages, such evidence may assist in elucidating some of the beliefs which lay behind the consumption of psychoactives during Bronze Age Cypriot ritual practices.

Opium, for example, is commonly described as inducing a feeling of overwhelming joy, bliss or euphoria and relaxing any tension or anxiety (Hayter 1968, 42; Rätsch 2005, 410). The sensation of flying or floating is common, with the combination of these two aspects commonly interpreted as an 'admission to paradise' (Hayter 1968, 42, 48). These experiential effects make opium an extremely strong sedative and soporific. Visual hallucinations from opium consumption can exaggerate, multiply, colour or giving fantastic shape to observed objects (Hayter 1968, 44). The possible aphrodisiac effects of opium consumption, however, are somewhat ambiguous (Meyer and Quenzer 2005, 248; Rätsch 2005, 410).

At low to moderate doses, alcohol generally produces feelings of relaxation and cheerfulness, reduces inhibitions and slightly impairs judgement and motor skills (Meyer and Quenzer 2005, 244). At higher doses alcohol can induce lethargy and confusion and reduce memory, severely impair motor skills and heighten a range of emotions including affection and aggression (Julien 2008, 107-109; Meyer and Quenzer 2005, 244). Extreme doses can cause a loss of bodily functions, unconsciousness and even death (Meyer and Quenzer 2005, 246).

As a number of these experiential characteristics correspond to those previously suggested to contribute to religious interpretations of ASCs, it is possible that alcohol and opium induced ASCs were somehow interpreted as encounters with the supernatural world. It is, therefore, unsurprising that such an association is also suggested in the previously mentioned Uguaritic textual references to the *marzēah*. In one mythological text (KTU1.114), the god El is described to collapse, 'like those who descend into the underworld' after consuming a large quantity of wine (McLaughlin 2001, 24-26). Due to the association between the *marzēah* and ancestor veneration ritual, this particular passage has been interpreted as El accessing the underworld via his drunkenness (Armstrong 1998, 104, 110; Wyatt 2002:404; 412, Note 43). Interestingly, it is the ability of alcohol to provide an individual with access to the underworld that is meaningful here, rather than its role in stimulating social interaction as usually emphasised in considerations of mortuary feasting (Hamilakis 1998; Steel 2002; 2004a; Webb and Frankel 2008).

In light of this interpretation, it is possible that the widespread evidence for the consumption of alcohol and opium in Cypriote mortuary ritual reflects a similar attempt to access the world of the dead. This may have particularly been the case with opium, whose soporific effects may have been viewed as a means of accessing the underworld, given the strong symbolic links between sleep and death in the East Mediterranean.[6] As the attempt to contact the underworld suggested in the consumption of psychoactives apparently coincides with the final interment of the body, it is possible that the Bronze Age Cypriotes considered direct contact with the world of the dead to be a necessary part of the mortuary rites in order to ensure that the spirit of the deceased was finally accepted into this realm. In this regard, it is particularly interesting to note that for certain intact burials, Base Ring juglets were found immediately next to the head of the deceased.[7] This may indicate the provisioning of the deceased with opium as a means of accessing the world of the dead for themselves.

As the ancestors appear to have been the primary recipients of Early and Middle Bronze Age ritual observance, ancestral spirits appear to be the most important, if not the only, supernatural forces recognised by the Cypriotes at this time. The complex treatment of skeletal remains, deposition of valuables such as jewellery and bronze weapons in tombs and apparent attempts to interact with the world of the dead reinforce the suggestion that the ancestors had significant power and influence. Furthermore, such beliefs also correspond well with the idea that ancestral lineage and family history were key to maintaining status and privilege within the relatively unstratified, kin-based agricultural communities of Early and Middle Bronze Age Cyprus.

---

6   Best exemplified by the twin Greek Gods Hypnos (sleep) and Thanatos (death).
7   In Ayia Irini Tomb 20 for example.

Non-mortuary Ritual

Soon after the start of the Late Bronze Age, however, sites identified as ritual in character begin to appear in contexts not obviously associated with mortuary practice. Evidence for the earliest of these is unfortunately quite meagre, with possible MCIII/LCIA (*c.* 1700-1600 BCE) extramural sanctuaries identified at Phlamoudhi-Vounari (Al-Radi 1983; Horowitz 2008; *Cf.* Webb 1999, 135-140) and Athienou-Bamboulari tis Koukounninas (Dothan and Ben-Tor 1983). At the LCI-IIA (*c.* 1600-1375 BCE) site of Kalopsidha Koufos (Åström 1966; Crewe 2010), although no architecture was uncovered, trial trenches uncovered a large number of miniature cups and jugs remarkably similar to those found in slightly later levels at Athienou, which is discussed further below.

Dating to the LCIIA period (*c.* 1450-1375 BCE), the earliest clear example of a non-mortuary ritual site is Ayios-Iakovos Dhima (Gjerstad *et al.* 1934, 356-361). This appears to be an isolated extramural sanctuary comprised of a roughly circular plaster floor layer around 10m in diameter, split by a low stone wall and probably surrounded by a wooden fence. The eastern area contained two circular stone podia, interpreted as altars and a clay bathtub was set into the floor of the western part of the sanctuary. Finds from the site lay in or around the bathtub and included gold and silver jewellery and other metal objects, local and imported fine-ware pottery and, interestingly, a faïence imitation of a Base Ring juglet. Animal bones found within the bathtub suggest meat consumption. The portable artefacts mirror those from contemporary tomb deposits, although tombs have not been discovered in the immediate vicinity. While it is possible that the rituals observed at the site were directed towards ancestral spirits, there is no evidence which clearly associates it with mortuary ritual, suggesting that other supernatural forces could equally have been the focus of attention.

The slightly later Level III of the extramural sanctuary at Athienou-*Bamboulari tis Koukounninas* 14th to 13th centuries BCE) consisted of a c.18m square open court bordered to the north and east by rectangular rooms (Dothan and Ben-Tor 1983). Within the courtyard were over 10,000 miniature vessels (Figure 18), described by the excavators as votive. These included miniature versions of common Late Cypriote and Aegean wares, although the majority were crudely hand-made miniature bowls and jugs. Also found in and around pits in the courtyard were nine Base Ring juglets, ten Bucchero juglets and scores of White Shaved juglets. Again there are parallels with mortuary ritual, particularly in the apparent consumption of opium, but the architectural setting within an open court and massive amounts of miniature vessels suggests a much greater number of participants, probably beyond the extent of a single kin group. Furthermore, large quantities of metallurgical debris were also found, although it is still uncertain whether smelting actually occurred at the site (Maddin *et al.* 1983, 136; *cf.* Muhly 1985, 33).

These new elements of Cypriote ritual practice, apparently introduced during the first half of the Late Bronze Age, surely relate to the disturbance of previous kin-based communities brought about by the movement of people out of their ancestral rural settlements into newly established coastal sites. These settlers needed to re-establish claims to authority in a competitive environment where the

Figure 18. Athienou-Bamboulari tis Koukounninas, 'votive' vessels in situ on the Stratum III courtyard surface (Dothan and Ben Tor 1983, Pl.24/1).

display of wealth was becoming an important way to gain status. Furthermore, as the development of the Cypriote economy would have required mobilisations of labour extending beyond the capabilities of an individual kin-group, forms of supernatural authority that similarly extended beyond an individual kin-group's ancestors were also likely to become the focus of ritual observance. While there is insufficient iconographic evidence from this early stage of the Late Bronze Age to suggest the nature of the recipient of the new rituals seen at these sanctuaries, it is unlikely that they had a direct kin association with the practitioners in the way that the recipients of mortuary observance probably did. A new social order not centred on kinship ties would have prompted the recognition of new supernatural entities of a more public nature.

At the same time, the presence of Base-ring juglets (and perhaps also Bucchero and White Shaved juglets)[8] at Athienou suggests that earlier methods of interacting with the supernatural via the consumption of psychoactives may have continued. Indeed, the relatively large quantity of such vessels suggests that opium was consumed here by numerous ritual participants. If so, such a group setting for the personal supernatural experience enabled through opium consumption may have been a particularly effective way of strengthening common religious beliefs and ideology.

---

8 As the Bucchero jug appears to replace the Base Ring juglet in the Cypriote ceramic repertoire some time during the 13th Century BCE, this vessel has also been associated with opium (Merrillees 1979, 169). The distinctive White Shaved juglet also appears in place the Base Ring juglet in certain ritual contexts, suggesting that this vessel may also have been associated with a strong psychoactive. Without any corroborating residue analysis evidence, however, these hypotheses will remain tentative at best.

Given the importance of such personal experiences to the formation and maintenance of belief systems (Dornan 2004), such activity may have played a central role in establishing beliefs relating to these relatively new public deities. Non-mortuary ritual practice appears to become increasingly common in the 13th century BCE, demonstrated by examples of intramural ritual architecture from Ayia Irini (Gjerstad *et al.* 1934, 642-824), Kition-*Kathari* (Karageorghis 1985; Karageorghis and Demas 1985) and Myrtou-*Pighades* (du Plat Taylor 1957). At Myrtou-*Pighades*, a large stepped altar in the courtyard was probably crowned with the so-called horns of consecration, whilst large amounts of animal bone including deer antler and ox scapula suggest animal sacrifice. Internal features such as hearths, benches and altars were also found at all three sites. Finds from these sites include ritual paraphernalia previously only seen in nearby regions such as the Aegean and Levant, such as ceramic offering stands, bronze tripods, bull figurines (which do appear occasionally in tombs) and conical rhyta. Elements of previous Cypriote ritual practices do continue, however, with pottery linked to liquid consumption, such as bowls, jugs and juglets, abundant. Vessels possibly associated with opium, such as Base Ring juglets at Kition and Ayia Irini and Bucchero jugs at Myrtou, were also present, although in much smaller numbers. Metallurgical debris was again found at Kition and Myrtou, while at Ayia Irini, an associated building was full of pithoi, implying the storage of agricultural produce.

Towards the end of the 13th and into the 12th century BCE, the construction of monumental temples using ashlar masonry, commonly featuring a pillared hall and associated courtyard, suggests the development of powerful religious institutions. These include the Sanctuary of Aphrodite at Kouklia-*Palaepahos* (Maier 1975; Maier and Karageorghis 1984), new temples constructed in the temple precinct at Kition-*Kathari* (Karageorghis 1985; Karageorghis and Demas 1985) and the Sanctuaries of the Horned and Ingot Gods at Enkomi (Courtois 1971, 1973; Dikaios 1969-1971; Webb 1999, 102-113, 2001).

Certain artefacts from the Kition temple precinct again suggest an association with opium. In addition to the Base Ring juglet mentioned above (discovered in a pit within the adyton of Temple 4) an ivory sceptre-head representing an opium poppy capsule (Figure 19) was discovered in a courtyard associated with Temple 1 (Karageorghis 1985,110, Pl.CXII, CXCI; Karageorghis and Demas 1985, 49). In relation to the possible consumption of opium here, Smith (2009, 160-162) points out that a number of the other artefacts from the precinct can be linked to divination rituals, including gaming pieces (clay balls and astragali), a possible gaming board and numerous notched ox scapulae. As such, opium may have been consumed to induce the 'liminal mindset' required for the reading and interpreting of scapula[9] (Smith 2009, 160) or to induce sleep in order to seek divine revelation through dreaming (Peatfield 1981). This possible role may also explain the evidence for the apparent restriction of opium consumption at Kition. If this substance was used to inspire divine revelation its use is likely to have been restricted to individuals who held a specific, and probably privileged, ritual role as oracles. As such, the ivory

---

9 Referred to as scapulomancy. See Webb 1985.

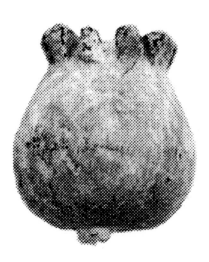

Figure 19. Poppy-shaped ivory sceptre-head. Kition-Kathari, Floor IIIA (Smith 2009, Fig.III.11a).

Figure 20. Bronze figurine of the 'Ingot God' (34.5cm high) (Knapp 2008: Fig.59).

sceptre-head may have been borne by just such an individual, emphasising ritual authority and a privileged relationship with the supernatural, inspired through opium consumption.

Finds from the two Enkomi sanctuaries are also of particular interest. Within the Sanctuary of the Horned God (Dikaios 1969-1971) were numerous animal bones including several ox skulls, gold leaf ox horns and objects of bronze including a bull figurine. Within one of the rooms opening off the main hall, 276 bowls were found stacked in 3 piles while the bronze figurine of the Horned God was also buried in this room. The sheer quantity of bowls found suggests the consumption of liquids by large numbers of ritual participants, while opium consumption is hinted at by the discovery of a Base Ring juglet in one of the bowl stacks, several Bucchero juglets and a rare Bucchero ware amphora from a nearby well. A comparable assemblage, including another Bucchero jug, scores of bucrania and notched scapulae and several ceramic wine-mixing craters, was found in the Sanctuary of the Ingot God (Courtois 1971, 1973; Webb 1999, 102-113), which was located in an adjacent quarter of the town. Divination and the consumption of alcohol and possibly opium again appear to have been important components of the rituals conducted in this sanctuary.

The Bronze figurine of the Ingot God (Figure 20), named after the oxhide-shaped ingot upon which he stands, was also discovered in this Enkomi sanctuary, within the northeast adyton. The strong association between cult and metallurgy suggested by this figurine is also exhibited at Kition, where a copper workshop opened directly onto the largest of the 12th century temples (Karageorghis 1985; Karageorghis and Demas 1985). Such associations and further iconographic references to metalworking have lead Knapp (1986; 1988; 1993) to suggest that ideology (presumably religious) was used to legitimize and maintain elite control of the Late Cypriote copper industry on Cyprus. The discovery of a possible textile workshop within the Kition Temple precinct (Smith 2009, 34-41), however, suggests that other industries may have also been subject to ideological control. Furthermore, the discovery of anchors and ship graffiti in the Kition temples suggest that maritime trade also had its own cult connections (Webb 1999, 44, 302).

The diverse range of religious institutions suggested by this 12th century BCE evidence implies continued competition for status, now between factions whose identity is tied to economic roles rather than kin relations. Furthermore, this period also sees the abandonment of ancestral chamber tombs in favour of simple, individual shaft burials, suggesting the reduced importance of ancestor worship. As such, it appears that temple based religious institutions had become the primary source of social and supernatural authority. At the same time, the sacred iconography of the period exhibits a combination of influences from both the Aegean and Near East (Webb 1999, 281). This suggests that the full incorporation of Cyprus into the international trading networks of the Late Bronze Age resulted in the adoption of foreign derived deities by an increasingly multicultural elite (Webb 1999, 307-308).

Despite the significant transformation of Cypriote ritual practice during the Late Bronze Age, the repeated discovery of vessels associated with opium and alcohol consumption and the remnants of sacrifice and subsequent meat consumption at Cypriote cult sites suggests that local aspects of ritual practice continued to be used during rituals dedicated to these new gods. In particular, the continued association of poppy-shaped vessels with cult sites on Cyprus implies that traditional methods of personally interacting with the supernatural world remained in use.

Conclusion

Changes in Cypriote religious ritual during the Late Bronze Age appear to be a response to, rather than a cause of, changes to other aspects of social life, which can ultimately be attributed to intensifying Cypriote contact with the pre-established states of the eastern Mediterranean. Despite the significant changes to the social, economic, political and religious lives of Cypriote during this period, however, it appears that certain aspects of ritual behaviour persist. In particular, psychoactive substances such as alcohol and opium continued to be consumed during ritual practice, with the ASCs they induced likely to have been consistently viewed as direct personal interaction with the supernatural. While the socio-political meanings of such practices and the precise nature of the supernatural they were associated with may have changed throughout the Late Cypriote period, at this general level, their symbolic meaning therefore seems to have remained relatively constant.

This serves to emphasise the conservative nature of ritual, even in the face of significant changes to other aspects of social life (Bell 1997, 211, 251). Indeed, the Late Cypriote evidence reviewed here further suggests that culturally embedded ritual practices can actually be more resistant to change than the religious beliefs with which they were associated. If ritual practice is inscribed onto and guided by material culture, then it may in fact be more enduring than beliefs that rely on imperfect human memory for their reproduction in prehistoric periods.

In addition to analysing more traditional forms of archaeological evidence for ritual behaviour, this paper has considered a broad range of evidence that enabled insights into some of the cognitive processes that guided and give meaning to these ritual practices. These included archaeological evidence suggesting the consumption of psychoactive substances, iconography, contemporary textual sources and ethnographic evidence. While inferences concerning religious beliefs will never be as secure or detailed as those made about most other aspects of the human past, this paper has demonstrated how such inferences can aid the development of richer and more nuanced interpretations of ancient ritual practices.

Acknowledgements

This paper is an extract from my PhD thesis submitted to the University of Nottingham in 2011. This research project was funded by a Ray and Edith Bennett Travelling Scholarship from the University of Melbourne, a University of Nottingham Scholarship for the Arts, Universitas 21, the Near Eastern Archaeological Foundation and the Department of Archaeology at the University of Nottingham. I would like to give particular thanks to my supervisor, Professor Bill Cavanagh, for his invaluable advice and guidance throughout the course of this research project. Special thanks also to Dr Anna Drummond for her comments and advice on this paper.

References

Aldenderfer, M. 1993. Ritual, Hierarchy, and Change in Foraging Societies. *Journal of Anthropological Archaeology* 12, 1-40.

Al-Radi, S.M.S. 1983. *Phlamoudhi Vounari: A Sanctuary Site in Cyprus.* Studies in Mediterranean Archaeology 65. Göteborg: Paul Åströms Förlag.

Armstrong, D.E. 1998. *Alcohol and Altered States in Ancestor Veneration Rituals of Zhou Dynasty China and Iron Age Palestine.* Lewinston, Queenston and Lampeter: The Edwin Mellen Press.

Åström, P. 1966. *Excavations at Kalopsidha and Ayios Iakovos in Cyprus.* Studies in Mediterranean Archaeology 2. Lund: Paul Åström.

Bell, C. 1997. *Ritual: Perspectives and Dimensions.* Oxford: Oxford University Press.

Bourguignon, E. 1973. Introduction: A Framework for the Comparative Study of Altered States of Consciousness, in: Bourguignon, E. (ed.). *Religion, Altered States of Consciousness, and Social Change.* Columbus: Ohio State University Press, 3-35.

Bradley, R. 2005. *Ritual and Domestic Life in Prehisotric Europe*. London and New York, Routledge.

Catling, H.W. 1962. Patterns of Settlement in Bronze Age Cyprus. *Opuscula Atheniensia* 4, 129-169.

Catling, H.W. 1994. Cyprus in the 11th Century B.C.- An End or a Beginning?, in: Karageorghis, V. (ed.). *Cyprus in the 11th Century B.C.* Nicosia: A.G. Leventis Foundation, 133-141.

Courtois, J.-C. 1971. Le Sanctuaire du Dieu au Lingot d'Enkomi-Alasia, in: Schaeffer, C. F. A. (ed.). *Alasia I*. Paris: Klinchsieck, 151-362.

Courtois, J.-C. 1973. Le Sanctuaire du Dieu au Lingot d'Enkomi-Alasia (Chypre) et les Lieux de Culte Contemporains en Méditerranée Orientale. *Comptes-Rendus des Séances de l'Année – Académie des Inscriptions et Belles-Lettres* 117/2, 223-246.

Crewe, L. 2004. *Social Complexity and Ceramic Technology on Late Bronze Age Cyprus: The New Evidence from Enkomi*, Unpublished Ph.D thesis, the University of Edinburgh.

Crewe, L. 2007. *Early Enkomi: Regionalism, Trade and Society at the Beginning of the Late Bronze Age on Cyprus*. British Archaeological Review International Series 1706. Oxford: Archaeopress.

Crewe, L. 2010. Rethinking Kalopsidha: From Specialisation to State Marginalisation, in: Bolger, D. and Maguire, L.C. (eds.). *The Development of Pre-State Communities in the Ancient Near East*. Oxford and Oakville: Oxbow Books, 63-71.

Dikaios, P. 1969-1971. *Enkomi Excavations 1948-1958 I-II*. Mainz am Rhein: Verlag Philipp von Zabern.

Dornan, J.L. 2004. Beyond Belief: Religious Experience, Ritual, and Cultural Neurophenomenology in the Interpretation of Past Religious Systems. *Cambridge Archaeological Journal* 14/1, 25-36.

Dothan, T. and Ben-Tor, A. 1983. *Excavations at Athienou, Cyprus 1971-1972*. Qedem 16. Jerusalem: The Hebrew University of Jerusalem.

du Plat Taylor, J. 1957. *Myrtou Pighades: A Late Bronze Age Sanctuary in Cyprus*. Oxford: Ashmolean Museum.

Fogelin, L. 2007. The Archaeology of Religious Ritual. *Annual Review of Anthropology* 36, 55-71.

Fogelin, L. 2008 (ed.). *Religion, Archaeology, and the Material World*. Carbondale, Illinois: Center for Archaeological Investigations, Southern Illinois University Carbondale.

Frankel, D. and Tamvaki 1973. Cypriot Shrine Models and Decorated Tombs. *The Australian Journal of Biblical Archaeology* 2, 39-44.

Fritz, J. 1978. Paleopsychology Today: Ideational Systems and Human Adaptation in Prehistory, in: Redman C. (ed.). *Social Archaeology: Beyond Subsistence and Dating*. New York: Academic Press, 37-60.

Geertz, C. 1973. *The Interpretation of Cultures*. London: Hutchison and Co.

Gjerstad, E., Lindros, J., Sjöqvist, E. and Westholm, A. 1934. *The Swedish Cyprus Expedition I. Finds and Results of the Excavations in Cyprus 1927-1931*. Stockholm: The Swedish Cyprus Expedition.

Glazier, S.D. 1997. Introduction, in: Glazier, S.D. (ed.). *Anthropology of Religion: A Handbook*. Wesport, Connecticut and London: Greenwood Press, 1-15.

Hamilakis, Y. 1998. Eating the Dead: Mortuary Feasting and the Politics of Memory in the Aegean Bronze Age Societies, in: Branigan, K. (ed.). *Cemetery and Society in the Aegean Bronze Age*. Sheffield: Sheffield Academic Press, 115-132.

Haviland, W.A. 2002. Culture and the Supernatural, in: Haviland, W.A., Walrath, D., McBride, B. and Prins, H.E.L (eds.). *Cultural Anthropology, 10th Edition*. Orlando: Harcourt Brace and Company, 360-380.

Hawkes, C. 1954. Archaeological Theory and Method: Some Suggestions from the Old World. *American Anthropologist* 56, 155-168.

Hayden, B. 2003. *Shamans, Sorcerers and Saints*. Washington: Smithsonian Books.

Hayter, A. 1968. *Opium and the Romantic Imagination*. London: Faber and Faber.

Herscher, E. 1997. Representational Relief on Early and Middle Cypriot Pottery, in: Karageorghis, V., Laffineur R. and Vandenabeele, F. (eds.). *Four Thousand Years of Images on Cypriote Pottery, Proceedings fo the Third International Conference of Cypriote Studies, Nicosia, 3-4 May, 1996*. Brussels, Liège and Nicosia: Leventis Foundation, 25-36.

Hill, J.D. 1995. *Ritual and Rubbish in the Iron Age of Wessex: A Study on the Formation of a Specific Archaeological Record*. Oxford: Tempus Reparatum.

Hodder, I. 2010 (ed.). *Religion in the Emergence of Civilization: Çatalhöyük as a Case Study*. Cambridge: Cambridge University Press.

Horowitz, M. 2008. Phlamoudhi-Vounari: A Multi-Function Site in Cyprus, in: J. S. Smith (ed.). *Views from Phlamoudhi, Cyprus*. Boston: American Schools of Oriental Research, 69-85.

Iacovou, M. 1989. Society and Settlements in Late Cypriot III, in: Peltenburg, E. J. (ed.). *Early Society in Cyprus*. Edinburgh: Edinburgh University Press, 52-58.

Iacovou, M. 1994. The Topography of 11th Century B.C. Cyprus, in: Karageorghis, V. (ed.). *Cyprus in the 11th Century B.C.* Nicosia: Leventis Foundation, 149-165.

Insoll, T. 2004. *Archaeology, Ritual, Religion*. London and New York: Routledge.

Julien, R.M. 2008. *A Primer of Drug Action: A Comprehensive Guide to the Actions, Uses, and Side Effects of Psychoactive Drugs*. New York: Worth Publishers.

Karageorghis, V. 1985. *Excavations at Kition 5. The Pre-Phoenician Levels, Part II*. Nicosia: Department of Antiquities, Cyprus.

Karageorghis, V. and Demas, M. 1985. *Excavations at Kition 5. The Pre-Phoenician Levels, Part I*. Nicosia: Department of Antiquities, Cyprus.

Keswani, P.S. 1989. Dimensions of Social Hierarchy in Late Bronze Age Cyprus: An Analysis of the Mortuary Data from Enkomi. *Journal of Mediterranean Archaeology* 21, 49-86.

Keswani, P.S. 1996. Hierarchies, Heterarchies, and Urbanization Processes: The View from Bronze Age Cyprus. *Journal of Mediterranean Archaeology* 9/2, 211-250.

Keswani, P.S. 2004. *Mortuary Ritual and Society in Bronze Age Cyprus*. London: Equinox.

Kling, B. 1987. Pottery Classification and Relative Chronology of the LC IIC – LC IIIA Periods, in: Rupp, D. W. (ed.). *Western Cyprus: Connections*. Studies in Mediterranean Archaeology 77. Göteborg: Paul Åströms Förlag. 97-111.

Kling, B. 1989. *Mycenaean IIIC:1b and Related Pottery in Cyprus*. Studies in Mediterranean Archaeology 87. Göteborg: Paul Åströms Förlag.

Knapp, A.B. 1986. *Copper Production and Divine Protection: Archaeology, Ideology and Social Complexity on Bronze Age Cyprus*. Studies in Mediterranean Archaeology Pocket Book 42. Göteborg: Paul Åströms Förlag.

Knapp, A.B. 1988. Ideology, Archaeology and Polity. *Man* 23, 133-163.

Knapp, A.B. 1990. Production, Location and Integration in Bronze Age Cyprus. *Current Anthropology* 31, 147-76.

Knapp, A.B. 1993. Power and Ideology on Prehistoric Cyprus, in: Hellström, P. and Alroth, B. (ed.). *Religion and Power in the Ancient Greek world: Proceedings of the Uppsala Symposium 1993*. Uppsala: Ubaliensis S. Academiae, 9-25.

Knapp, A.B. 1996. Settlement and Society on Late Bronze Age Cyprus: Dynamics and Development, in: Åström, P. and Herscher, E. (eds.). *Late Bronze Age Settlement in Cyprus: Function and Relationship*. Studies in Mediterranean Archaeology Pocket Book 126. Jonsered: Paul Åströms Förlag.

Knapp, A.B. 2008. *Prehistoric and Protohistoric Cyprus: Identity, Insularity, and Connectivity*. Oxford: Oxford University Press.

Koschel, K. 1996. Opium Alkaloids in a Cypriote Base Ring I Vessel (Bilbil) of the Middle Bronze Age from Egypt. *Ägypten und Levante* 6, 159-166.

Kyriakidis, E. 2007. In Search of Ritual, in: Kyriakidis E. (ed.). *The Archaeology of Ritual*. Los Angeles: Cotsen Institute of Archaeology, University of California, Los Angeles, 1-8.

Kyriakidis, E. 2007 (ed.). *The Archaeology of Ritual*. Los Angeles: Cotsen Institute of Archaeology, University of California, Los Angeles.

Lewis-Williams, J.D. 1999. Wrestling with Analogy: A Methodological Dilemma in Upper Palaeolithic Art Research, in: Whitley, D.S. (ed.). *Reader in Archaeological Theory: Post-processual and Cognitive Approaches*. London and New York, Routledge, 157-175.

Maddin, R., Muhly, J.D. and Wheeler, T.S. 1983. Metal Working, in: Dothan T. and Ben-Tor, A. (eds.). *Excavations at Athienou, Cyprus 1971-1972*. Qedem 16. Jerusalem: The Hebrew University of Jerusalem, 132-138.

Maier, F.G. 1975. The Temple of Aphrodite at Old Paphos. *Report of the Department of Antiquities, Cyprus*, 69-80.

Maier, F.G. and Karageorghis, V. 1984. *Paphos. History and Archaeology*. Nicosia: Leventis Foundation.

Manning, S. 1998. Changing Pasts and Socio-political Cognition in Late Bronze Age Cyprus. *World Archaeology* 30/1, 39-58.

Marcus, J. and Flannery, K.V. 2004. The Coevolution of Ritual and Society: New 14C Dates from Ancient Mexico. *Anthropology* 101/52, 18257-18261.

McLaughlin, J.L. 2001. *The Marzeah in the Prophetic Literature, References and Allusions in Light of the Extra-Biblical Evidence*. Leiden: Brill.

Merrillees, R.S. 1962. Opium Trade in the Bronze Age Levant. *Antiquity* 36, 287-292.

Merrillees, R.S. 1971. The Early History of Late Cypriote I. *Levant* 3, 56-79.

Merrillees, R.S. 1979. Opium Again in Antiquity. *Levant* 11, 167-171.

Meyer, J.S. and Quenzer, L.F. 2005. *Psychopharmacology: Drugs, the Brain, and Behavior*. Sunderland, Massachusetts: Sinauer Associates.

Morris, B. 2006. *Religion and Anthropology: A Critical Introduction*. Cambridge: Cambridge University Press.

Muhly, J.D. 1985. The Late Bronze Age in Cyprus: A 25 Year Retrospect, in: Karageorghis, V. (ed.). *Archaeology in Cyprus 1960-1985*. Nicosia: Leventis Foundation, 20-46.

Muhly, J.D. 1989. The Organisation of the Copper Industry in Late Bronze Age Cyprus, in: Peltenburg, E.J. (ed.). *Early Society in Cyprus*. Edinburgh: Edinburgh University Press, 298-314.

Negbi, O. 1986. The Climax of Urban Development in Bronze Age Cyprus. *Report of the Department of Antiquities, Cyprus*, 97-121.

Parker Pearson, M. 1999. *The Archaeology of Death and Burial*. College Station: Texas AandM University Press.

Peatfield, A. 1981. Review of Karageorghis, J. 1997. La grande déesse de Chypre et son culte, à travers l'iconographie, de l'époque néolithiqueau Vième s. a.C. *Journal of Hellenic Studies* 101, 185.

Peltenburg, E.J. 1996. From Isolation to State Formation in Cyprus, c. 3500-1500 B.C., in: Karageorghis, V. and Michaelides, D. (eds.). *The Development of the Cypriot Economy from the Prehistoric Period to the Present Day*. Nicosia: University of Cyprus, 17-43.

Pope, M.H. 1972. A Divine Banquet at Ugarit, in: Efird, J. M. (ed.). *The Use of the Old Testament in the New and Other Essays. Studies in Honour of Franklin Stinespring*. Durham: Duke University Press, 170-203.

Rätsch, C. 2005. *The Encyclopedia of Psychoactive Plants: Ethnopharmacology and its Applications*. Rochester: Park Street Press.

Renfrew, C. 1985. *The Archaeology of Cult: The Sanctuary at Phylakopi*. Athens: The British School of Archaeology at Athens.

Renfrew, C. 2007. The Archaeology of Ritual, of Cult, and of Religion, in: Kyriakidis, E. 2007(ed.). *The Archaeology of Ritual*. Los Angeles, Cotsen Institute of Archaeology, University of California: Los Angeles, 109-122.

Schachner, G. 2001. Ritual Control and Transformation in Middle-Range Societies: An Example from the American Southwest. *Journal of Anthropological Archaeology* 20, 168-194.

Shanks, M. and Tilley, C. 1982. Ideology, Symbolic Power and Ritual Communication, in: Hodder, I. (ed.). *Symbolic and Structural Archaeology.* Cambridge: Cambridge University Press, 129-154.

Smith, J.S. 2009. *Art and Society in Cyprus from the Bronze Age into the Iron Age.* Cambridge: Cambridge University Press.

South, A.K. 2008. Feasting in Cyprus: A View from Kalavasos, in: Hitchcock, L.A., Laffineur, R. and Crowley, J. (eds.). *DAIS, The Aegean Feast, Proceedings of the 12th International Aegean Conference, 25-29 March 2008, The University of Melbourne.* Aegaeum 29. Liège: Université de Liège, 309-315.

Spiro, M.E. 1987. *Culture and Human Nature.* Chicago: Chicago University Press.

Stacey, R. 2008. *Email sent to D. Collard 3 December 2008.*

Steel, L. 1998. The Social Impact of Mycenaean Imported Pottery in Cyprus. *Annual of the British School at Athens* 93, 285-296.

Steel, L. 2002. Wine, Women and Song: Drinking Ritual in Cyprus in the Late Bronze and Early Iron Ages, in: Bolger, D. and Serwint, N. (eds.). *Engendering Aphrodite: Women and Society in Ancient Cyprus,* Boston: American Schools of Oriental Research, 105-119.

Steel, L. 2004a. A Goodly Feast... A Cup of Mellow Wine: Feasting in Bronze Age Cyprus, in: Wright, J.C. (ed.). *The Mycenaean Feast.* Princeton: American School of Classical Studies at Athens, 161-180.

Steel, L. 2004b. *Cyprus Before History.* London: Duckworth.

Steel, L. 2010. Late Cypriote Ceramic Production: Heterarchy or Hierarchy, in: Bolger, D. and Maguire, L.C. (eds.). *The Development of Pre-State Communities in the Ancient Near East.* Oxford and Oakville: Oxbow Books, 106-116.

Swiny, S. 2008. Of Cows, Copper, Comers, and Cult: The Emergence of the Cypriot Bronze Age. *Near Eastern Archaeology* 71/1-2, 41-51.

Trigger, B. 2003. *Understanding Early Civilizations: A Comparative Study.* Cambridge: Cambridge University Press.

Wasilewaska, E. 1994. The Search for the Impossible: The Archaeology of Religion of Prehistoric Societies as an Anthropological Discipline. *Journal of Prehistoric Religion* 8, 62-75.

Webb, J.M. 1985. The Incised Scapulae, in: Karageorghis, V. and Demas, M. (eds.). *Excavations at Kition 5. The Pre-Phoenician Levels, Part I.* Nicosia: Department of Antiquities, Cyprus, 314-328.

Webb, J.M. 1992. Funerary Ideology in Bronze Age Cyprus: Toward the Recognition and Analysis of Cypriote Ritual Data, in: Ioannides, A.G. (ed.). *Studies in Honour of Vassos Karageorghis.* Nicosia: Leventis Foundation, 87-99.

Webb, J.M. 1999. *Ritual Architecture, Iconography and Practice in the Late Cypriot Bronze Age.* Studies in Mediterranean Archaeology Pocket Book 75. Jonsered: Paul Åströms Förlag.

Webb, J.M. 2001. The Sanctuary of the Ingot God at Enkomi: A New Reading of its Construction, Use and Abandonment, in: Fischer, P.M. (ed.). *Contributions to the Archaeology and History of the Bronze and Iron Ages in the Eastern Mediterranean. Studies in Honour of Paul Åström.* Vienna: Österreichishes Archäologisches Institut, 69-82.

Webb, J.M. and Frankel, D. 2008. Fine Ware Ceramics, Consumption and Commensality: Mechanisms of Horizontal and Vertical Integration in Early Bronze Age Cyprus, in: Hitchcock, L.A., Laffineur, R. and Crowley, J. (eds.). *DAIS, The Aegean Feast, Proceedings of the 12th International Aegean Conference, 25-29 March 2008, The University of Melbourne.* Aegaeum 29. Liège: Université de Liège, 287-295.

Whitley, D.S. and Hays-Gilpin, K. (eds.). 2008. *Belief in the Past: Theoretical Approaches to the Archaeology of Religion.* Walnut Creek, California: Left Coast Press.

Wyatt, N. 2002. *Religious Texts from Ugarit, 2nd Edition.* London: Sheffield Academic Press.

Wylie, A. 1985. The Reaction Against Analogy, in: Schiffer, M. (ed.). *Advances in Archaeological Method and Theory. Vol.8.* Orlando: Academic Press, 63-111.

Chapter 7

Colonial entanglements and cultic heterogeneity on Rome's Germanic frontier

Karim Mata[1]

Abstract

Roman expansion into the Rhineland was followed by centuries of religious entanglements that involved the interactions of individuals and communities with a variety of backgrounds, interests and agendas, and, over time, an array of cultic narratives and practices was maintained, transformed and abandoned. The notion of cultic heterogeneity used in this discussion is informed by the perception that all social constructs are reproduced through continuous affirmation vis-à-vis extent alternatives. Cultic discourse is inherently heterogeneous due to the discrepant attitudes, abilities and actions of situated agents. This will be explored by considering the symbolic narratives and ritual practices associated with the Hercules *Magusanus* cult on Rome's Germanic frontier.

Keywords: *cult, ritual, discourse, heterogeneity, Hercules, Roman, colonialism.*

Introduction

In the eighth century AD, the Dutch central river area formed a contested border zone between a Christianized South and pagan North. It was a time when faithful servants of the Christian God traversed hostile lands with the aim of converting the Frisian people (Talbot 1954; Heidinga 1999). Under the leadership of Willibrord, an Anglo-Saxon monk from Northumbria who would become known as the 'apostle to the Frisians', such efforts involved the destruction of pagan ritual spaces and the creation of Christian sites of worship. These incursions did not go uncontested of course, and, not infrequently, missionaries were killed and churches destroyed.

---

1 Department of Anthropology, University of Chicago, 1126 East 59th Street Chicago, IL 60637 USA kmata@uchicago.edu.

Apart from harboring an understandable hesitance for abandoning long-held beliefs, the Frisians undoubtedly understood that the evangelizing missions into their territory were part of a wider effort by the Christian Franks to gain political dominance over the region. Such missionary work was done by one of Willibrord's disciples, an Irish Benedictine monk by the name of Werenfried, who would come to be associated with an 8th century church at present-day Elst. Its location offered a strategic point of access into Frisian territory. Upon his death, the monk was buried there, and the tomb of St. Werenfried would become a place of pilgrimage for those looking to relieve arthritic pains or improve horticultural efforts. In the role of patron saint, Werenfried would come to play an important part in the historical narratives produced by communities throughout the region.

This brief impression of Early Medieval religious entanglements reveals the interaction of individuals and communities with different identities and backgrounds, the politicization and contestation of religious narratives, rituals and spaces, as well as the involvement of personal convictions and public imaginaries. We can expect equally complex situations to have arisen in Roman times. Roman expansion into the Rhineland was followed by centuries of religious entanglements that involved the interactions of individuals and communities with a variety of backgrounds, interests and agendas, and, over time, a range of cultic discourses was produced, transformed and abandoned. My contribution to this collection of papers on the archaeology of ritual failure involves an exploration of the heterogeneity of symbolic narratives and ritual practices as this pertains to the Hercules *Magusanus* cult on Rome's Germanic frontier.

In this discussion, cult refers to a religious community whose members engage with a certain set of representational rituals, beliefs, objects and spaces for the fulfilment of spiritual and secular needs. Cults are socially reproduced and historically situated communities that operate within a larger system of shared moralities and worldviews. When enmeshed in political struggles, cults may be used for the explicit communication of dominant ideologies and the implicit reproduction of existing relations of power. At the same time, myriad opportunities arise for subordinate individuals and groups to reproduce, transform or abandon the form, content and meaning of these social constructs. Such dialectic interactions between dominant and subordinate discourses produce both diachronic change and synchronic variability, or, in other words, cultic heterogeneity. This notion of cultic heterogeneity is mainly informed then by the realization that any social discourse, whether understood as dominant or subordinate, is reproduced through continuous affirmation vis-à-vis real or imagined alternatives, and therefore always 'at risk' of being transformed by the structured improvisation of situated agents (Bourdieu 1977; Comaroff and Comaroff 1991).[2] Such heterogeneity tends to frustrate the reductive tendencies of archaeologists seeking to understand social discourses, and the circumstances that gave rise to them. Our disciplinary interests and practices drive the search for patterns, and we are quick to normalize the

---

2   Claims of discursive homogeneity are commonly made in social discourses, but ignoring their actual heterogeneity risks channelling the political programs of our historical subjects.

observable and simplify the complex. Archaeological narratives are produced with a body of evidence that is as biased as our shifting interests, and the tendency to ignore or reduce past complexities has proven tenacious (Trouillot 1995, 19; Insoll 2004, 12; Johnson 2006, 123).

It so happens that Werenfried's church was built on the exact spot where a temple of Hercules *Magusanus* stood centuries before (Bogaers 1955; Derks 2002). The distribution of mostly archaeological and epigraphic evidence for his cult extends throughout the Lower Rhineland where an earliest association between a native *Magusanus* and Roman Hercules seems to have been made in the early first century AD (Derks 1991, 251). So far, three ritual sites have been associated with this deity, and all are located in the territory of the Batavians (Figure 21), an identity that arose during the tribal reshuffling of the Rhineland in the decades following Caesar's Gallic wars (58-50 BC). The *Magusanus* cult has been given an important role in shaping the ways this community forged a place for itself in the Roman Empire (Roymans 2004). Its sanctuaries are assumed to have been sites where communal feasts were staged to commemorate communal origins, where elites competed for social standing, and where men engaged in martial rites-of-passage and personal votive rituals (Derks 1998, 98; Roymans 2009, 232).[3]

Recent research on Hercules *Magusanus* (Derks 1998; Roymans 2009) has been characteristically Marxist-structuralist in outlook, such that it emphasizes the importance of enduring value-systems grounded in economic modes of existence. From this perspective, archaeological distributions of cult practice have been associated with more-or-less distinct landscapes[4], whereby the appeal of Hercules in the lowlands of the Roman-Germanic frontier zone is explained by themes commonly associated with this particular deity – martiality, masculine prowess, pastoral lifeways and adventurous exploration. Hercules seems to have been ideally suited to serve as the patron of native soldiers and pastoralists, and as mediator between Roman civilization and Germanic barbarity (Roymans 2009, 233).

Foundation myths are also viewed as important elements in the construction of imagined histories that served to define the collective identities and self-image of local groups. A '*mythological anchoring of Celto-Germanic groups in the Roman world*' occurred through a syncretic process whereby local deities were identified

---

3   Archaeological investigation in the Batavian homeland paints a picture of a society largely dominated by the military sphere, whereby the role of pre-Roman martial and pastoral ideologies, and the 'suitability' of the Batavian community for Roman military recruitment, has featured importantly (Roymans 2004).

4   Derks (1998), for example, observes that the distribution of syncretic Mars dedications is primarily restricted to a southern agricultural zone while those to Hercules *Magusanus* are mainly found across the pastoral lowlands of the northern river and coastal areas.

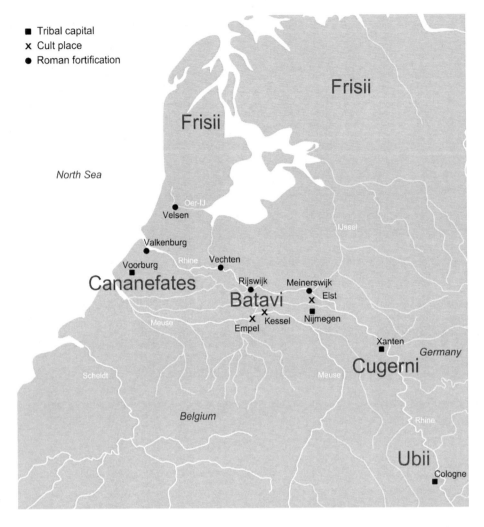

Figure 21. Paleogeographic reconstruction of the Netherlands in the first century AD, with sites and tribal groups mentioned in the text.

with those from the Greco-Roman pantheon (Roymans 2009, 235).[5] While an association with Rome's foundation myth has not been considered in the case of *Magusanus*, the Batavians may well have claimed descent from Hercules himself (Derks 1998, 111). It is furthermore held that descent myths were not imposed by Rome, but were willingly and actively appropriated by local aristocrats who were in the best position to learn about Greco-Roman mythology (Roymans 2009, 225).

---

5   The use of syncretism here differs little from mid 20th century anthropological formulations. Herskovits, for example, argues how syncretism occurs at times of cultural interaction and results from '*the tendency to identify those elements in the new culture with similar elements in the old one, enabling the persons experiencing the contact to move from one to the other, and back again, with psychological ease*' (Herskovits 1966, 57; see Apter 2004 for a discussion). Roman archaeologists have come to embrace the concept ever since nativists have urged for a reassessment of the widely used *interpretatio Romana* concept (the recognition of divine responsibility and capability in local deities by Roman outsiders) which ignores indigenous perceptions.

In other words, native elites are treated as the primary promoters of the dominant discourse, and the community-wide adoption of new narratives and rituals.[6]

The post-colonial perspectives that influenced Roman archaeology during the 1980s and 1990s have shaped interpretations in the Lower Rhineland as well (Brandt and Slofstra 1983; Blagg and Millett 1990; Millett 1990; Derks 1991; Roymans 1995). Archaeologists working from a nativist point-of-view typically underscore Roman laissez-fair attitudes while emphasizing the role of native elites in acculturation processes. In the Lower Rhineland specifically, a distinction tends to be made between non-intervention in ideological and economic domains on the one hand and political and military imposition on the other (Derks 1999, 355). Despite this added nuance, elites and native soldiers continue to draw scholarly attention for their perceived centrality in Romano-Batavian relations and the production of ethnic discourse. While this centrality of elites in local transformation processes in the region is problematic due to their near absence in the archaeological record (Van Driel-Murray 2002, 200), a restrictive focus on the assertive role of particular social groups (*e.g.* military men) remains problematic from a theoretical point-of-view as well (Mata 2012, 36). By placing the responsibility of syncretic identifications squarely in the hands of assertive local elites, nativists have downplayed the interests of colonial authorities and neglected the heterogeneity of social constructs.

In considering the contributions of indigenous populations to colonial entanglements, post-colonial archaeologists have argued that the arrival of 'colonial' materials in local contexts cannot simply be explained in terms of the adoption of associated values and behaviours (Mattingly 1997; Webster 1997). In other words, the presence of 'Roman' materials and practices cannot speak to their social role in local contexts in any clear-cut way. While this is a crucial point, it is also true that local transformations occurred under imposed conditions, and, especially in a military frontier zone, must be examined with Roman politico-military strategies and ideological discourses in mind. At the same time, colonial authorities and their agents are rarely able to ensure the acceptance of dominant discourses by social subordinates, even under conditions of extreme imposition. This complexity has been recognized by those archaeologists who treat colonial encounters as intricate entanglements of embedded interests and strategies pursued by a wide variety of individuals and groups (Van Dommelen 2002; Stein 2005; Dietler 2010).

Under colonial conditions, cultic, ethnic and other social discourses are reproduced in heterogeneous ways due to the understandings, capacities and actions of local agents with different socio-cultural backgrounds and dispositions (Shennan 1989; Jones 1997). Those with the highest archaeological and historical

---

6   An 'ideological core' is thought to have persisted after a formative period of Batavian ethnogenesis despite the social and economic transformations that followed (Derks 2009, 268). Such continuity is argued for because large-scale settlement of foreign veterans never seem to have taken place in the region where the only sanctuaries of Hercules *Magusanus* were located, while the monumentalization of the sanctuaries around 100 AD is taken as a testament to their continued importance for the Batavian community. In contrast, the foundation of Roman colonies, the influx of foreigners, and the establishment of a public Mars cult in the German Rhineland are thought to have caused the marginalization of Hercules there (Roymans 2009, 230).

visibility are colonial authorities, local elites, and the artists and intellectuals they employ. This visibility results from the successful imposition and normalization of their authority and their dominance over political, military and religious institutions. However, their constructs are always open to wider interpretation and appropriation because these are cultivated in the public domain (Streets 2004, 145). Subalterns ignore, adopt, or transform dominant discourses for their own benefit, with their content interpreted and appropriated in accordance with local logics. Such dynamics allow for their survival beyond the formative circumstances under which they were forged, while simultaneously assisting the production of alternatives. In response to such challenges, dominant discourses are continuously reformulated in order to remain politically effective. It is through such dialectics that we may expect symbolic narratives and ritual practices to persist, fail or transform.

Herculean Multivalence

Multivalence was an inherent aspect of Roman religion. This is clearly shown by the wide variety of participants in any single cult, but also in the way symbolic narratives and ritual practices had no real constancy; as situational constructs, they were ever-adjusted to local and historical circumstances. Hercules was continuously appropriated and reinvented, with discourses becoming increasingly politicized due to the power struggles and imperialist endeavors of the Late Republic period (Galensky 1972; Ritter 1995).[7] Different thematic associations were made by a wide variety of groups and individuals. For Romans, Hercules for a long time had primarily been a protector of commercial activities. It seems the divine hero who epitomized the search for rewards from perilous labor was easily associated with the uncertainties inherent in commerce and travel, and his sanctuaries are commonly found along trade and transhumance routes, and near emporia, markets and fairs (Bowden and Rawlings 2005). Cultic rituals involved merchants dedicating a portion of their profits (*decuma*) to Hercules, to ensure his protection.

As Rome's military enterprises expanded during the Republican period, Hercules increasingly became associated with the martial sphere, such that the cults of Hercules *Invictus* (Unconquered Hercules) and Hercules *Victor* (Hercules the Conqueror), both located in the *forum Boarium*, rose to prominence. As Rome's most ancient forum, this sacred space increasingly witnessed the organization of public triumphs and lavish banquets (*epulum*) staged by prominent Roman leaders who competed for prestige and popular support (Plutarch *Crassus* 12.2; Kondoleon

---

7   The thematic repertoire found throughout the Western Mediterranean is highly varied. Hercules was associated with a broad range of themes, including health, springs, youth, strength, immortality, commerce, cattle-breeding, travel, even eloquence (Bowden and Rawlings 2005). Furthermore, syncretic constructs of the Classical Hercules and local divinities can be found throughout the Italic peninsula (Marzano 2009, 83), with references made to a wide variety of elements drawn from Herculean myth. For example, traders in olive oil could refer to the mythical fact of Hercules *Olivarius* importing the olive plant from Hyperboria (Pausanius, *Description of Greece* 5.7.7), and similar notions will have been entertained by salt traders (Hercules *Salarius*), quarrymen (Hercules *Saxanus*) or boxers (Hercules *Pugilis*).

and Bergman 1999; Beard 2007).[8] Such events could involve triumphant Roman generals dedicating a portion of the spoils of war to Hercules (Marzano 2009, 86).

This growing emphasis on the martial characteristics of Hercules involved the appropriation of Herculean myth by the heroes and foes of Late Republican imperialism (Ritter 1995, 56).[9] Literary and numismatic sources frequently link Hercules to individuals such as Hannibal, Caesar, Antonius, and Octavian, and it is clear that the divine hero featured importantly in the personal lives of prominent political figures (Cassius Dio *Roman History* 37.52). An important aspect of this development is the manner in which these individuals became personally involved with local communities; like Hercules before them, Roman leaders founded new communities, and, not infrequently, inserted themselves into local lineages.[10] The benevolence of Hercules was publicly vied over then, and, in terms of ritual, could involve *evocatio* ceremonies that served to call away his protection over the enemy (Millett 1995, 99; Marzano 2009, 88).

The imperial domination over religious affairs during the Augustan age was the culmination of this Late Republican trend whereby public discourses and institutions became increasingly politicized by private individuals. Under Augustus (63 BC-19 AD), new narratives were produced through poetry and iconography in order to position the emperor as the divinely- sanctioned founder of a new age of peace and prosperity achieved through his Herculean efforts (Dobbin 1995).

---

8 The political importance of such events becomes clear when we consider the legislative restrictions placed on public banqueting by politicians who sought to monopolize the *epulum* (Marzano 2009, 85). Writers at the time understood their political significance (Plutarch *Aemilius Paulus* 28.5), as did Augustus, who restricted their occurrence to celebrations of the emperor and his family, thereby situating himself as the ultimate benefactor of Rome.

9 Hannibal portrayed himself as Hercules and was following in the divine hero's footsteps when crossing the Alps (Rawlings 2005). We also find him dedicating spoils of war in Gaditanus (Cadiz in southern Spain), at a prominent Hercules sanctuary (Livy *History of Rome* 21.21.9; Mierse 2004). The idea of Hercules returning from Spain and having prepared barbarian lands for conquest occurs in association with later figures such as Pompey, Caesar and Augustus. Claims to direct descent from Hercules were also made, by Antonius, for example, which affected how he presented himself to his followers and probably helped promote his long-held popularity among the legions (Plutarch *Antonius* 4.1; Spencer 2001, 262). Also interesting is that Caesar (like his conquering predecessor Alexander the Great) seems to have suffered from the 'sacred disease' (possibly epilepsy), also known as the 'madness of Hercules' (*heraklei nosos, morbus herculeus*). Such identifications may have led Caesar as a young boy to write a poem in honor of Hercules (*Laudes Herculis*, Praises of Hercules). The personal interests and involvement of these important individuals in shaping imperialist discourses and public imaginaries should not be underestimated.

10 New communities arose around military sites and wherever military veterans were settled, but, also more drastically, whenever conquered groups were uprooted and placed in new territories such as was common along the Germanic frontier. Plutarch suggested that it was Rome's destiny to spread noble blood through the world, a fate fulfilled by Antonius and Caesar in good Herculean fashion (Plutarch *Antonius* 36.4). Undoubtedly, this resulted in many politically motivated claims of descent within local communities (Tacitus *The Histories* 4.55).

Hercules came to occupy a central place in Rome's mythical history with the *forum Boarium* becoming the epicenter of Rome's mythical past (Barry 2011, 15).[11]

The militarization and masculinization of Roman society also produced sociopolitical constructs of gender distinction that emphasized male politico-military engagement and female exclusion from the public sphere (Spencer 2001, 261). While women generally seem to have been barred from attending military celebrations in the *forum Boarium*, they were not universally excluded from the Hercules cult (Holleman 1977; Schultz 2000). Not only do female characters feature strongly in Herculean myth, he seems to have played an important role in the lives of Roman women as well.[12] Interesting in terms of political narrative is the role of female oracles and muses. Literary sources refer to prophetesses based in sanctuaries dedicated to Hercules[13], while the Roman cult of the muses centered on the temple of Hercules *Musagetes* (*aedes Herculis Musarum*) in Rome. It was this temple Augustus chose to rededicate in an atmosphere of political reconciliation after the battle at Actium, where his triumph over Antonius and Cleopatra made him the sole ruler of Rome. In this way, Hercules, the deified hero most often associated with male virility, adventure and conquest, was simultaneously linked, in equally gendered terms, to themes of culture, concord, and arbitration (Hardie 2007).

Hercules on the Germanic frontier

The evidence for the syncretic Hercules *Magusanus* comes primarily from votive inscriptions found throughout the Rhineland and the materials excavated at three ritual sites in the Batavian territory. Excavations at Elst, Empel and Kessel (Figure 21) have provided information about the contexts, materials and practices associated with his cult. All three sites show evidence for pre-Roman activity, a fact that has been used to argue for the existence of a local deity that came to be identified with the Roman Hercules.[14] The sanctuaries at Empel and Elst can be

---

11 In the *forum Boarium*, no fewer than six sites were dedicated to the worship of Hercules (Spencer 2001, 265). This was the location where Hercules arrived with Geryon's cattle which the brute Cacus attempted to steal (Dionysius of Halicarnassus *Roman Antiquities* 1.39). Vergil attributes the foundation of the *ara maxima* to Hercules himself, and predates it to the arrival of Aeneas in Latium (Vergil *Aeneid* 7-8).

12 In Rome, Hercules was traditionally viewed as the guardian of wedded life and women tied their wedding dress (*tunica recta*) with the 'knot of Hercules', which symbolized protection, fertility and love.

13 A reference to rituals of divination is made by Pausanius in his description of Hercules *Buraicus* (*Description of Greece* 7.25.10). Caesar purportedly consulted a prophetess at the temple of Hercules *Gaditanus* in Spain (Seutonius *Caesar* 7), while Augustus conferred with the Tiburtine sibyl whose sanctuary in Tivoli is associated with a temple dedicated to Hercules *Saxanus*. There, an association (*collegium*) known as the *Herculanei Augustales* engaged in a cult of the divine emperor (Bourne 1916, 64).

14 This makes *Magusanus* the only occurrence of an indigenous Hercules north of the Alps (Roymans 2004, 242). Since Hercules syncretisms were common throughout the Italic peninsula, it is worth considering how Hercules *Magusanus* might be associated with the arrival of Italic groups in the Lower Rhineland. A similar process may be behind the presence of the great number of *matronae* dedications in the region (Derks 1991, 245; Garman 2008).

linked to Hercules directly[15], while all three sites have provided materials primarily associated with martiality, votive rituals, and commensal practices (Roymans and Derks 1994; Derks 1998; Roymans 2009).

Pre-Roman depositions at Elst, Empel and Kessel cannot be dated earlier than the first century BC. Because of this, the rise of these ritual sites can perhaps best be interpreted in light of Roman state expansion and subsequent Celto-Germanic tribalization and militarization (Ferguson and Whitehead 1992; Millett 1995, 99). One can think here of the increased participation of Rhineland communities in political and military conflicts across Gallia and Germania. In this context, new cultic practices were not simply the latest manifestations of pre-existing 'cultural mentalities' but resulted from the formation of new group identities and the widespread militarization of Celto-Germanic communities.[16] As noted above, the Hercules cult at Rome became increasingly linked to triumphal celebrations that involved the sacrifice of spoils of war. That such practices were not uniquely Roman is shown by war booty depositions found throughout northern Europe that resulted from similar commemorative rituals (Grane 2007). The pre-Roman depositions in the Lower Rhineland are perhaps best understood in such terms as well.[17]

Against a background of military conquest and territorial consolidation we can expect Roman authorities to have been acutely interested in the formation of symbolic landscapes. Roman political and ideological interests will have driven the colonization of existing sites of symbolic importance and the active construction of sacred landscapes on the edge of Empire. A crucial aspect of the *Magusanus* sanctuaries is their strategic distribution in a riverine frontier landscape. The sanctuary at Empel was located on the southern bank of the Meuse on one of the highest levees in the area, near the mouth of the Dieze River (Roymans and Derks 1994). The sanctuary at Kessel was located *c.* 10 km east of Empel near the confluence of the rivers Meuse and Waal, reportedly a site of strategic importance

---

15 At Empel, a votive inscription to *Magusanus* was found dated to the Trajanic period and left by a veteran of the *Legio X*. The remains of a statuette of Hercules (Hercules *Bibax*, 'the drinker') were also found there and it resembles one discovered at *castellum Flevum* (Velsen), a fort built north of the Rhine during Early Roman military offensives (Swinkels 1994, 85). At Elst, an altar dedicated to Hercules was found, as well as the remains of a Hercules statuette (Roymans 2004, 242; Derks *et al.* 2008, 138).

16 Coin distribution analysis has shown how the earliest coins in the Lower Rhineland arrived in the mid second century BC, increase significantly in number at the time of Caesar's wars, peak during the period of Augustan campaigns, and decline thereafter. Similar distributional fluctuations have been noted for the ritual depositions of weapons and military gear (Roymans and Aarts 2005). Such patterns reflect the ebb and flow of political interactions and violent conflict across the Celto-Germanic world and not merely the continuation of pre-Roman warrior ideologies.

17 The Late Iron Age materials found at Kessel and Empel (Roymans 2004) could certainly also have resulted from a single military event. Such a battle-ground thesis is made likely by literary references to Caesar's defeat of Germanic groups (Usipetes and Tencteri) in the vicinity (Caesar *Gallic War* 4.4-15). The presence of human bones and domestic materials can be explained by the reported fact that these groups consisted of men, women and children intent on settling new territory, while the wide range of Late La Tène weapon types encountered there may be explained by the fact that Celto-Germanic warriors were not uniformly equipped, carrying weapons of variable origin and age. Whether the evidence resulted from a single battle or recurring rituals associated with a martial cult, these would have been sites of symbolic significance.

for the Romans (Roymans 2004, 131). The Elst sanctuary was located between, and at a short distance from, the Batavian capital (Nijmegen) and the Rhine frontier. The nearest frontier post was *castra Herculis* (Meinerswijk), a legionary fort positioned to guard a connecting waterway between the Rhine and the northerly flowing IJssel.[18]

Monumentalization of the three sanctuaries was likely the result of Roman initiatives.[19] Roman interests for constructing a symbolic frontier resulted in the construction of one of the largest known Gallo-Roman temples at Elst, a monumental structure worthy of renovation before being permanently abandoned around 170 AD. Roman interests will likewise have ensured that the Empel sanctuary recovered from a destructive fire that occurred *c.* 200 AD, and for the site to have remained in use until the first half of the third century. It is not clear when the sanctuary at Kessel was abandoned, but fortifications from the second half of the fourth century (built in part from materials recovered from an earlier temple structure) testify to the continued importance of that location to Roman interests. Not surprisingly then, evidence suggests that these symbolic sites were contested spaces, with signs of destruction at Elst dated to the Batavian revolt of 69 AD, and literary and numismatic references pointing at important military events near Empel and Kessel.[20] Their association with Roman imperial power is likely the main reason why these sanctuaries were commonly targeted by Germanic groups whose incursions increased over the course of the late second and early third century.

At a time of recurring Roman expeditions into Germania the sanctuaries will have been used for regular calendar events faithfully observed by military communities, as well as for staging the occasional triumph. Such events involved processions of military men in parade armor carrying banqueting implements and the sacrificial spoils of war. Sacrificial ceremonies were followed by communal feasts that allowed soldiers to share in the achievements of their military leaders, and be reminded of the power and glory of Rome and her divinely-sanctioned

---

18   This fort was likely built during the offensive campaigns of Germanicus (14-16 AD), a popular Roman general and nephew to Emperor Tiberius. Its importance to Rome is also shown by the fact that the fort was rebuilt several times up until the fourth century (Ammianus Marcellinus *Rerum Gestarum* 18.2.4). This interest for sites of strategic importance is also shown by the location of *castellum Fectio* (Vechten) on a northerly branch of the Rhine that allowed access north to the river Oer-IJ where *castellum Flevum* (Velsen) was located.

19   Not only is there evidence for the involvement of the Roman military (Van Enckevort 2005; Van Enckevort and Thijssen 2005), but the late date of monumentalization also speaks against it having resulted from native initiative. This occurred long after martiality as an ideological focus of tribal warriors became mundane due to the regularization of military service, a trend suggested by the decline in coin and *militaria* depositions at the sanctuaries, and their increased presence in settlement contexts (Nicolay 2007). Furthermore, it remains to be adequately explained why the sanctuaries of female deities, which significantly outnumber those of male deities in the Rhineland, did not experience such monumentalization (Derks 1998, 122); if such efforts involved the initiatives of Romanized elites, why this neglect of the founding mothers of native communities?

20   Caesar defeated Germanic armies near Kessel where the rebel Julius Civilis would later battle his nephew Julius Briganticus during the Batavian uprising of 69 AD (Roymans 2004, 144). Of further interest are the coin emissions of the Gallic Emperor Postumus (259-268 AD) which reference Hercules *Magusanus/Deusonius* (Hercules of the Dieze River). Postumus may have been referencing important battles fought against invading Franks near Empel.

emperor (Marzano 2009, 91). We have seen how such events became associated with the Hercules cult in the *forum Boarium,* and this will likely have been the case for the sanctuaries in the Lower Rhineland as well.[21]

There is little doubt that Caesar's conquest of Gallia inspired the actions of those who came after, while Early Imperial military adventures into the unknown regions of the North shaped public narratives for generations. New communities and landscapes were formed during a period of repeated military operations beyond the Germanic frontier, and, in the public imagination, the deeds of great men paralleled Herculean labors.[22] Literary sources show how links were being made between Hercules and Rome's subduers of Germanic barbarity, and such associations can also be found articulated in the symbolic landscapes that were being formed throughout the Rhineland.[23] We can expect narratives of conquest and nation-building to have taken shape in the early Roman period, feeding the public imagination and political discourses for some time.

Religious cults and their sanctuaries will have been sites of intense politicization, symbolic battle grounds for the hearts and minds of colonizer and colonized alike. While the *Magusanus* cult may have served the legitimization of the Batavian ethnic identity (Roymans 2004, 249), the fact that it had come about due to Roman imposition will have been at once inescapable and contested. Narratives of

---

21 The ceramic assemblage includes high numbers of drinking wares, along with oil *amphorae* and *mortaria* (Klomp 1994). The range of metal objects includes coins, brooches, weapons, armor and horse gear (Roymans 2004). At Empel, the remains of a wagon stand out along with the metal fittings that may have embellished it (Roymans and Derks 1994); these include the military dress boot of a general or emperor possibly pointing at triumphal celebrations, and a small head of the Titan goddess Luna whose symbolic repertoire includes themes of rebirth and eternal youth. Her presence in the context of triumphal celebration may also have symbolized the conquest of Greco-Roman Gods over the Titans (*i.e.* civilization over barbarity), or her role as caretaker of the Nemean Lion killed by Hercules. Comparable Luna figures were found in Nijmegen near the camp of *Legio X* (Swinkels 1994, 89). The bronze statuette of Hercules *Bibax* ('the drinker') may also be understood as referencing triumphal banqueting or immortality (Swinkels 1994).

22 Caesar was the first Roman general to venture across the Rhine into Germanic territory, where his personal ambitions resulted in the brutal annihilation and displacement of local groups. Agrippa, serving Augustus as governor of Gaul (39-38 BC), conducted further operations across the Rhine and settled the Ubii on the west bank near Cologne. Agrippa also likely was the one who settled the Batavi, a splinter group of the trans-Rhenian Chatti, in the Dutch river area. After the defeat of Lollius by Germanic groups in 16 BC, Drusus (stepson to Augustus and brother to Tiberius) arrived in the Rhineland and to him we may ascribe the military reorganization of the Upper and Lower Rhineland. He ordered the construction of roads and canals, established army bases at Nijmegen, Xanten and Cologne, and campaigned across the Rhine between 12-9 BC. His brother, the future emperor Tiberius, settled the Cugerni on the west bank near Xanten and he campaigned extensively across the Rhine from 9 BC-12 AD. Next, Germanicus (son of Drusus) campaigned across the Rhine (14-16 AD), and it is certain that he made use of Batavian troops.

23 A good example of the motivation behind such monumental landscapes is the Tiberius column from the Batavian capital (Nijmegen) which has been linked to triumphal events staged in 17 AD in honor of Germanicus, and can perhaps best be understood as a symbolic celebration of the triumph of Roman civilization over barbarity (Panhuysen 2002). The Trophy of Augustus in the sanctuary of Heracles *Monoikos,* located along the Via Julia that connected Gaul with the Italic peninsula, communicates a comparable message (see www.monuments-nationaux.fr). It celebrates the subjugation of Alpine tribes by Augustus, through the achievements of Drusus and Tiberius. Cassius Dio mentions how Augustus frequently received the appellation of imperator thanks to the victories of Drusus and Tiberius (Cassius Dio *Roman History* 54.33).

contestation will have dominated discourses during times of violent conflict between Rome and trans-Rhenian communities. Reportedly, Hercules was one of the main divinities of interest among Germanic groups (Tacitus *Germania* 3.1), such that we can expect *ovatio* rites, for securing the protection of Hercules and calling him away from the Germanic side, to have taken place at the sanctuaries.[24] The struggles for his benevolence, between Romans and their Batavian allies, and between Romans and their Germanic foes, will have been an important part of the discourse that surrounded *Magusanus*.

We have no direct evidence for the existence of an emperor cult being associated with Hercules *Magusanus*. Epigraphic evidence from the German Rhineland shows how individuals active in the priesthoods of syncretic Mars cults were also active in the imperial cult (Derks 1991, 252), but such evidence has so far not been found for Hercules. However, that links between his cult and imperial rulers were made certainly seems possible when we consider the unique relationship between the Julio-Claudian dynasty and the native soldiers who loyally served their Roman patrons for generations (Speidel 1994; Roymans 2004). It would not have been forgotten that these communities owed their very existence, and continued good fortune, to their colonial masters. The *Magusanus* cult will have provided ways for individuals and communities to place this special relationship in sacred terms, and perform rites to ensure its survival.

Equally significant is the fact that, over the course of decades, many individuals had received honorable 'membership' in the Julio-Claudian house. It seems wholly possible, therefore, that these new members of Rome's ruling clans came to consider themselves heirs of empire.[25] Hercules comes into play here because he was perceived as the initial civilizer of the North. Of course, imperial discourses such as these served to legitimize Roman conquest of Gallic and Germanic barbarity, but the appropriation of Roman foundation myths also made it possible for local communities to make similar claims of inheritance. Such claims, expressed through cultic discourse, can be understood as the ultimate exploitation of imposed conditions by the colonized.[26]

---

24 A ritual likely performed on the Germanic side as well (Tacitus, *The Annals* 2-12).
25 Such attitudes are perhaps reflected in the bold claims of individuals such as Julius Sabinus of the Gallic Lingones tribe who instigated his own rebellion during the period of the Batavian revolt. He claimed high birth through blood-descent from Caesar himself – Sabinus' great-grandmother apparently could be added to the Roman general's list of conquests (Tacitus *The Histories* 4.55). British pre-conquest rulers actually presented themselves as Hercules (Roymans 2004, 244), and, in doing so, were probably communicating political claims in symbolic terms understood by an adversary bent on conquest.
26 This is furthermore suggested by the circumstances that surround the Batavian Revolt of 69 AD. The end of the Julio-Claudian dynasty followed the death of Emperor Nero (37-68 AD), an event in which the Batavian guard played a crucial role. The Germanic provinces feature importantly in the ensuing period of political strife. Of particular interest is the fact that the Rhineland troops who refused to support Emperor Galba (68-69 AD), declared their commander Vitellius (69 AD) 'emperor of the Germanic provinces' by handing him the sacred sword of Caesar (Suetonius *Vitellius* 8). Such initiatives not only reflect a desire to establish new bonds with the next emperor in terms of the old alliance with the Julio-Claudians, but also local feelings of responsibility and entitlement. Batavians, Ubians and other communities in the Rhineland must have considered themselves important players in the political struggles of the Empire. When Vespasianus (69-79 AD) came to power by successfully ending all opposition, no members of the imperial horse guard were recruited in the Rhineland for the next three decades.

But what happened when expansion into Germania came to a halt and Rome instead focused on territorial consolidation and the construction of a permanent frontier system along the Rhine? As Roman rulers opted for defensive policies, discourses in the Rhineland will have adjusted to fit new realities. The Early Roman narratives that centered on military success and the deeds of conquering generals were gradually adjusted to emphasize themes of immortality and prosperity such as we find them in a wide variety of representations from the second and third century AD (Speidel 1994; Derks 1998; Garman 2008). The multivalence of Hercules allowed for the continued relevance of his cult on the frontier, with 'Hercules the conqueror' of barbarity gradually becoming 'Hercules the protector' of a prosperous and eternal Roman Empire.

Despite changes in imperial policies, interest for Hercules did not waiver, and, as a result of the concerns of individual Roman rulers, could even flourish (Hekster 2005). Some examples may illustrate how this manifested itself in the Lower Rhineland. Few Roman legions are known to have claimed Hercules as patron deity, and it seems telling that two of those (*Legio XXII Primigenia* and *Legio XV Primigenia*) were founded for service along the Germanic frontier (Keppie 2000)[27]. Equally suggestive is the fact that another legion of Hercules (*Legio Traianus Fortis*) was founded by Emperor Trajan (98-117 AD) who, before ascending to the imperial throne, served as governor of Lower Germany (*Germania Inferior*) where he oversaw substantial construction efforts (Hessing 1999).[28] Once emperor, he reinstated the Batavian horse guard to serve as his personal bodyguard and elevated the administrative status of two tribal capitals in the province – *Colonia Ulpia Traiana* (Xanten) and *Ulpia Noviomagus Batavorum* (Nijmegen). Importantly, the monumentalization of the *Magusanus* sanctuaries can be dated to Trajan's reign. His successor Hadrian (117-138 AD), who like Trajan was of Spanish descent, had served as an officer in one of the legions of Hercules (*Legio XXII*) and seemed to have shown a keen interest in the half-god as well (Barry 2011, 23). Building activities in the Lower Rhineland have been dated to his reign, while the capital of the

---

27 Evidence in the form of brick stamps suggests that soldiers from the *Legio XXII* were stationed at *castellum Fectio* (Bogaers 1965, 106). The discovery of an altar stone near the fort points at cult practices centered on Hercules *Magusanus* in the vicinity (Van Es 1994, 53). Intensive archaeological investigation in the area has shown the existence of a densely occupied rural landscape where military veterans likely settled. Equally significant in this light are the indications for a nearby sanctuary dedicated to Haeva/Hebe, Hercules' consort (see comments below).

28 When considering the background and motivation of those involved in the cult of Hercules *Magusanus*, it is difficult to ignore the potential role of Hispanic communities. The Iberian peninsula features importantly in Herculean myth, and Hercules sanctuaries there are numerous. Trajan was from Hispania and is known to have minted coins depicting Hercules *Gaditanus/Invictus* between 100 and 115 AD (Barry 2011, 21). The construction of the famous Tower of Brigantium (*farum Brigantium*) on the Gaelician coast was built during his reign. It purportedly marked the spot where Hercules had vanquished Geryon. Furthermore, Dio Chrysostom's discourses on kingship were written with Trajan in mind, who he compared to Hercules (Dio Chrysostom *Orations* 1-4). In addition to the two Italic legions of Hercules, at least five legions (*Legio V Alaudae, Legio XXI Rapax, Legio XX Valeria Victrix, Legio I Germanica,* and *Legio IIII Macedonica*) known to have served in the Rhineland had also seen active duty in Hispania during the Cantabrian wars (29-19 BC). If soldiers belonging to these legions were unfamiliar with the land where Hercules once labored, service on the Spanish frontier will undoubtedly have ensured familiarity, if not genuine interest.

Cananefates was renamed *Municipium Aelium Cananefatium*, colloquially known as *Forum Hadriani* (Voorburg). Such were the ways Rhineland communities would have felt the impact of the personal interests and activities of important political figures, which undoubtedly affected cultic discourse.

Beyond the interests and actions of Roman imperial patrons, a variety of other agents contributed to these discourses as well. The epigraphic evidence shows how *Magusanus* is mentioned in at least twenty-one inscriptions, of which fifteen have been found in the Lower Rhineland (Derks 1991, 255). The earliest inscription comes from the Batavian territory, while the vast majority of dedications occur in the German Rhineland and date to the second and third century AD.[29] Dedications were predominantly made by military men and tend to concentrate near military camps, but they also include those made by priests, traders and parents.

Such variability in the identity and background of dedicators speaks to the inherent multivalence of Hercules, but also to the multicultural and socially dynamic character of the Rhineland. The Batavian district where the three sanctuaries were located for a long time housed a large community of soldiers and civilians where an interest for Hercules, guardian of the Germanic frontier, was maintained (Roymans 1995, 56; Vossen 2003, 415).[30] We should expect a Roman-sanctioned discourse centered on a syncretic half-god to have coexisted, then, with a range of public and private alternatives. Indeed, votive dedications found throughout the region were typically made by a wide variety of individuals and groups to an equally diverse range of Roman, local and syncretic deities.

As noted earlier, the Augustan era witnessed a proliferation of sociopolitical constructs of gender difference that encouraged increased exclusion of women from the public sphere. These undoubtedly shaped imperial discourses and colonial policies on the Germanic frontier as well, and epigraphic evidence may actually reflect how this was expressed through cultic discourse. The distribution of dedications shows how the vast majority of goddesses are local, while male gods are almost always Roman in origin (Derks 1998). Furthermore, all syncretic deities are male and of regional significance, while native female deities are typically of micro-regional importance. The latter are also exclusively concerned with aspects of health and reproduction. We see then that the epigraphic habit reflects a striking contrast between female and male spheres, a colonial discourse that may, or may not, have mirrored social realities, but certainly will have concerned the Hercules cult as well.

Nothing comparable to Hercules *Musagetes* seems to have existed on the Germanic frontier. That particular symbolic narrative may never have been appropriate for communicating cultural reconstruction and political reconciliation

---

29 The earliest inscription dates to the first half of the first century AD and concerns a dedication by a Batavian *civitas* official. The next datable inscription comes from the Trajanic period and was dedicated by a veteran from the *Legio* X (Roymans 2004, 248).

30 Latin, Celtic and Greek names have been found inscribed on ceramics, while epigraphic evidence points at the presence of Spanish veterans of the *Legio X Gemini* (Haalebos 2000, 467). Over time, a great number of military units and appended communities would occupy the Rhineland, with veterans and civilians permanently settling there as well (Alföldy 1968; Holder 1999).

on the frontier, such as happened in Rome under Augustus.³¹ There are, however, credible indications for the role of female oracles in the Rhineland, and these may have been associated with Hercules. Literary sources refer to women of divine status and with the power of foresight. They seemed to have held significant political authority and served as arbiters in local conflicts.³² However, as in Rome, we probably should not expect women to have participated in triumphal banquets and other such ceremonies staged by Roman authorities at the three sanctuaries as these will have been restricted to men and soldiers. That women did make offerings to the half-god is shown by an altar stone dedicated to Hercules *Magusanus* and Haeva by a husband and wife requesting divine protection over their children (Roymans 2009, 233). Haeva's association with Hercules, together with the content of the dedication, suggests that she is to be equated with Juventas, Roman goddess of youth. In Rome, invocations to Juventas were made in a temple of Hercules and involved appeals for the safety of military youths (*velites*).

It is furthermore possible that Haeva was a local transcription of Hebe, the Greek equivalent of Juventas. Her presence in the area is corroborated by the name of the Roman fort *Levefanum* (Rijswijk) situated near the confluence of the Rhine and Lek (Bechert and Willems 1995, 80). *Levefanum* may be a transcription of *Hebefanum*, thereby referring to a sanctuary of Hebe in the vicinity. If true, it may be another instance of symbolic manufacturing by the colonial power, and again involving Hercules, though in this instance by way of his female consort. Because *castellum Levefanum* was built (*c.* 50AD) after the period of Early Roman offenses in Germania, the choice of Hebe over Hercules himself may have been an early attempt by Roman authorities to emphasize themes of imperial longevity at a time when policies were shifting towards territorial consolidation and the formation of a permanent frontier. Mythological narratives surrounding Hebe, as cupbearer of the Olympian gods, primarily centre on themes of rejuvenation and immortality.

This isn't to say that dedicators to Hercules and Hebe stationed at *Levefanum*, such as the members of a Thracian mounted unit (*cohors I Thracum equitata*), would not construct their own narratives while freely and frequently referencing well-known myths. Indeed, those associated with a homeland will have been closely nurtured by troops stationed abroad, even becoming part of regimental discourse.³³

---

31 Though see Swinkels (2009) for depictions of Hercules and the muses on a terra sigillata cup from Nijmegen, dated to the early first century AD.

32 The Bructerian prophetess Veleda in particular had a crucial part to play in the Batavian Revolt (Tacitus *Germania* 8; *The Histories* 4.61, 4.65, 5.22). Upon her capture, her status seems to have proven a challenge to Roman authorities, and, rather than falling victim to violent retribution for her part in the uprisings, was placed into exile south of Rome where she spent her remaining days as a temple servant (AE 1953, 25).

33 For example, for members of Thracian mounted units stationed along the Germanic frontier (Derks 2009, 254) one can think of Hercules' eighth labor, wherein he defeats the king of Thrace (Diomedes) and tames his man-eating horses. There is also a curious episode that tells of Thracian women being the only females allowed in a shrine of Hercules (Pausanius Description of Greece 7.5.8). Furthermore, Ares/Mars, being born in Thrace and worshipped as this community's patron deity, was Hebe's brother. It was Hebe who healed her brother's wounds on the battle field. The symbolism surrounding her husband's apotheosis to Olympus, will also have had great appeal to a military community; immortality being the promised reward for their earthly labors.

Hercules and his consort possibly occupied a prominent place in the cultic life of Thracian units (*cohors IV Thracum*) stationed at the Valkenburg fort (*praetorium Agrippinae*) as well. There, the remains of a Hercules statue were found, which was likely erected during Trajan's reign when other Hercules sanctuaries on the Germanic frontier were monumentalized (De Hingh and Vos 2006, 151).

Having emphasized the changing face of a Roman-sanctioned discourse, along with some of the alternatives maintained by a large community of individuals with mixed identities and backgrounds, something can also be said about their demise. The abandonment of the sanctuaries occurred before the Batavian identity disappeared due to the Late Roman ethnic reconfiguration of the Lower Rhineland. The end of associated discourses was likely the result of the increased frequency of cross-border raiding by Germanic groups during the third century AD, culminating in the permanent settlement of the Franks. The association of Hercules with frontier defense is suggested by the numismatic evidence from the reign of Postumus who founded the short-lived Gallic Empire (260-274 AD) in direct response to Germanic invasions (Drinkwater 1987). Postumus, reportedly of humble Batavian descent, is known to have issued coins depicting Hercules *Magusanus/Deusonius*. This symbolic reference to the sacred guardian of the Lower Rhineland frontier is easily understood in this third century context. However, due to the frequent collapse of frontier defenses, it became impossible for Hercules to retain this status. The permanent inability of Rome to go on the offensive, in turn, precluded a revisiting of Herculean themes of victorious conquest.

The fall of the Roman Empire led to the formation of the Frankish kingdoms south of the old frontier, with the Early Medieval period marked by the internal struggles of the Merovingian dynasty and conflicts with the Frisians for control of the Lower Rhineland. The rise of Christianity within Frankish society, and the political purposes to which it was put, ensured the permanent removal of Hercules from the dominant discourse. Ritual failure in this context, then, may be understood as involving the abandonment of particular narratives and rituals by dominant political powers. However, here as well, the reality of cultic heterogeneity can be shown by the way Hercules remained relevant in the lives of people in the region. Evidence for this comes from the Frisian territory with dates covering the Late Roman and Early Medieval periods (Therkorn 2004; Therkorn *et al.* 2009).[34] It suggests the survival of a cultic discourse confronted by Christian missionaries and eventually prohibited (or creatively negotiated) by church authorities as pagan folk practice and superstition. With the completion of Frisian conversion unrealised until the twelfth or even thirteenth century, the possibility that Werenfried's church at Elst represents a Christian colonization of an ancient site of lingering symbolic potency may not be altogether farfetched.

---

34 Research by Therkorn (2004, 88) suggests that star constellations (symbolizing Hercules and other deities) were marked out in settlement space. Further evidence comes in the form of Hercules amulets that were predominantly worn by women and children (Therkorn 2009, 107). Thematically, Hercules remained associated with fortune, fertility, and protection.

Conclusion

While archaeologists are ideally placed to study the material traces of ritual behaviour, it has been the character and availability of archaeological evidence that has shaped the methodological preferences of archaeologists in distinct ways. Since the 1980s, post-processual approaches have increasingly focused on such things as symbolic content, social function, and subjective experience (Insoll 2004; Barrowclough and Malone 2007; Fogelin 2007). What these approaches have in common is the way they tend to distinguish analytically between content (myths and symbols), form (practices, objects, and structures), and context (spatio-temporal and social). Those studying symbolic systems tend to focus on the examination of literary, representational and comparative sources, while those interested in practice-oriented, functionalist and phenomenological approaches restrict their gaze to the material traces of ritual behaviours and spaces. Furthermore, ritual practices also often demonstrate stronger historical endurance than the more transient symbolic narratives they are associated with. We can see this, for example, in the wide distribution of like ritual forms across cultural boundaries in prehistoric Europe, as much as in the ways indigenous rituals continued when new symbolic narratives arrived under Roman colonial rule. Because of this, separating ritual practices from symbolic systems, as archaeologists are prone to do, clearly has analytical merit.

For the purposes of this discussion on cultic heterogeneity, I have approached ritual practices and symbolic narratives (*i.e.* cultic discourse) as historically situated and socially reproduced constructs that are embedded in broader cultural moralities and worldviews. In recognizing the complexity of past entanglements, and the heterogeneity of cultic discourse, my aim was to produce a thick description of those surrounding a single cult. This I have attempted to do by considering the narratives, rituals and contexts engaged by various groups and individuals, along with their motives and perspectives, and by using multiple lines of evidence – literary, representational, archaeological and historical.

Research on Hercules *Magusanus* has so far largely focused on the symbolic construction of community, whereby the formative period of the Batavian identity, and the role of *Magusanus* for the self-definition of this community vis-à-vis Rome, has dominated discussions. A structuralist focus on environment and modes-of-existence have also made native ideological endurance a central aspect, while Marxist views on the instrumental manipulation of ideology has placed elites at the center of interpretive arguments. Though offering a compelling framework for thinking about local cultic experience, this combination of post-colonial and Marxist-structuralist perspectives risks reducing past complexities, because it neglects colonial and subordinate interests. Before we can evaluate the meaning of a sacred inscription on a ceramic cup, bronze ring or altar stone, or can begin to understand the social significance of rituals in a variety of spatio-temporal contexts, it serves to consider a broad range of situated narratives, practices, and actors. The heterogeneous nature of cultic discourse, such as described here for a syncretic deity under colonial conditions, is worth exploring in other contexts as well, when evidence allows for this.

Acknowledgments

I would like to thank Vasiliki Koutrafouri and Jeff Sanders for organizing a stimulating TAG session on the archaeology of ritual failure, and for laboring to see the publication of this volume realized. Participation was made possible by financial assistance in the form of a Doolittle-Harrison Fellowship and Lichtstern Travel Grant (University of Chicago). I am also grateful for the advice and insights offered by friends and colleagues at the University of Amsterdam and the University of Chicago. Though these have certainly helped shape my arguments, any factual errors or logical fallacies remain my own.

References

Primary Sources

AE, *L'Année Épigraphique*.

Ammianus Marcellinus. 1986. *The Later Roman Empire (A.D. 354-378)*. Harmondsworth: Penguin Books.

Caesar. 1996. *Seven Commentaries on the Gallic War*. Oxford: Oxford University Press.

Cassius Dio Cocceianus. 1987. *The Roman History: The Reign of Augustus*. Harmondsworth: Penguin Books.

Dio Chrysostom. 1932. *Dio Chrysostom*. London: W. Heinemann, ltd.

Dionysius. 1937. *The Roman Antiquities of Dionysius of Halicarnassus*. Cambridge: Harvard University Press.

Livy. 1912. *The History of Rome*. London: J.M. Dent.

Pausanias. 1965. *Description of Greece*. New York: Biblo and Tannen.

Plutarch. 1992. *Plutarch: The Lives of the Noble Grecians and Romans.* New York: Modern Library.

Suetonius. 1980. *The Twelve Caesars*. New York: Penguin Books.

Tacitus. 1999. *Germania*. Oxford: Clarendon Press.

Tacitus. 2004. *The Annals*. Indianapolis: Hackett Pub.

Tacitus. 1997. *The Histories*. Oxford: Oxford University Press.

Velleius Paterculus. 2011. *The Roman history: from Romulus and the foundation of Rome to the reign of the Emperor Tiberius*. Indianapolis: Hackett Pub. Co.

Virgil. 1986. *The Aeneid*. Manchester: Carcanet New Press and Mid Northumberland Arts Group.

Secondary Sources

Alföldy, G. 1968. Die Hilfstruppen der romischen Provinz Germania inferior. *Epigraphische Studien*, VI.

Apter, A. 2004. Herskovits's Heritage, Rethinking Syncretism in the African Diaspora, in: Leopold A. M. *et al.* (eds.). *Syncretism in Religion, a reader.* New York: Routledge, 160-184.

Barrowclough, D.A. and Malone, C. 2007 (eds.). *Cult in Context, Reconsidering Ritual in Archaeology*. Oxford: Oxbow Books.

Barry, F. 2011. The Mouth of Truth and the Forum Boarium, Oceanus, Hercules, and Hadrian. *The Art Bulletin* XCIII 1, 7-37.

Beard, M. 2007. *The Roman Triumph*. Cambridge: Belknap Press of Harvard University Press.

Bechert, T. and Willems, W.J.H. 1995 (eds.). *De Romeinse rijksgrens tussen Moezel en Noordzeekust.* Utrecht: Matrijs.

Blagg, T.F.C. and Millett, M. (eds). 1990. *The Early Roman Empire in the West.* Oxford: Oxbow Books.

Bogaers, J.E. 1955. *De Gallo-Romeinse tempels te Elst in de Over-Betuwe.* Den Haag: Staatsdrukkerij- en Uitgeverijbedrijf.

Bogaers, J.E. 1965. Romeins Nijmegen, Exercitus Germanicus Inferior. *Numaga* XII/3, 98-106.

Bourdieu, P. 1977. *Outline of a Theory of Practice.* Cambridge: Cambridge University Press.

Bourne, E. 1916. *A Study of Tibur – Historical, Literary and Epigraphical – from the Earliest Times to the Close of the Roman Empire.* Menasha: George Banta publishing company.

Bowden, H. and Rawlings, L. 2005 (eds.). *Herakles and Hercules: Exploring a Graeco-Roman Divinity.* Swansea: The Classical Press of Wales.

Brandt, R. and Slofstra, J. 1983 (eds.). *Roman and Native in the Low Countries: Spheres of Interaction.* BAR International Series 184. Oxford: British Archaeological Reports.

Comaroff, J. and Comaroff, J.L. 1991. *Of Revelation and Revolution.* Chicago: University of Chicago Press.

De Hingh, A. and Vos, W. 2006. *Romeinen in Valkenburg (ZH): de opgravingsgeschiedenis en het archeologisch onderzoek van Praetorium Agrippinae.* Hazenberg Archeologie Leiden.

Derks, T. 1991. The perception of the Roman pantheon by a native elite, the example of votive inscriptions from Lower Germany, in: Roymans, N. *et al.* (eds.). *Images of the Past, Studies on Ancient Societies in Northwestern Europe.* Studies in pre- en protohistorie. Amsterdam: Instituut voor Pre- en Protohistorische Archeologie Albert Egges van Giffen, 235-265.

Derks, T. 1998. *Gods, Temples, and Ritual Practices: The Transformation of Religious Ideas and Values in Roman Gaul*. Amsterdam: Amsterdam University Press.

Derks, T. 1999. Between daily existence and divine order. The landscapes of Roman Gaul, in: Fabech, C. et al. (eds.). *Settlement and Landscape, Proceedings of a Conference in Århus, Denmark, May 4-7 1998*. Jutland Archaeological Society publications. Moesgård: Jutland Archaeological Society, 343-352.

Derks, T. 2002. De tempels van Elst (Gld). Nieuw archeologisch onderzoek rond de N.H. kerk. *Archeologisch Instituut Vrije Universiteit Brochure* 9.

Derks, T., van Kerckhove, J. and Hoff, P. 2008 (eds.). Nieuw archeologisch onderzoek rond de Grote Kerk van Elst, gemeente Overbetuwe (2002-2003). *Zuidnederlandse Archeologische Rapporten* 31.

Derks, T. 2009. Ethnic identity in the Roman frontier. The epigraphy of Batavi and other Lower Rhine tribes, in: Derks, T. et al. (eds.). *Ethnic Constructs in Antiquity, The Role of Power and Tradition*. Amsterdam: Amsterdam University Press, 239-282.

Dietler, M. 2010. *Archaeologies of Colonialism, Consumption, Entanglement, and Violence in Ancient Mediterranean France*. Berkeley: University of California Press.

Dobbin, R.F. 1995. Julius Caesar in Jupiter's Prophecy, "Aenied", Book 1. *Classical Antiquity* 141, 5-40.

Dommelen, P. van 2002. Ambiguous Matters: Colonialism and Local Identities in Punic Sardinia, in: Lyons C. L. et al. (eds.). *The Archaeology of Colonialism*. Issues and Debates. Los Angeles: Getty Research Institute, 121-150.

Driel-Murray, C. van 2003. Ethnic Soldiers: The Experience of the Lower Rhine Tribes, in: Grünewald T. and Seibel S. (eds.). *Kontinuität Und Diskontinuität, Germania Inferior Am Beginn Und Am Ende Der Römischen Herrschaft*. Ergänzungsbände zum Reallexikon der Germanischen Altertumskunde 35. Berlin: De Gruyter, 200-217.

Driessen, M. 2005. Monumentality for Roman Nijmegen, in: Visy Z. (ed.). *Limes XIX, Proceedings of the XIXth International Congress of Roman Frontier Studies Held in Pécs, Hungary, September 2003*. Pécs: University of Pécs, 315-322.

Drinkwater, J.F. 1987. *The Gallic Empire: Separatism and Continuity in the North-Western Provinces of the Roman Empire, A.D. 260-274*. Stuttgart: Franz Steiner Verlag Wiesbaden.

Enckevort, H. van and Thijssen, J. 2005. *In de schaduw van het Noorderlicht. De Gallo-Romeinse tempel van Elst-Westeraam*. Nijmegen: Uniepers/Bureau Archeologie Gemeente Nijmegen.

Enckevort, H. van 2005. The Significance of the Building Activities of Trajan and the Legio X Gemina for the Integration of the Batavians into the Roman Empire, in: Visy Z. (ed.). *Limes XIX, Proceedings of the XIXth International Congress of Roman Frontier Studies Held in Pécs, Hungary, September 2003*. Pécs: University of Pécs, 85-94.

Es, W.A. van 1994. De Romeinse Vrede, in: Es, W.A. van and Hessing, W.A.M. (eds.). *Romeinen, Friezen en Franken in het Hart van Nederland. Van Traiectum tot Dorestad 50 v. C.–900 n. C.* Amersfoort: Rijksdienst voor het Oudheidkundig Bodemonderzoek, 48-63.

Ferguson, R.B. and Whitehead, N.L. (eds). 1992. *War in the Tribal Zone, Expanding States and Indigenous Warfare*. Sante Fe: School of American Research Press.

Fogelin, L. 2007. The Archaeology of Religious Ritual. *Annual Review of Anthropology* 361, 55-71.

Galinsky, G.K. 1972. *The Herakles Theme: The Adaptations of the Hero in Literature from Homer to the Twentieth Century*. Oxford: B. Blackwell.

Garman, A.G. 2008. *The Cult of the Matronae in the Roman Rhineland: An Historical Evaluation of the Archaeological Evidence*. Lewiston: Edwin Mellen Press.

Giddens, A. 1984. *The Constitution of Society, Outline of the Theory of Structuration*. Berkeley: University of California Press.

Grane, T. 2007. The Roman Empire and Southern Scandinavia – a Northern Connection. Ph.D. Dissertation, University of Copenhagen.

Haalebos, J.K. 2000. Die wirtschaftliche Bedeutung des Nijmegener Legionslager und seiner canabae, in: Grünewald, T. *et al.* (eds.). *Germania Inferior, Besiedlung, Gesellschaft Und Wirtschaft an Der Grenze Der Römisch-Germanischen Welt*. Ergänzungsbände zum Reallexikon der germanischen Altertumskunde 28. Berlin: De Gruyter, 464-479.

Hardie, A. 2007. Juno, Hercules, and the Muses at Rome. *American Journal of Philology* 128/4, 551-592.

Heidinga, H.A. 1999. The Wijnaldum excavation: Searching for a central place in Dark Age Frisia, in: Besteman J. C. (ed.). *The excavations at Wijnaldum: reports on Frisia in Roman and Medieval times*. Rotterdam/Brookfield: A.A. Balkema.

Hekster, O. 2005. Propagating Power. Hercules as an Example for Second-Century Emperors, in: Bowden H. *et al.* (eds.). *Herakles and Hercules: Exploring a Graeco-Roman Divinity*. Swansea: The Classical Press of Wales, 205-221.

Herskovits, F.S. 1966 (ed.). *The New World Negro: Selected Papers in Afroamerican Studies*. Bloomington: Indiana University Press.

Hessing, W.A.M. 1999. Building programmes for the Lower Rhine Limes. The impact of the visits of Trajan and Hadrian to the Lower Rhine, in: Sarfatij, H., Verwers, W.J.H. and Woltering, P.J. (eds.). *In discussion with the past. Archaeological studies presented to W.A. van Es, Amersfoort*, 149-56.

Holder, P.A. 1999. Exercitus Pius Fidelis, The Army of Germania Inferior in AD 89. *Zeitschrift fur Papyrologie und Epigraphik* 128, 237-250.

Holleman, A.W.J. 1977. Propertius IV 9, an Augustan View of Roman Religion. *Revue Belge De Philologie Et D'histoire. Recueil Trimestrial* 551, 79-92.

Insoll, T. 2004. *Archaeology, Ritual, Religion*. London: Routledge.

Johnson, M.H. 2006. On the Nature of Theoretical Archaeology and Archaeological Theory. *Archaeological Dialogues*, 13/02, 117-132.

Jones, S. 1997. *The Archaeology of Ethnicity: Constructing Identities in the Past and Present*. London: Routledge.

Keppie, L.J.F. 2000. *Legions and Veterans: Roman Army Papers 1971-2000*. Stuttgart: Franz Steiner Verlag.

Klomp, A. 1994. Feestgelagen en het gebruik van aardewerk, in: Roymans N. *et al.* (eds.). *De tempel van Empel, een Hercules-heiligdom in het woongebied van de Bataven.* 's-Hertogenbosch: Stichting Brabantse Regionale Geschiedbeoefening, 152-161.

Kondoleon, C. and Bergmann, B.A. (eds). 1999. *The Art of Ancient Spectacle.* Washington: National Gallery of Art.

Marzano, A. 2009. Hercules and the Triumphal Feast for the Roman People, in: Bernárdez B. A. *et al.* (eds.). *Transforming Historical Landscapes in the Ancient Empires, Proceedings of the First Workshop, December 16-19th 2007.* BAR International Series 1986. Oxford: John and Erica Hedges Ltd, 83-97.

Mata, K. 2012. Anthropological Perspectives on Colonialism, Globalization and Rural Lifeways: Expanding the Limits of Archaeological Interpretation in the Lower Rhineland, in: Duggan, M., F. McIntosh and D.J. Rohl (eds.). *TRAC 2011: Proceedings of the Twenty First Annual Theoretical Roman Archaeology Conference in Newcastle (UK) 14-17 April 2011.* Oxford: Oxbow Books, 33-47.

Mattingly, D.J. 1997 (ed.). *Dialogues in Roman Imperialism: Power, Discourse, and Discrepant Experience in the Roman Empire.* Portsmouth, R.I: JRA.

Mierse, E. 2004. The Architecture of the Lost Temple of Hercules Gaditanus and Its Levantine Associations. *American Journal of Archaeology* 108/4, 545-575.

Millett, M. 1990. *The Romanization of Britain: An Essay in Archaeological Interpretation.* New York: Cambridge University Press.

Millett, M. 1995. Re-Thinking Religion in Romanization, in: Metzler J. *et al.* (eds.). *Integration in the Early Roman West: The Role of Culture and Ideology.* Dossiers d'archéologie du Musée national d'histoire et d'art. Luxembourg: Musée national d'histoire et d'art, 93-100.

Mitchell, J.P. 2007. Towards an Archaeology of Performance, in: Barrowclough D. A. *et al.* (eds.). *Cult in Context, Reconsidering Ritual in Archaeology.* Oxford: Oxbow Books, 336-340.

Nicolay, J. 2007. *Armed Batavians: use and significance of weaponry and horse gear from non-military contexts in the Rhine Delta (50 BC to AD 450).* Amsterdam: Amsterdam University Press.

Panhuysen, T. 2002. *De Romeinse Godenpijler van Nijmegen.* Nijmegen: Vereniging van vrienden van het Museum Kam.

Rawlings, L. 2005. Hannibal and Hercules, in: Bowden H. *et al.* (eds.). *Herakles and Hercules, Exploring a Graeco-Roman Divinity.* Swansea: The Classical Press of Wales, 205-221.

Ritter, S. 1995. *Hercules in Der Römischen Kunst Von Den Anfängen Bis Augustus.* Heidelberg: Verlag Archäologie und Geschichte.

Roymans, N. 1995. Romanization, cultural identity and the ethnic discussion. The Integration of the lower Rhine populations in the Roman Empire, in: Metzler J. *et al.* (eds.). *Integration in the Early Roman West, The Role of Culture and Ideology.* Dossiers d'archéologie du Musée national d'histoire et d'art. Luxembourg: Musée national d'histoire et d'art, 47-64.

Roymans, N. 1996. The sword or the plough. Regional dynamics in the romanisation of Belgic Gaul and the Rhineland area, in: Roymans N. (ed.). *From the Sword to the Plough, Three Studies on the Earliest Romanisation of Northern Gaul.* Amsterdam: Amsterdam University Press, 9-126.

Roymans, N. 2004. *Ethnic Identity and Imperial Power: The Batavians in the Early Roman Empire.* Amsterdam: Amsterdam University Press.

Roymans, N. 2009. Hercules and the Construction of a Batavian Identity in the Context of the Roman Empire, in: Derks *et al.* (eds.). *Ethnic Constructs in Antiquity: The Role of Power and Tradition.* Amsterdam: Amsterdam University Press.

Roymans, N. and Aarts, J. 2005. Coins, soldiers and the Batavian Hercules cult. Coin deposition in the sanctuary of Empel in the Lower Rhine region, in: Haselgrove C. *et al.* (eds.). *Iron Age Coinage and Ritual Practices.* Studien zu Fundmünzen der Antike. Mainz am Rhein: Von Zabern, 337-359.

Roymans, N. and Derks, T. 1994. Het heiligdom te Empel. Algemene beschouwingen, in: Roymans N. *et al.* (eds.). *De tempel van Empel, een Hercules-heiligdom in het woongebied van de Bataven.* 's-Hertogenbosch: Stichting Brabantse Regionale Geschiedbeoefening, 10-38.

Schultz, C.E. 2000. Modern Prejudice and Ancient Praxis, Female Worship of Hercules at Rome. *Zeitschrift fur Papyrologie und Epigraphik* 133, 291-297.

Shennan, S. 1989 (ed.). *Archaeological Approaches to Cultural Identity.* London: Unwin Hyman.

Speidel, M. 1994. *Riding for Caesar: The Roman Emperors' Horse Guards.* Cambridge: Harvard University Press.

Spencer, D. 2001. Propertius, Hercules, and the Dynamics of Roman Mythic Space in Elegy 4.9. *Arethusa* 34/3, 259-284.

Stein, G. 2005 (ed.). *The Archaeology of Colonial Encounters, Comparative Perspectives.* Santa Fe: School of American Research Press.

Streets, H. 2004. *Martial Races: The Military, Race and Masculinity in British Imperial Culture, 1857-1914.* Manchester: Manchester University Press.

Swinkels, L. 1994. Een vergoddelijkte Hercules en enkele andere bronsfiguren, in: Roymans N. *et al.* (eds.). *De tempel van Empel, een Hercules-heiligdom in het woongebied van de Bataven.* 's-Hertogenbosch: Stichting Brabantse Regionale Geschiedbeoefening, 82-90.

Swinkels, L. 2009. Hercules and the Muses on a terra sigillata cup from Nijmegen, in: Enckevort, H. van (ed.). *Roman Material Culture. Studies in honour of Jan Thijssen.* Nijmegen: Museum Het Valkhof Nijmegen, 103-114.

Talbot, C.H. 1954. *The Anglo-Saxon Missionaries in Germany, Being the Lives of SS. Willibrord, Boniface, Sturm, Leoba, and Lebuin, Together with the Hodoeporicon of St. Willibald and a Selection from the Correspondence of St. Boniface.* London: Sheed and Ward.

Therkorn, L.L. 2004. *Landscaping the powers of darkness and light. 600 BC - 350 AD settlement concerns of Noord-Holland.* Doctoral Dissertation, University of Amsterdam.

Therkorn, L.L. *et al.* 2009. *Landscapes in the Broekpolder: excavations around a monument with aspects of the Bronze Age to the Modern.* Beverwijk and Heemskerk: Amsterdams Archeologisch Centrum.

Trouillot, M.-R. 1995. *Silencing the Past: Power and the Production of History.* Boston: Beacon Press.

Vossen, I. 2003. The possibilities and limitations of demographic calculations in the Batavian area, in: Grünewald T. and Seibel S. (eds.). *Kontinuität Und Diskontinuität, Germania Inferior Am Beginn Und Am Ende Der Römischen Herrschaft.* Ergänzungsbände zum Reallexikon der Germanischen Altertumskunde 35. Berlin: De Gruyter, 414-435.

Webster, J. 1997. Necessary comparisons, a post-colonial approach to religious syncretism in the Roman provinces. *Culture Contact and Colonialism* 28/3, 324-338.

Chapter 8

The dead acrobat

Managing risk and Minoan iconography

Evangelos Kyriakidis[1]

Abstract

Uncertainty in ritual is a topic that sounds like a contradiction in terms, as ritual is closely associated with invariance and repetition (Bell 1997, 138-169). This invariance is one characteristic which distinguishes ritual from sport (Kyriakidis 2005, 39 and *forthcoming*). Yet, as we shall see below, uncertainty does exist in rituals in all kinds of forms and guises. Moreover, in cases of institutionalised rituals, this uncertainty is managed. Sport, like any other games, is a very similar type of action to ritual, but one that is also distinguished from it through the type, frequency and management of risk.

Keywords: *Minoan Crete, ritual risk, institutionalised ritual, ritual learning.*

Ritual is a category of action that has had many definitions and almost every researcher terms it in a different way. Although some have praised the lack of a definition (*e.g.* Bell 2008, 277-288), this is a major handicap for the study of ritual as it is difficult to compare ideas without a firm grasp of what two scholars mean when they make reference to the term. The slippery definition is a result of both the intangibility of ritual as well as the large number of people who have an opinion on the matter: everyone knows a lot about rituals. Seeking common denominators, or the crowd-sourcing of definitions (Brabham 2008, 75-90) cannot lead to a satisfactory solution until we have a number of scholars who actually state what they mean by the term and have written on the topic. For the purposes of this paper I will use my own definition of the term which I have been using for the past 5 years. According to this definition (Kyriakidis 2008, 289-294):

> *Ritual is an etic* (Lett 1990, 127-129) *category that refers to set activities with a special (not-normal) intention-in-action, and which are specific to a group of people.*

---

1   University of Kent.

The fact that ritual is a set category is, I believe, a factor that can distinguish ritual from sport. Like ritual, sport and games are set in that they are rule-governed and repeated activities with an undetermined ending, *i.e.* nobody knows who will win (this is why game fixing is a crime). Ritual, on the other hand, is set also in that it has a pre-determined outcome.

The fact that ritual is a set category that has a predetermined course of action may make it seem to be free of risk. There are several reasons why this is not the case:

Firstly, we have already mentioned that ritual is an etic category, *i.e.* an observer's category, not primarily an initiate's/insider's category. It is mainly for the observer that ritual is a set category. For initiates, and especially lower-level or new initiates, rituals can often give a false sensation of uncertainty as to what happens next. Only those who can see outside the box, often in the higher echelons of initiation, may be aware of ritual invariance.

Secondly, the successful performance of the ritual is not itself predetermined, and all performance-based activities, both sport and ritual are risk prone (Shieffelin 1996, 60). It can not be known in advance whether a liturgy will be completed, or whether a bull will be sacrificed. We are not sure whether the Orthodox Patriarch in Jerusalem will come out of the inner chamber of the Church of the Holy Sepulchre, apparently the tomb of Christ, with the 'Holy Fire' one day before Easter as he has been doing every year for the last millennium (Peters 1985, 262). Ritual failure refers mainly to this type of uncertainty.

It is important here to explain what we mean by ritual failure. A specific ritual, *e.g.* a Sunday church liturgy can be seen as a category in its own right. Categories have specific traits that are necessary for an item's classification as such, which are called definitive criteria: Sunday church liturgies have to occur both on a Sunday and in church; otherwise, if planned under that rubric and do not satisfy these two conditions, they cannot be classified as such and will fail. A human sacrifice, to use an extreme, has two main ingredients, the involvement of a human, and death; if a rabbit is slaughtered instead or if a human is involved but does not die, the ritual fails as such.

There are also traits in a given category that are not crucial for membership in that category: the priest does not have to read all the hymns correctly to the letter in order for the Sunday church service to be classified as such. Failing in one of the non-crucial traits of ritual does not constitute ritual failure, but rather a deviation. We must make clear however, that ritual failure does not refer to ritual dissolution (*e.g.* see Chao 1999, 505-534 and esp. 534), the death of a ritual, though it may indeed contribute to such dissolution.

Moreover, ritual is often associated with risk, although ritual itself may not be uncertain. We are uncertain whether a sacrifice will be accepted by the gods, even if the performance of the sacrifice itself has been completed successfully. We are not sure whether the performance of a divination ritual will have the desired result. It is impossible to know in advance wether a magic spell will have the intended effect. In this respect risk is not part of the ritual but associated to it, it is an aftermath of ritual. It is this association with risk that is the most common in rituals.

If we bundle various actions into packages, large or small, we will soon discover that there are ritual packages which include mundane actions, and, conversely, mundane packages that include ritual actions. Very often rituals are embedded in packages that are not themselves ritual. For example the package 'mundane dining' may include a prayer ritual, the package 'university study' may include matriculation, graduation and other rituals. Also, non-rituals are sometimes embedded in ritual packages: liturgy in a church may be interrupted by a passing of the basket activity for contributions by the community; or a funeral may include coffee drinking, chatting, quarrelling with the cemetery authorities for all sorts of reasons, or even sports – as the ones Achilles organised for the funeral of his friend Patroclus in *Iliad 23*. Risk therefore may exist in a mundane activity that is thus associated with ritual. This type of risk is extrinsic to ritual.

Howe (2000, 69) identifies extrinsic and intrinsic types of risk, the former being "risks which accompany the enactment of a ceremony but are not built into the structure of the rite" and the latter being "integral to the rite itself, part of its very essence."[2] Although I do not follow Howe's definitions, since there is no disjunction between the enactment of the rite and its performance, I do agree that there is a valid distinction between intrinsic risk, risk that is built into the rite itself (will the performance of the rite be successful, will the ritual be a ritual or not?), and extrinsic risk, *i.e.* risk that is associated with the rite but is not part of it (will the gods appreciate the sacrifice or not?).

There is often an effort to manage risk in rituals (*e.g.* Schieffelin 2007, 1-20), particularly those that are institutionalised (*i.e.* when there is a group of people/institution responsible for their performance –see Kyriakidis 2005, 74-79). Attention is given primarily to managing the intrinsic risks, but also to a lesser extent the extrinsic ones, so that on the one hand their effects are 'guaranteed', and on the other performers do not suffer. Early Chinese oracle bone divination rituals (see Flad 2008, 403-419) for example, showed a development that helped manage that risk. Drill holes in the bones that were used for these rituals ensured controlled cracking that would help the performers produce desirable results, thus both protecting the performers and ensuring that the 'clients' were sufficiently enthralled and satisfied by the rites.

It is important here to remind ourselves that ritual is not irrational, unreasonable, illogical or non-contiguous to its performers. To them, ritual is very similar to technology (see Marcus 2006, 221-254; Nikolaidou 2008, 183-208; Kyriakidis 2008, 291), *i.e.* a set way to do things, be that invoking rain, communicating with the gods, or curing disease. Ritual as a technology is a collection of learning mechanisms through every one of its characteristics, as I have argued elsewhere (Kyriakidis 2005, 69-72). In fact risk, or uncertainty, probably constitutes one of the most important traits for ritual in terms of its function as a learning mechanism, although this is a trait which I have not previously discussed.

---

2 For more on the various types of ritual risk see Grimes 1996, 279-293. Grimes employs Austin's speech theory (1962, 12-24) to refine the classification of ritual failure, or rather ritual infelicities.

Risk or rather uncertainty is recognised as one of the strongest learning facilitating mechanisms. The concept of blocking (Kamin 1969, 242-259) in psychology was crucial for identifying the value of uncertainty in conditioning (learning). Blocking is the process by which the association of a reinforcer with a second stimulus is blocked (or hindered) once there already has been an association between that reinforcer with another stimulus. For example, the association between a bell (stimulus) and food (reinforcer) arriving is hindered if there has already been an association between a light (a second stimulus) and food arriving (reinforcer).

Pearce and Hall 1980, 532-552) have extensively argued that the effects of 'blocking' do indeed take place but due to a different mechanism from the one just mentioned. They have argued that the first time the light-stimulus appears there is heightened attention (and therefore faster learning) by the beholder due to the uncertainty of what this stimulus is to be associated with. Once a stimulus has been associated with a reinforcer (food), then attention is reduced and further associations are hindered. According to Pearce and Hall, therefore, uncertainty about what comes next is a mechanism that heightens attention and facilitates learning. Their argument is too complicated to present here fully, but it suffices to say that 'the more uncertain an animal is about a stimulus, the faster it learns about that stimulus' (Dayan and Yu 2003, 176-177).

Risk in other words, is a strong learning mechanism. This characteristic could arguably make rituals not risk averse, as one may imagine, but risk prone. It is this 'learning' facet of risk that is a desirable effect in most rituals and needs to be maintained. Thus the challenge for managing risk in rituals lies in how to avert the potentially detrimental risk for the performers (especially in the higher echelons of initiation), while on the other hand keeping this beneficial learning aspect of risk and a number of strategies may be formulated to that end (*e.g.* internalising risk, see Schieffelin 1996, 59-89, or attempting to explain this failure in terms of the ritual itself, see Schieffelin 2007, 1-20 and Michaels 2007, 121-132).

Returning to the distinction between sport and ritual, we have now seen that not only sports, but also rituals can have an uncertain outcome. This would apparently eliminate this difference between ritual and sport. There is a significant difference however. In sport each performer may want a specific outcome, *i.e.* winning (in some even cases they may be certain of it!) but observers always see a different end; during each 'performance' one cannot predict the outcome. In ritual performers often may not know the end, yet observers can see an invariance (albeit fragile in some cases), a stable performance with a predictable end that, if nothing goes wrong, occurs every time.

I would also argue that risk, and especially intrinsic risk, is managed differently between the two types of activity. Managers of sport may stress the uncertain ending of sport which in fact is the essence of the whole activity (beyond the rules): 'Which team will win? Who will run the fastest? Who will beat whom in the boxing match?' 'Come and find out for yourselves'. Managers of ritual, as we saw above, would not stress this unknown end in describing a ritual. People are invited to go to a matriculation ceremony, or a wedding ceremony. Potential failure is

Figure 22. The boxer's Rhyton (Courtesy R. Koehl), note only extant figure bull-leaping being gored from the horns of the bull. Boxer rhyton (HM 342, 498, 676), Seprentinite, Reconstruction drawing by R. Porter, Koehl number 651, Koehl Type III S Conical, LMI, (Koehl 2006, 164-166), from Hagia Triada, portico 11, Piazzale Superiore (Banti et al. 1977, 82-83, 201). Courtesy R. Koehl

not part of the narrative (though it does happen sometimes). Although there is an internal risk that these rituals will not be completed and will fail, or that there will be deviations from the 'norm' such as that performers will not behave according to the rules, these un-prescribed failures or deviations are rarely advertised, rather it is the success and the end result (in the rituals in which there is one) that is usually stressed, especially to outsiders or non-performers.

This distinction offers an insight into the Minoan sport of bull leaping. Bull leaping is widely depicted in Minoan iconography, and is found in most of the Minoan iconographic media: seals and signet rings, three-dimensional clay figurines, gold cups, stone vessels and wall-paintings. A considerable amount of scholarship has been dedicated to this subject, and it is not our aim to review it here (MacGillivray 2000, 53-55; Papageorgiou, *forthcoming*; Mavroudi, *forthcoming*). Bull leaping is widely recognised as a Minoan ritual, yet one of its most important characteristics is that it sometimes fails, and this failure is glorified, *i.e.* it is recorded in art. For example in the so-called Boxer's Rhyton (Koehl 2006, frontispiece, p.i), a bull leaper is gored to presumably death by the horns of a bull, and others are trampled by bulls. This is a clear intrinsic failure on the part of the performer, in that the performance of a successful jump over the bull has failed. The fact that this, apparently mortal, failure has been advertised through art, but also that this is a difficult, particularly risky physical activity that requires an enormous amount of skill, strength and practice, point to the interpretation that this is indeed a sport

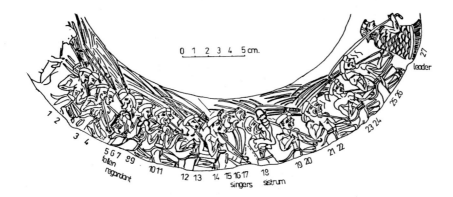

Figures 23 and 24. Harvester Vase (courtesy J. Younger). Note human figure 5 in the centre of the picture that has fallen and the other to his right (human figure 6) that is turning backwards to see. Harvester Vase (Herakleion Museum 184). Warren 1969, 88, 174-176, 178-181; fig 3, 4, Koehl 2006, 90-91, Koehl number 110, LMI, from Hagia Triada room 4 (Banti et al. 1977, 72). Courtesy J. Younger.

and not a ritual. It may belong to a ritual package which may include the capture of the bull, bull leaping and perhaps sacrifice (Kyriakidis 2002, 78-80; Papageorgiou, *forthcoming*) but the activity of bull leaping itself seems to be a sport.

By contrast, other depictions in Minoan art may be ritual, such as the offerings to the seated lady (see Rehak 2000, 169-276), or processions (Papageorgiou, *forthcoming*) such as that depicted on the 'Sacred Grove' fresco from Knossos. The most prominent depiction of offerings to a seated lady is attested in Xeste III at Akrotiri (Doumas 1992, fig. 122) in which a blue monkey offers saffron gathered by ladies to the seated lady. In no depiction of offerings to a seated lady do we have any hints of failure.

In procession scenes however we do have depictions of deviations from the 'norm'. In the West 'Sacred Grove' fresco (Davis 1987, 157-161) at Knossos, several women are depicted in procession. There, some of the women assume the same stance, whereas a number of others are depicted as either not assuming the 'prescribed' position, or even turning back to look at the others. Neither of these, however, constitute failure but mere deviation, despite the fact that not all women seem to fully follow the 'rule'. The same is the case in the Harvester's Cup Rhyton (Herakleion Museum stone finds number 184; Warren 1969, 88, 174-176, 178-181; fig 3, 4). In this depiction, all men seem to be marching in a rhythm following the music of a double wind instrument and three singers. All figures move in exactly the same fashion, almost with military discipline, with one exception. He probably lost his pace and fell down distracting the man in front who turns to look what happened. His failure to march does not constitute ritual failure (except as far as he is concerned), as all the others are marching successfully and the procession continues.

Both occasions of ritual deviation in Minoan art as well as the failure to jump over the bull in the sport of bull-leaping are one aspect of Minoan naturalism in art in that they demonstrate the depiction of real events rather than of merely idealised scenes. And they remind the viewer that rituals may easily drift from the prescribed performance. They also remind us that bull-leaping is a very dangerous sport (and not a ritual).

In Minoan art therefore, as elsewhere, rituals are depicted as having risks. These depictions, as they appear there however, do not feature ritual failure but rather ritual deviation, *i.e.* minor deviations from the rule-governed norm. Thus, rituals do have uncertainties and risks of various kinds, both extrinsic and intrinsic. That are starker in the perception of the performer than that of the observer. In institutionalised rituals that are managed by a group of people, this uncertainty is also managed, since it constitutes one of the common effects of rituals, *i.e.* it enhances learning. Through Minoan art we can see that in Minoan rituals this uncertainty is shown only when it does not put into doubt the succes of rituals. Outsiders should never know, after all, that ritual failure is an option.

References

Austin, J. 1962. *How to do Things with Words*, Cambridge MA: Harvard University Press.

Bell, C. 1997. *Ritual Perspectives and Dimensions*, Oxford: Oxford University Press.

Bell, C. 2008. Response: Defining the need for a definition, in: Kyriakidis E. (ed.). *The Archaeology of Ritual*, Los Angeles CA: The Cotsen Institute of Archaeology Publications, 277-288.

Brabham, D. 2008. Crowdsourcing as a Model for Problem Solving: An Introduction and Cases. *Convergence: The International Journal of Research into New Media Technologies,* 14/1, 75-90.

Chao, E. 1999. The maoist Shaman and the Madman: Ritual Bricolage, Failed Ritual, and Failed Ritual Theory, *Cultural Anthropology* 14/4, 505-534.

Davis, E. 1987. The Knossos Miniature Frescoes and the Function of the Central Courts, in: *R. Hägg and N. Marinatos* (eds.). *The Function of the Minoan Palaces. Proceedings of the Fourth International Symposium at the Swedish Institute in Athens, 10-16 June, 1984.* [Swedish Institute in Athens, Series in 4°, 35] Stockholm: Skrifter Utgivna av Svenska Instituet i Athen, 157-161.

Dayan, P. and Yu, A. 2003. Uncertainty and learning, *Neuroscience* 49/2, 171-181.

Doumas, C. 1992. *The Wall-Paintings of Thera.* Athens: The Thera Foundation, Petros M. Nomikos.

Flad, R. 2008. Divination and Power, A Multiregional View of the Development of Oracle Bone Divination in Early China. *Current Anthropology* 49/3, 403-437.

Grimes, R. 1996. Infelicitous Performances and Ritual Criticism, in: Grimes, R. (ed.). *Readings in Ritual Studies.* Upper Saddle River, New Jersey: Prentice Hall, 279-293.

Hüsken, U. 2007 (ed.). *When Rituals Go Wrong: Mistakes, Failure, and the Dynamics of Ritual,* Boston MA: Brill.

Kamin, L. 1969. Predictability, surprise, attention, and conditioning, in: Campbell, B. and Church, R. (eds.). *Punishment and Aversive Behavior,* New York: Appleton-Century-Crofts, 242-259.

Koehl, R. 2006. *Aegean Bronze Age Rhyta,* Philadelphia PA: INSTAP Academic Press.

Kyriakidis, E. 2002. *Ritual and its Establishment: the case of some Minoan Open-Air Rituals,* PhD University of Cambridge.

Kyriakidis, E. 2005. *Ritual in the Aegean: the Minoan Peak Sanctuaries,* London: Duckworth.

Kyriakidis, E. 2008. The Archaeologies of Ritual, in: Kyriakidis, E. (ed.). *The Archaeology of Ritual,* Los Angeles CA: Cotsen Institute of Archaeology Publications, 289-306.

Kyriakidis, E. *forthcoming*. Ritual, Games and Learning, in: Renfrew, C., Morely, I. and Boyd, M.J. (eds.). *Play, ritual and belief in animals and early human societies. forthcoming.*

Lett, J. 1990. Emics and Etics: Notes on the Epistemology of Anthropology, in: Headland, T., Pike, K. and Harris M. (eds.). *Emics and Etics. The Insider/ Outsider Debate* (Frontiers of Anthropology vol. 7, Newbury Park, CA: Sage Publications, 127-42.

MacGillivray, J.A. 2000. Labyrinths and Bull-Leapers. *Archaeology* 53/6, 53-55.

Marcus, J. 2006. The roles of ritual and technology in Mesoamerican water management, in: Marcus J. and Stanish, C. (eds.). *Agricultural Strategies,* [Monograph 50] Los Angeles: Cotsen Institute of Archaeology Publications, 221-254.

Mavroudi, N. 2011. Άνδρες, γυναίκες και ένας... πίθηκος στην κρητική εικονογραφία της Εποχής του Χαλκού. Proceedings of the 11th Cretological Conference, *forthcoming.*

Michaels, A. 2007. Perfection And Mishaps In Vedic Rituals, in: Hüsken, U. (ed.). *When Rituals Go Wrong: Mistakes, Failure, and the Dynamics of Ritual,* Boston MA: Brill, 121-132.

Nikolaidou, M. 2008. Ritualised Technologies in the Aegean Neolithic? The Crafts of Adornment, in: Kyriakidis E. (ed.). *The Archaeology of Ritual,* Los Angeles CA: Cotsen Institute of Archaeology Publications, 221-254.

Papageorgiou, I. 2011. Η προπαγάνδα της εικόνας: Χώροι εισόδου σε δημόσια αιγαιακά κτήρια της Ύστερης Εποχής του Χαλκού και ο συναφής τοιχογραφικός διάκοσμος, Proceedings of the 11th Cretological Conference, *forthcoming.*

Pearce, J. and Hall, G. 1980, A model for Pavlovian learning: Variation in the effectiveness of conditioned but not unconditioned stimuli. *Psychological Review* 87, 532-552, 1980.

Peters, F. 1985. *Jerusalem: The Holy City in the Eyes of Chroniclers, Visitors, Pilgrims and Prophets from the Days of Abraham to the Beginning of Modern Times.* Princeton NJ: Princeton University Press.

Schieffelin, E. 1996. On Failure and Performance. Throwing the Medium out of the Seance, in: Laderman, C. and Roseman, M. (eds.). *The Performance of Healing*, London: Routledge, 59-89.

Schieffelin, E. 2007. Introduction, in: Hüsken, U. (ed.). *When Rituals Go Wrong: Mistakes, Failure, and the Dynamics of Ritual,* Boston MA: Brill, 1-20.

Rehak, P. 2000. The Isopata Ring and the Question of Narrative in Neopalatial Glyptic, in: Müller, W. and Pini, I. (eds.). *Minoisch-mykenische Glyptik: Stil, Ikonographie, Funktion. V. Internationales Siegel-Symposium Marburg, 23-25 September 1999,* Berlin: Gebr. Mann Verlag, CMS Beiheft, 269-276.

Warren, P. 1969. *Minoan Stone Vases*, Cambridge: Cambridge University Press.

Discussion: Defining moments

Richard Bradley[1]

Edited collections are usually of two kinds. Sometimes they are tightly integrated and conform to a single thesis. In archaeology a famous example is Kent Flannery's book *The Early Mesoamerican Village* (Flannery 1976). The various contributions pursue a line of argument which amounts to much more than the sum of its separate parts. The alternative is for an editor to select a theme of wider interest and to accept – and even encourage – the diversity of approaches taken by the individual authors. A typical instance is Neil Price's *The Archaeology of Shamanism* (Price 2001). Both provide worthwhile models, but they result in entirely different kinds of volume. It is obvious that *Ritual Failure* belongs to the second group.

Discussants also take two forms. Some regard themselves as peer reviewers, praising some papers at the expense of others and passing judgement on the individual chapters. At times they have the irritating habit of telling the reader how they could have provided a more persuasive analysis than the authors of the book. I ally myself with a second group which is more interested in the issues treated by the contributors. Commentators of this kind do not arrange the chapters in order of merit. Instead the emphasis is on the potential of particular ideas and the ways in which they can be developed. The more disparate the contents of any collection, the more such observations may be helpful. In this piece I wish to focus on some questions of definition raised by the separate chapters. Then I turn to the difficult question of what rituals were meant to do and the ways in which they became implicated in the politics of the past. Only by investigating all these matters can we consider how some of them failed.

The diversity of these chapters is a source of strength, but the authors' conceptions of ritual are almost equally varied. This requires some thought. Some writers are more explicit than others, but there is little acknowledgement that the concept of ritual is not favoured by all social anthropologists today. At the same time the contributors employ Catherine Bell's notion of ritualisation in so many different ways that it hardly appears as the radical reformulation that she originally intended (Bell 1992). Is it to be regarded as a strategic process that affects dealings with the supernatural, or can it extend to mundane activities that are conducted with an unusual degree of formality? It would have been useful to employ Colin

---

[1] Department of Archaeology, University of Reading.

Renfrew's distinction between *ritual* and *cult*. It could be helpful here (Renfrew 1985).

In fact the process of ritualisation need not imply an appeal to supernatural agency. Just as there are sacred rituals, there are secular rituals, too. They may play a political role in some societies, but not necessarily in others. Nor is it clear to what extent they can be distinguished from habitual behaviour of the type considered by Pierre Bourdieu (1977). In some ways these distinctions reflect the kinds of society considered by the authors, and the degree to which religious specialists played a significant role. Some of the case studies consider the archaeology of early states. Is the same approach appropriate where communities were organised in a different way? When was the boundary crossed, or was there never a boundary in the first place? Just as I have found it difficult to distinguish between rituals and some of the conventional practices of domestic life (Bradley 2005), is it possible to make comparisons between the beliefs of the first farmers and those of the urban societies which were their ultimate successors? And if that does appear a useful exercise, is it possible to discuss it without resorting to notions of social evolution that are fundamentally teleological?

There is also a question of scale. Just as particular rituals may be placed along a continuum extending from the sacred to the secular, they may also be considered as either public or private – in fact they may involve a subtle combination of both. Public rituals are more likely to affect the political process, and to that extent they may succeed or fail in fulfilling the intentions of the participants. Private rituals, on the other hand, may be conducted with other aims in view and their success or failure will have less drastic consequences.

In the case of public rituals there are two distinct possibilities to consider. They may be a method of maintaining social cohesion, or they may represent an expression of political power. To a certain extent those models are at odds with one another, although each can be transformed over the course of time. One example would be the provision of feasts (Dietler and Hayden 2001). Were they employed as a levelling mechanism intended to prevent social inequalities from developing? That view has been employed in the archaeology of hunter gatherers. Alternatively, feasts may have provided an arena for competition. They were organised as a way of emphasising differences of status and wealth. They could even have been a method of creating obligations that would never be reciprocated – in that sense they inflicted debts. In each case the provision of feasts may have accompanied public rituals, but the motives of those taking part may not have been the same.

Any reference to *failure* involves a choice between these models. If rituals were intended to promote social stability they would have failed if they provided a route by which particular groups or individuals rose to positions of power. If, on the other hand, they were intended as a vehicle for competition they would be unsuccessful if the social order remained unchanged. Without a clear conception of what particular ceremonies were intended to do, it is difficult to talk of 'ritual failure'. There is the same problem unless it is known who was entitled to take part and the audiences to whom such events were presented.

In fact some of the authors do not provide definitions of ritual failure, nor do they relate their own discussions of this theme to any wider discussions in the social sciences. Rather than follow the lines laid down in Ute Hüsken's edited volume of 2007, they identify several different kinds of failure in the communities they discuss. On the one hand, failure may be identified by the mistakes made in conducting a ritual or by administrative inefficiency in organising public events. On the other, ritual failure is postulated simply because archaeologically recognisable rituals appear to have gone out of fashion. In other cases they seem to have been transformed. At times the artefacts and monuments associated with rituals in the past were deliberately destroyed and the ideas connected with them were rejected. Iconoclasm provides the most compelling evidence that particular rituals had failed. The fact that other rituals changed their character over time suggests that they were more resilient.

None of this needs be true of private rituals, the success or failure of which might not leave any obvious evidence behind. That is true whether or not they were directed to the supernatural. Only where written evidence, such as a curse tablet, survives is it possible to take the discussion much further. Otherwise the usefulness of a concept of ritual failure is closely connected with the objectives of participants, their numbers, and the scale on which particular events had been organised. Only large scale rituals are likely to leave much trace, and, in particular, those that were conducted sufficiently often for such activities to be recognised by archaeologists.

There is a paradox here, for the individual authors describe how the power of particular rituals was undermined or transformed, yet the social anthropologist Maurice Bloch (1977) defines ritual in terms of its resistance to change. For him, it has certain characteristics. It can be conducted using special forms of speech or song; it may require a range of unusual bodily postures and movements; sometimes it involves oratory; and it may take place in a specialised language which is quite different from the everyday. For Bloch, the fact that rituals communicate in such a specialised manner makes them unusually difficult to challenge, especially whilst they are happening. They can refer to the remote past and involve the use of archaic forms of language. In some ways it is more important to conduct these rituals correctly than it is to understand their meanings (Humphrey and Laidlaw 1994).

Yet Bloch himself has shown how the same forms of ritual, while adhering to the traditional formula, can be conducted in completely different political contexts, so that they can alter their scale, as well as their wider political significance. Thus in his own study area, Madagascar, the same rituals, involving similar utterances and similar forms of conduct, could be associated with the institution of kingship during one period and with resistance to colonial rule during another phase (Bloch 1986). Only by observing the setting of these events as well as their apparent contents could their true significance be recognised.

It has never been easy for archaeologists to identify unambiguous evidence of ancient rituals, but they do have a distinct advantage over social anthropologist, for they are used to dealing with extended periods of time: with sequences that can be measured in centuries rather than the human generations that are so important to social theorists. It means that in principle they can observe continuities or discontinuities in the histories of particular rituals in relation to their wider cultural context. Did rituals remain the same as the societies that performed them changed? Or were those rituals modified whilst other parts of the archaeological record remained the same? Where an accurate chronology is available it is possible to ask more searching questions. Did public rituals develop at a different pace from other aspects of life in the ancient world? And did those rituals come to an end quite rapidly, or were they only gradually transformed? Were they abandoned altogether, or did their elements re-emerge in different configurations or different settings? As the papers in this volume demonstrate, virtually all these sequences were followed in particular places. There is so much diversity that a single model of 'ritual failure' cannot accommodate them all.

In truth the idea of something *ending* presupposes a longer sequence, and that is what archaeology is uniquely equipped to provide. The great merit of these papers is that they play to this strength. Like so many ideas, we owe the notion of ritual failure to scholars working in other disciplines. What the contributors to this collection demonstrate is that archaeologists can provide a distinctive perspective of their own. Problems of definition will always arise when we investigate the ancient world, but our particular time scale is entirely our own. We can take comfort from that.

References

Bell, C. 1992. *Ritual Theory, Ritual Practice*. New York: Oxford University Press.

Bloch, M. 1977. The past and the present in the present. *Man* 12, 278-292.

Bloch, M. 1986. *From Blessing to Violence. History and Ideology in the Circumcision Ritual of the Merina of Madagascar*. Cambridge: Cambridge University Press.

Bourdieu, P. 1977. *Outline of a Theory of Practice*. Cambridge: Cambridge University Press.

Bradley, R. 2005. *Ritual and Domestic Life in Prehistoric Europe*. Abingdon: Routledge.

Dietler, M. and Hayden, B. 2001 (eds.). *Feasts: Archaeological and Ethnographic Perspectives on Food, Politics and Power*. Washington DC: Smithsonian Institute Press.

Flannery, K. 1976 (ed.). *The Early Mesoamerican Village*. New York: Academic Press.

Humphrey, C. and Laidlaw, J. 1994. *The Archetypal Actions of Ritual*. Oxford: Clarendon Press.

Hüsken, U. 2007 (ed.). *When Rituals Go Wrong. Failure and the Dynamics of Ritual*. Leiden: Brill.

Price, N. 2001 (ed.). *The Archaeology of Shamanism*. London: Routledge.

Renfrew, C. 1985. *The Archaeology of Cult: the Sanctuary at Philakopi*. London: British School of Archaeology at Athens.